Creech
Cross

By

S. E. England

ISBN: 979-8-8574-5181-6

1st Edition
www.sarahenglandauthor.co.uk

Tales of The Occult by Sarah E. England

About the author

Sarah England is a UK author with a background in nursing and psychiatry, a theme which creeps into many of her stories. At the fore of Sarah's body of work is the bestselling occult horror trilogy, *Father of Lies, Tanners Dell,* and *Magda,* followed by a spin-off from the series, *The Owlmen.* Other novels include *The Soprano, Hidden Company, Monkspike, Baba Lenka, Masquerade, Caduceus, Groom Lake* and *The Droll Teller. The Witching Hour* is a collection of short stories; and *Creech Cross* is her latest book.

If you would like to be informed about future releases, there is a newsletter sign-up on Sarah's website. Please feel free to get in touch – it would be great to hear from you!

www.sarahenglandauthor.co.uk

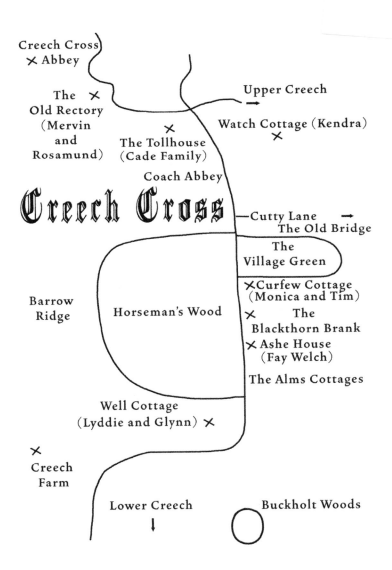

Chapter One

*'All of the old paths interweave and interlock,
criss-crossing into the mizmaze'*

Not long after we moved to Creech Cross I started a diary,
a log of events, perhaps to reassure myself the insanity
wasn't mine. A journey so mired in misconceptions,
superstition and trickery, it became almost impossible to see
the truth, to know who to trust. Why were we blind for so
long? I think, to be honest, humour got us through on
occasion, because there were genuinely moments so bizarre,
so weird, as to be comical. But in order to understand, it is
necessary to tell the story from the beginning, to go back to
2002 when Glynn and I first arrived, and once more take
the road past the red post, over the old stone bridge, and
into the other world that is Creech Cross...

The village is a small one, situated between Dorset and
Somerset in the southwest of England, on a border as
jagged as the path of a hare, leaping from side to side in a
jumble of hills, neither fully in one county or the other.
Drive along the boundary road and you'll be welcomed to

Dorset or Somerset a dozen times or more. But sooner or later, there'll be a red signpost on the right-hand side marking the way to Creech Cross, a road rarely travelled except by residents and couriers. In fact, it could be said that if a person wished to vanish, then that was the place to go. For sure, many who'd ventured in were never seen again.

Centuries ago, there were no lanes in the area at all, nothing formal outside of the straight Roman roads connecting the main towns; and the ones that did exist required a toll in order to pass. With the county of Dorset largely comprised of softly undulating downs, the locals managed to successfully avoid those tolls, but on the lane running through Creech Cross there stands a tollhouse, and so it seems the village had once been a thoroughfare and more important than the backwater it became. Evident, no doubt, by the many tracks snaking into the hills, by the small family farms still in existence, and a long-closed public house.

We knew nothing about the place beforehand. To us, it was simply an idyllic village, and by the time we found it at the tail end of the previous year, a godsend, because we desperately needed somewhere to live. Glynn had been transferred by his company from Yorkshire to the South West of England, had to visit clients across several counties, and his new job began in January. Meanwhile, I'd managed to secure a temporary nursing job at a nearby cottage hospital for care of the elderly. But we'd run into a problem, and that was finding a house. Not that we were finnicky. We genuinely couldn't find anything suitable we could afford.

Unrealistically, what we'd both had in mind was a

pastoral idyll, a thatched cob cottage with an inglenook fireplace, a garden with apple trees, maybe a stream; but quickly sobered up to the realisation that our dream house was way out of our price range. Therefore, reluctantly, after several increasingly frantic months, we settled on a 1960s bungalow. Although it needed a serious upgrade, there was a generous garden with access to fields at the back – green space being a priority because of Skip, our springer spaniel. *Bags of potential*, said the agency sales blurb, along with, *scope to put your own personal stamp on it.*

But just as we were about to put in an offer, another agent rang asking if we'd like to view Well Cottage in Creech Cross. We were half an hour away at the time, in a café in Blandford Forum, deciding what we could afford for the bungalow while still having enough to modernise it.

"What do you think, Lyds?" Glynn asked, putting his hand over the phone.

It was a Friday afternoon in late October, and a decision had to be made. Our buyers were becoming increasingly impatient, demanding an imminent exchange or they'd go elsewhere. On the other hand, if we didn't bid on the bungalow that day we'd lose it.

I pulled a face. *Oh God, what to do?*

"It's what we wanted," he whispered. "Traditional cottage. Rural. Backs onto open country."

"Can we see it this afternoon? Now?"

He nodded, spoke to the agent again. "Yes, we could be there in half an hour."

The adrenalin was up. We raced out of the café and I had the map open before Glynn had started up the engine.

After that, everything unfolded very quickly. As if it was all inevitable, meant to be, no stopping it.

I remember standing in the kitchen as the sun dropped over the horizon, gazing out of the window at an oddly-shaped hill with a huddle of spidery, wind-bent trees on top, aware of a fizz of excitement in my stomach. My God, the place was magical, stunning, otherworldly…

"That's Barrow Ridge," the agent said. "There are several round here."

"Several what?" Glynn asked.

Anna, the viewing agent, a middle-aged woman in a green Barbour jacket with a matching hat, seemed astonished at the question.

"Barrows, Mr Spicer. Ancient burial mounds."

We were looking into each other's eyes, Glynn and I, and I knew he felt the same as I did. There would, we were told, be a huge amount of interest when the cottage was advertised tomorrow, but the owner wanted to sell as soon as possible and would accept the asking price for a quick sale.

"And as you can see, there's a little gate leading into the woodland at the bottom of the garden. It's so quiet round here, completely unspoilt…"

I barely heard her.

The light was fading rapidly, dusk descending on the valley.

We'd lose the bungalow if we didn't put our bid in within the hour.

"Could you give us a minute?" Glynn asked.

But we both knew we'd go for it. We wouldn't get better in our price range. The search had been going on for three months, and our excitement, our disbelief at this flip-switch of luck, was infectious.

After a few exchanged whispers, Glynn said, "We want

to offer."

"Quite sure?" Anna asked.

I nodded.

"Absolutely," said Glynn.

Having already spent hours going over the figures that afternoon, we knew it would take every last penny, but unlike the bungalow this one didn't need upgrading. It smelled of new paint, the kitchen white, pristine. Ditto the bathroom. We could move straight in.

"I'll buzz the owner – see if we can get it tied up today," said Anna.

We could hardly believe it.

She put a hand over the receiver as the phone rang. "Her name's Kathleen Ettrick – they've got a farm over at Lower Creech."

I willed there to be an answer, for the deal to be sealed there and then. I wanted to live there, for that view to be the first thing I saw every morning, for this to be home. My heart was thundering along.

"Mrs Ettrick? Oh, good afternoon. Anna Bradley-Holt here…"

She wandered into the dining room. Location-wise, the cottage was perfect; convenient but rural, as if the hectic modern world no longer existed, yet it was really only on the other side of the old stone bridge we'd just crossed. Town was a twenty-minute drive away.

Left alone in the kitchen, we stared out of the window at Barrow Ridge. At the stillness of the woods beyond the garden gate, the trees mired in autumnal fog. Silently, covertly, praying.

It was a strange phenomenon, that feeling of ancient and modern, of two parallel timelines. After leaving the main road at the red signpost, the lane had twisted and turned for several miles, flanked by trees leaning over from bordering banks – gnarled, blackened hooks that met in the middle, forming a spiky corridor. Damp coppery leaves lay piled in the ditches, coating the lane, the woods either side hazy with autumnal fog. Then quite abruptly it dipped, levelled, and with a flood marker preceding it, a dilapidated stone bridge appeared before us. It felt like crossing a threshold, the lane from that point onwards narrow with no passing places, until we came to the junction with Coach Lane, and the mesmerising glory of the valley

Reminiscent of Glastonbury Tor, of Avalon, Barrow Ridge rose out of low-lying fog in the burnished gold of an October afternoon, the landscape mystical, almost spectral… and from that very first moment we were both utterly, hopelessly enchanted.

Coach Lane is the main road cutting through the valley. Long, winding, and full of blind bends, it begins and ends nowhere in particular, but meanders, at intervals, into further lanes and coombs, the landscape a maze of downs, hillocks, meadows and streams – the kind of place you'd have to be born to in order to internalise its complex web of tracks, paths and hamlets, some of which were comprised of only three or four whitewashed cob dwellings, with names like Wryneck Cottage and Widow's Penny. It reminded me of Tolkien's 'shires' more than Hardy's Wessex. A place unique, peculiar, belonging to neither one county nor the other, but perhaps only to itself.

Anna's throaty, confident voice carried from the other room.

"They've got cash buyers behind them pushing for an exchange. No chain. Yes, we have – they've got that sorted." She laughed. "No, they're not, definitely not!"

Glynn looked at his watch. "We've still got time to go for the bungalow if she pisses us about."

I was worrying about Skip if this woman said no. What if we didn't get the bungalow, either? It was really difficult finding rented accommodation that would take a dog. Nor could we increase the offer. We honestly had no more.

Please, please, please…

Anna was walking back.

"You've just bought yourselves an amazing house. Asking price accepted. Thought it would be." She dropped the phone into her bag. "Do you need to whizz round again?"

I don't remember the rest of what was said. I was so excited, so relieved, the whole thing was a blur. And as I slipped my hand in Glynn's I sensed his pulse had quickened, too.

Not for one second did either of us ever think to question anything other than the price, the ease of location for work, the appeal of the cottage. It never occurred to us we might not be safe there. Why would it? And the slight smile playing around the lips of the agent didn't register with me at all, not until months and months had passed, when comprehension started to kick in.

Thing is, you are safe. You are. Until you're not. And then everything changes.

***

Chapter Two

Well Cottage is located at the tail end of the village, set back from the lane where it sweeps around on a hairpin bend towards Lower Creech. At some point it had been rebuilt over the original foundations, although it was not clear when, and the extension was recent. Before that, however, it had been derelict for hundreds of years.

A small church is silhouetted on the brow of the hill at Upper Creech, and there's another below, in Lower Creech, which could be walked to by way of the bridlepath directly opposite our cottage. I took Skip that way the day after we moved in, when I met Keith Cribbs, and I'll come to that shortly, but it struck me how many churches there were for so few inhabitants, in addition to an abbey – Creech Abbey – which now lies in ruins.

The original cottage must have been tiny, the extension effectively doubling the size. Where a single room had once sufficed for both cooking and living, now there's a good farmhouse style kitchen, with what Anna had termed a dog and boot room between that and the back garden. The extension to the side encompasses a comfortable lounge complete with a wood-burning stove, and a dining room, or study as we were going to use it, at the front.

Upstairs, there's a master bedroom, one of the nicest bathrooms I'd ever seen – white, fully tiled, with an Edwardian slipper bath – plus what can only be described as a box room. The agents had stretched credulity in describing that as a second bedroom, but the cottage suited us perfectly. We were thrilled with it. And in the second week of January, we moved in, the sale having gone through without a single hitch.

We let ourselves into a silent, empty house. A white vacuum.

"Bloody hell, it's cold in here!"

"Been empty too long," I said. "Can we get the fire going?"

At a guess, we were about an hour ahead of the removal guys, so we hunted around for logs, rubbing our hands together, hoping there'd be a few in the shed or the garage. Unfortunately, there was nothing.

"Never mind," said Glynn. "Let's get the heating on – just need to go check the oil tank. Where's the kettle? Can we get some coffee going?"

I looked out of the dining room window as dusk fell. "Hope they can find us. It'll be dark soon."

"Don't worry, they said it'd be done today. At least there isn't much to unload."

I left him giving Skip a quick walk and hurried upstairs with the cases. I was tired and tetchy, but excited, too. It had been an exceptionally long and stressful day. The buyers had been parked outside waiting for us to leave since eleven that morning, and it'd been a whirl of frantic packing and cleaning right to the last minute, followed by a five-hour drive, mostly motorway. I'd find a log supplier next day. It could wait. Everything could wait.

"Oil tank's empty," Glynn shouted up.

I wandered onto the landing and looked down. "What, nothing? No central heating?"

"A few litres, that's all. Enough for hot water for a few days if we're careful."

"Crap!"

"I know. I never thought to ask and the bloody solicitor didn't, either."

He raked his hair back and forth.

"It could be days before we can get a delivery. Still, at least the cooker's electric, that's something." "Yeah, and the shower, thank God."

"I've just thought – there's a fan heater in one of the boxes in my car. Same one as the kettle and toaster if you can find it. And there's a bag with the duvet and pillows in. Could you bring that? I'll make the bed up top priority when the van arrives."

He looked drained, worried. Then suddenly he grinned. "Champagne and cheese on toast, then? Followed by an early night? I know how we can keep warm."

"Class!" I ran downstairs. "You bought champagne? Really?"

He took me in his arms. "We're here! We did it, Lyds! We really did it!"

"We did, didn't we?"

The moment is still clear in my mind. God, we were so naïve.

Later, we lay in bed listening to the all-consuming silence of the night. We weren't used to that. Where we'd lived before was quiet, but there'd been the hum of distant traffic, an occasional raised voice from a neighbour, sometimes footsteps on the pavement outside.

Here, the silence, like the blackness, was total. No light came through the curtains. No outline of furniture. We could have been in outer space.

Unable to drop into sleep, tired but wired, the events of the day flashed before me. It all seemed so surreal. Downstairs, Skip whined, his claws pitter-pattering on the kitchen floor. Probably wondering where the hell he was? Eventually, I got up with the intent of going down to reassure him. It must have been about one or two in the morning, and my breath clouded like ectoplasm on the chill night air.

Careful not to disturb Glynn, I swung my legs over the side of the bed, then, with hands outstretched into what was coalface blackness, began to inch towards the bedroom door, groping blindly for the dressing gown I'd hung on the back. But the door no longer had a hook on it, there was no gown, nothing, in fact, but a flat board. Panic rose up. I was completely disorientated. When into the corner of my vision there floated the most extraordinary thing. An electric-blue orb. As bright as a Christmas tree light.

At first I didn't acknowledge its presence, being far more worried about the lack of a door handle. I was shivering, cold to the bone, and stared at it without comprehension. Suspended in mid-air, the orb was the size of a toy marble, its glow iridescent, and the longer I looked, the more I realised it wasn't the only one. There were dozens of them. One or two were orange, most were blue. I blinked and blinked again, refusing to believe the evidence of my own eyes. There was no fear. Not then. Just incredulity. Stunned surprise.

And then the lamp flicked on.

"What on earth are you doing?" Glynn said.

A fitted wardrobe door was in front of me, a closet instead of the landing.

"Were you sleepwalking?"

"No. I heard Skip pacing up and down in the kitchen and couldn't see. I thought this was the bedroom door. I was–"

"You must have been dreaming. Skip's in the dog and thingy room, remember?"

"Boot room. Oh, yes. Well, he must have pushed open the door because he's been scampering about down there for ages. I'll go check."

I hurried down to the kitchen and switched on the light.

It took a moment to register.

The door to the dog and boot room, a stable door with a bolt, was firmly shut. And through the inset window, I could see Skip fast asleep on his bed. Sensing he was being observed, his head jutted up and I quickly tiptoed away. He'd had a stressful day, too. Needed to sleep. It was odd, though. I could have sworn I heard the patter of nails. Perhaps I had been dreaming, after all?

It was only the next day, after Glynn had set off at seven for the office in Exeter, after I'd had breakfast, showered, phoned for an oil delivery, and was several minutes into the walk with Skip, that I remembered the mysterious coloured orbs.

The need to be outside had been paramount, to ground, recover, settle us both in. And so I took the nearest path, the bridleway opposite the cottage, which leads through the fields towards Lower Creech. About halfway along, there's a small wood on the right, fenced off by a ring of barbed wire, a perfect circle of densely packed trees.

And I was partly focusing on that, on its incongruity, while also wondering what those orbs had been, when I became aware of a man on the path ahead. And that he'd stopped dead in his tracks.

Keith Cribbs, approximately seventy, and his daughter, Cicely, were not incomers. It's possible they'd been embedded in that village for centuries, thousands of years even, reincarnating into the same family, the same groove, over and over and over.

Well, that day my heart bumped uncomfortably at the sight of him, and Skip stiffened, slowing his stride. About fifty yards away, rifle slung over one shoulder, he was standing with his hands in his pockets watching my approach. Keith Cribbs, I realised, was actually waiting for me to walk up to him, a half-smile on his face, the sort a predator wears when it spots prey – keen, focused, gleeful.

There really was nothing else I could do but keep walking.

***

Chapter Three

I read recently that intuition is the subconscious downloading information your conscious mind hasn't yet processed. But I didn't listen to it. Keith Cribbs had actually been quite friendly, and my first impression was probably wrong. Besides, Glynn was buzzing when he came home that night, chatting about the team he was working with, that he'd been out to lunch with his new boss, and I didn't want to spoil the mood by saying how creepy I'd found our new neighbour, how... reptilian...

Keith was a widower, lonely, a fact made obvious by how much he talked – the kind of talk that didn't require any input from the listener. Yet he'd watched my face. He'd watched it intently. There was a wily, inquisitive intelligence behind those pale, rheumy, blue eyes, an alertness at odds with the slow drawl of his speech. It was as if he'd wanted to keep me there, pinned, enthralled, almost hypnotised with the drone of his voice. And I was oddly tired when we finally parted company.

"You're miles away, Lyds," Glynn said. "So, how's your day been? Did you sort the oil?"

"Good, and yes, I did. Friday morning, all being well."

Glynn was the most optimistic I'd ever seen him. He's

the kind of bloke who'll go along with whatever makes everyone else happy. He doesn't like to make waves or be disliked. Everyone's friend, is how I'd describe Glynn. I didn't want to bring him down in any way that evening, nor could I either consolidate or articulate the feeling I'd had about Keith Cribbs, largely because it sounded as though I was looking for a problem when there wasn't one. And there wasn't. Everything was fine, I told myself, because it was.

"I really think I'm going to love it here," Glynn was saying.

I'd cobbled together a tuna pasta and he'd bought a bottle of wine on the way home.

"Me, too."

"I can't get over it. Everyone was so friendly. I've got a major workload, no denying that – a lot's in Bristol and a fair amount on the south coast, but I'm really looking forward to it. There's a course they want me to do too, Lyds. But I'll talk to you about that later."

"Oh?"

"Not for a while yet, don't worry. You'll be settled into the new job and have loads of friends in the village, by then. Anyway, what's it been like here? I see you've been unpacking."

"Yes, that's taken most of the day. Oh, I met our neighbour, Keith Cribbs. He's at Creech Farm, on the right as you drive round the hairpin bend."

"Dairy?"

"Yes."

"What's he like?"

I gave him an overview. Keith was mid-seventies, I reckoned. Pale, rheumy eyes, bulbous nose covered in purple veins, crew-cut grey hair, wiry build but with a beer belly – long, rubbery veins standing proud on his hands. He'd worn overalls, checked shirt and lace-up boots, smelled a bit sour like he only had strip-washes.

Glynn's eyebrows raised. "Blimey, your attention to detail! I never notice all this stuff."

"I know you don't. I bet you can't remember what I was wearing yesterday?"

He laughed. "You're right, I can't. But I can reel off at least twenty phone numbers and rarely forget a significant number plate."

"There you go! I'll forget a number plate instantly – can't even remember my own. Anyway, he offered to take me on a tour of the area. It's got quite a history. Apparently they used to hang people at the top of Barrow Ridge – you know, where that line of trees is? It was so the bodies could be seen swinging from the noose for miles around. It served as a warning. And Buckholt Wood is the ringed cluster of trees you come to between here and Lower Creech, about halfway along the bridlepath. That's where I met him, level with that. He said the fields either side were the scene of a bloody battle between Wessex men and invading Vikings, and Buckholt Wood is a sealed-off graveyard, the roots of the trees grown from blood and bone. Dogs won't go in there, he said, because they can smell death, and people have seen ghosts of decapitated, dismembered soldiers. It's fenced off because someone committed suicide in there recently."

Glynn put down his fork. "Jeez!"

"Told me all this ever so cheerfully. He'd make a perfect tour guide for one of those gruesome museums – you know, old gaols where they use effigies to recreate mass murderers? And then there's a place called Dagger's Gate if you go back up the lane towards the Village Green. A farmer was stabbed to death with a dagger there on his way home from the pub, and is said to haunt the gate on the track to his farm. Everyone's seen him, Keith said. Oh, and he told me not to take Skip onto the marsh fields between here and Barrow Ridge because there are bottomless bogs. Folk have disappeared. Quite a few, apparently."

"You going on this special tour of his?"

I shook my head. "Got to be joking. I have to say he was very nice, though. Said if we wanted any information on anything, to just go round. Oh, but not through his fields. That's something he was adamant about. Said to be sure to use the drive."

"Anything else?"

I was on a second glass of wine, and more of what Keith said was coming back to me. He'd actually packed in a lot of information in the half hour we'd stood on the path.

"Have you seen the sign outside one of the houses on the lane? It's an old pub sign – The Blackthorn Brank?"

"Yes, there are a few of those around. I suppose the inns get bought up for houses but people like to keep the history."

"Haunted, apparently. He said centuries ago, if a man couldn't stand his nagging wife, a gaoler would come and clamp her jaws together in an iron brank, like a scold's bridle, and chain her by it to the mantelpiece until she changed her ways. The pub was originally called The Cat and Chapel and the innkeeper had his wife locked into one. A woman called Margaret Faldo, it was. Only he beat her up, let customers rape her, then left her there, still in the brank, to starve to death."

"Bloody hell!"

"It was still a public house until the 1940s, when a war veteran got blind drunk and was thrown out after closing time. Pitch-dark and pouring with rain, the poor man got mizmazed, he said, and must have slumped down asleep somewhere."

"Mizmazed?"

"Yes, confused. Anyway, no one thought anymore about it until a fox was seen running through the farmyard a week later with a human hand in its mouth."

"Oh, for fuck's sake, Lyddie. And he told you all this the first time you met him?"

"To be honest, I got the feeling he was waiting for a reaction. I was going to tell him I was a nurse and not remotely squeamish, but here's the weird thing – he never once asked me who I was or where I lived, let alone what I did for a living."

"You must have introduced yourself?"

"Well, that's just it. I didn't. I barely said a word. Me and Skip had been walking along the path when he waylaid us. Just stopped and waited. Then said, 'Bootiful morrnen, innet?'"

Glynn laughed. "It's nice, isn't it – the accent?"

"And then he goes, 'Keith Cribbs. I'm your neighbour at Creech Farm.' Everything he said was really slow, very deliberate. I hardly spoke, but if I did say anything, it was as if I hadn't – just, you know, zero interest. And the thing was, he was talking so much, packing so much in, that I didn't realise until later I'd never told him my name. Yet he knew it. When I said I'd best get on and started to pull away, he said, 'Nice to meet you, Lydia. See you again.' I'd got all the way to Lower Creech before it hit me I hadn't actually told him."

"Small village. Hot wires. He already knew."

I was quiet for a while.

"He was friendly, anyway. That's the main thing."

"Yeah, and remember it's different in villages like this; everyone knows everyone. It was a bit like that where I grew up, before they built that massive estate."

"Just took me by surprise, I suppose. That he knew who I was by sight. We've only been here a day."

Glynn refilled our glasses.

"By the way, you know how you tried to get into the wardrobe last night?"

"Uh-huh!"

"Just an idea, but shall we leave a lamp on in the hall downstairs? In case one of us needs the bathroom."

"Definitely, yes. Especially as there's a step between the old part and the new. I nearly fell down that, as well."

We both laughed and then he held my gaze. I knew that look.

We were a little bit tipsy, a little bit high, everything still slightly unreal. Glynn, dark-haired, grey-eyed, had his face tilted towards mine, one hand pulling me gently towards him. The hum of the fan heater and the spatter of wintry rain on the windows was hypnotic as his chianti-sweet lips touched mine, pressing harder, his fingers in my hair. The moment consumed us in an instant. We were engrossed, quickly lost in each other, melting into one…

when the brass doorknocker was rapped three times, sharp and loud, a matter of feet away, echoing around the stillness of the house long after it stopped.

We jumped apart, the effect like a bucket of ice in the face.

"I'll go," he said.

"What if it's Keith Cribbs with…?"

But Glynn had already opened the door. And I heard a woman's voice. Strident, confident, well-spoken, very similar to Anna, the agent's. At first, I thought she'd come back for some reason. But it wasn't her. Instead, Glynn ushered in a tall, striking-looking woman wrapped in a turquoise pashmina, raven hair cut pixie-style. She had hazel button eyes, rose-pink cheeks and a wart at the outer corner of her upper lip, frankly impossible to miss.

Behind her, Glynn was clutching a bottle wrapped in lilac tissue paper as, thrusting a huge bouquet of Waitrose flowers at me, she lunged in for an air kiss.

"Welcome! Welcome! To our quaint little village. I'm Fay Welch. Duncan and Aiden are working this evening but I didn't want to delay. We're absolutely delighted you're here. Super-thrilled. And look, I'm really sorry but I've got to dash, do you mind? Only I'm on my way to the history society and it's all been arranged."

"Not at all. Thank you for dropping in, this is so kind of you."

"And we'd love it if you'd come over for dinner on Saturday?"

Glynn was already nodding enthusiastically, trying to hold Skip back from sniffing the backs of Fay's ankles.

"Lyddie?"

"Thank you," I said. "That'd be lovely."

I liked her immediately. She seemed eccentric, the eclectic mix of clothes – long red skirt, black court shoes with purple tights, checked shirt, green tweed jacket and the pashmina with tassels – resembling a frenzied plunge into a dressing-up box. None of the colours or styles matched. It could be said she was one of the worst dressed people imaginable, yet somehow she pulled it off. Glamorous and generous. That's what came across in those first few minutes – an explosion of drama, like an exotic bird bursting out of the back of a thrift shop. And she really was eye-catchingly pretty.

"Anything you want, anything you need," she quipped, fleeing the scene with a wave of her hand. "We're at Ashe House, the little crooked one with steps down the side, about halfway up the lane. Oh, and don't bring anything, don't dress up – just come as you are! No dogs, though. Sorry, but I'm allergic."

I followed her to the door.

"Oh, before you go, I don't suppose you'd be able to recommend a log supplier, would you? Only we haven't got any and–"

The full glare of the porch light was in her face and I saw she was older than first impressions suggested. Maybe mid-fifties? The wart was huge, though – conker brown and quivering like jelly.

"A lot of people get theirs from Keith Cribbs but I definitely wouldn't recommend you going round there."

"Oh."

"We go to Zach. Zach Stipple – Agnus's boy. Do you have a pen?"

"Yes, just a sec."

"I'll get Aiden to drop you some of ours tomorrow," she said, scribbling down Zach's number. "Just to tide you over. Don't worry if you're not in. He'll leave them by the garage."

"Thank you. Thank you ever so much, Fay."

I waved her off into thick fog, waiting until her

footsteps muffled and the sound of her car started up.

"Told you," Glynn said, closing the door. "Told you this is going to be the best thing we've ever done. She's lovely. We're going to be so happy here, I can feel it. Welcome to your new life, Lyds!"

And we were happy. For ages and ages we were. Even when everything became increasingly strange, progressively more bizarre as the weeks passed. I do remember being puzzled though, after she'd merged into the night, wondering why she'd said not to go over to Keith Cribbs. Why?

"Don't ask me," Glynn said. "Maybe he fancies her?"

I shuddered inwardly. "Poor Fay."

He frowned. "Something's just come to mind, don't ask me why, probably your description of Cribbs. But one of our neighbours when I was a kid, kept pigeons – he was a widower, late seventies – anyhow, I must have been about thirteen or so when I went into that pigeon shed of his. The whole place was plastered with hard porn. Pictures cut out of magazines and stuck on the walls. Not the usual porn, either. But specially ordered, cross-the-line, puke-making, stomach-turning stuff."

We looked at each other.

He shrugged. "Just that maybe she knows something we don't?"

***

Chapter Four

That night we kept the lamp on in the hall downstairs. The glow of light around the doorframe relieved the intensity of the darkness, plus we were far less likely to break our necks searching for the bathroom. The scratching, rustling and creaking noises were also less alarming in the presence of that light. But the all-pervading, absolute silence did take some getting used to, and for the second night in a row I lay unable to sleep.

Sometime in the early hours, though, I must finally have dropped off.

When into the deathly hush came a terrible, agonised scream.

Instantly, I jumped awake. "What the hell was that?"

Glynn murmured some expletive at being woken, but reached for my hand. "Shh!"

A few minutes later, though, it came again and I felt him tense.

The primeval, blood-curdling cry rent the freezing night air, echoing across the valley, an eerie sound that stirred up a deep well of ancient fears.

"A vixen," Glynn said, after a while. "Just a vixen."

I lay wide awake again, heart thumping, fixated on the

border of light around the doorway, thankful I didn't live in an age when there were only candles... where being born into a family there, especially as a girl, meant no escape to the world beyond the bridge. Here was all that was known, their madness her madness, their rules, her rules... God, the nights must have felt so long! What had they done for all those hours after the winter sun went down? Poor, cold, malnourished, unable to read... And what of those alone in the endless, silent blackness of night? Widowed? Bereaved? Or shackled to a brutal, murderous husband? What did they do for all that time?

A strange train of thought, indeed – drifting back through centuries, momentarily trapped as if I was there. The coldness in the cottage had the feel of a cave, and I fancied I could smell mildew, pipe smoke, wet earth and straw, aware on some level of humming, half dreaming about a young girl, a maid, weaving, twining something around her hands, more than one girl... and a chant repeated, a rhyme. My eyes sought the light around the door. There was history here, I told myself. That was all, centuries of lives... a stone well... and maids in a ring...

The next thing I knew it was morning, and the valley was a haze of breath-taking beauty. An icy mist hovered over the low-lying fields, the clump of trees atop Barrow Ridge skeletal against a rose-tinted sky. Glynn had opened the curtains to the stunning view, and vaguely I recalled his words before he left for work, that there'd been a heron over the marsh, the majestic span of its wings flapping slowly, calmly, as it lifted off over the fields, a relic from a prehistoric age.

For a while I lay peacefully, in a cocoon of serenity. Until a truck crunched onto the gravel drive outside and a door slammed.

Footsteps clomped heavily around the side of the house, followed by the solid tumble of logs hitting the ground. Oh, of course! Fay said Aiden, presumably her husband, would bring us some of theirs. We'd be able to have a fire that night. Still, my body was tense, breath tight, shallow. What if he banged on the door and I had to go down like this? If he was like Keith Cribbs? Looking me up and down, smirking, as I stood at the door in my nightdress? I lay rigid with indecision as footsteps thudded back and forth. Then the engine started up again and the truck reversed out in a spray of gravel.

Relief washed over me, the oddly disconcerting dream from the night before already fading. All was well, no need for anxiety, and there was loads of time yet before starting the new job, to settle in, and go for walks with Skip. Time I was immensely grateful for, something of a honeymoon period as it turned out.

We didn't have a huge amount to unpack. I was twenty-eight, Glynn in his early thirties. We'd only been together for three years, and before meeting him I'd rented various flats and bedsits. Mostly it was just clothes, CDs, lots and lots of books – I loved reading, especially ghostly thrillers, mysteries and historical fiction – and jointly there were household items and plants, quite a lot of those. We were going to buy new furniture for the cottage, to seek out unusual and unique items, probably reclamation pieces and paint them ourselves. As such, we'd brought with us only the bed, sofa, and kitchen table and chairs from the last house. I did my best to hang curtains that didn't fit, planning what colours and textures to replace them with, but for the time-being at least, it began to look more like home. And on Friday I ventured into town.

Mid-morning and the mist had lifted, a low, wintry sun swimming in and out of the clouds. Donna Summer was on the CD, *Love to love you, baby*, on full blast as I put my foot down on an open road. It was exciting, my heart was soaring, I was just so happy, so high, the zero point of all future potentials exquisite. What would this journey in life be like? Because it felt like it had only just begun.

The town was Sherbourne, with its mellow, grey-gold stone buildings, an abbey, expensive boutiques, and private schools that had turrets and a church, originally stately homes with mile upon mile of walls bordering the playing fields, woods, river frontage, and estate cottages. A vastly different world to the one I'd been brought up in, it felt hushed, genteel, an old England I'd only ever seen in films. For ages I wandered around, food-shopping mostly, until lunchtime when schoolchildren swarmed into the town centre, and I decided to head for home.

I was dreaming, I suppose, imagining what it must have been like to go to a school resembling a palace, when I almost missed the red signpost for Creech Cross. And that was when I properly acknowledged it, I think – driving back over the bridge into the village – how the atmosphere changed. There wasn't anything visible to mark the spot, no dramatic alteration in the terrain, nothing that could be described, other than coming through the tunnel of trees, the lane dipping down, then going over the bridge and briefly being transported into a liminal, transitional space. After which there was a discernible, perceptible difference.

Suddenly the music, Stevie Nicks singing *Gold Dust Woman*, seemed too loud and I switched it off. I don't know, it was weird, but I didn't feel quite myself, instead slightly queasy and mildly dizzy. As before, there was a distinct sense of not being in the present time. Of having passed through a gateway. But it was nothing I could define without sounding insane, even to myself, so I dismissed it as nonsensical, putting it down to disorientation following the move, and proceeded to drive slowly down the lane. I wanted to have a good look at the village.

The sign for The Blackthorn Brank was about halfway down on the left. It hung outside a Devon longhouse, a building with no facing windows and a gravelled courtyard at the back. I wondered who lived there now it was no longer an inn.

That day, all was quiet and still, no one around. I was looking for the little crooked house described by Fay. *Ashe House*, however, definitely wasn't little. I knew what a little house was and it was what I'd grown up in – not three storeys with huge bay windows, stone steps spiralling into a courtyard, and an iron-studded front door bigger than that of a church. There were hotels smaller than this house.

It was slightly set back from the lane, at the end of a short, curved driveway. I'm not sure why she'd called it crooked, except it was very tall, with tiny windows on the top floor, a cluster of chimney pots, and several flights of steps… But it was definitely Fay's house. Beyond that, was a row of alms cottages covered in ivy, and several traditional thatches with cream cob walls. Most of the village houses, however, were hidden from view, either behind hedges and trees or at the end of long, private muddy tracks, with mailboxes on the lane. There really wasn't much else to see.

Then on the opposite side to Fay's house, extending all the way down to our cottage, was woodland. This completely obscured the view, so I didn't see the red

Shogun truck parked on the drive until I'd rounded the bend. A young lad in a baseball cap was at the wheel, the back piled with logs. We'd had no word.

"I'm ever so sorry, have you been here long?"

Without answering, he jumped out and walked to the tail end of the truck.

"Where do you want them?"

"Are you Zach? Zach, erm…?"

"Stipple," he mumbled.

"Yes, yes, of course. Thank you for being so quick. We didn't know when you were coming."

There was no conversation forthcoming from Zach. At least six-two, he was skinny with lank dark hair, and avoided eye contact.

I led the way round to the side of the cottage.

"Could you put them here by the log store, please? With the others, the ones, erm… round here, anyway…"

He worked without stopping, and when he'd finished unloading I handed him the cash Glynn had left in the kitchen, which he counted out in front of me.

About eighteen, I thought. Absolutely no social skills at all. Not bad looking, deep-set green-grey eyes, even features, deathly pale though… Drugs?

When suddenly his head jerked up and he looked straight at me, so piercingly my heart nearly missed a beat.

"You should be careful not to judge. It isn't what it looks like round here. Don't judge, Lydia. It's important."

Lydia?

I was so shocked I couldn't think how to respond.

His voice was deep, powerful, authoritative and articulate, the expression and demeanour that of an older man, a much older man, and at complete odds with all that had gone before.

Don't judge!

Judge?

Who had I judged?

I was still standing there with my mouth open when he jumped back into the truck and drove off.

Suddenly, my whole being plummeted into shame. My face was burning. He was right. I'd always done it! Keith Cribbs I'd deemed sinister. Even Fay's dress sense I'd quietly judged. I saw that in an instant. I had always judged, quick summaries made in seconds. And somehow, that gauche young man had seen through to the core of me, at how horrible I was inside. His words had the effect of a gong hitting the solar plexus, reverberating through my body, an echo ping-ponging around my skull. I felt terrible, as if the darkest part of my soul had been illuminated for all to see.

Don't judge!

Who was he? What the hell just happened?

I could not have known though, could never have guessed, not then, that the boy's meaning was so entirely different to the way I'd interpreted it.

***

Chapter Five

I couldn't tell Glynn about Zach Stipple. No way. I just couldn't bring myself to. How the boy had changed so completely. It was as if... it's hard to describe... but as if another person had emerged.

After he drove off, my heart continued to thump so hard it was pulsing in my ears. I stood in the driveway looking towards Buckthorn Woods, the trees a cluster of sentinels guarding the gloomy interior. And a familiar feeling, an age-old bête noir, began then, to rise like a troll from a well. I recognised it instantly, the panicky feeling of having been rocked from a position of emotional surety, to flailing around in thin air, forced to acknowledge there were things beyond the limitation of my understanding, things unseen, inexplicable.

Yet I could not deny what I'd just seen and heard. I could not lie to myself. Zach had momentarily been transformed from a sullen teenager – one who'd barely looked up or responded – to a commanding authority with the knowing expression of a far older man. My stomach lurched uncomfortably as I forced myself to face the truth. That's what had made it so disturbing; the boy's entire demeanour had seemed so very, very old, the message not coming from him but rather *through* him. From another. From some ancient being.

I can't tell Glynn. He'll think I'm mad.

I must have let myself into the house, put away the shopping, made up a fire and cooked a meal, but I don't recall doing any it. Instead, I repeatedly examined what had just happened. Had I imagined it? Like I'd imagined the change of atmosphere driving over the bridge, the blue orbs in the bedroom, and the sound of a dog scampering around in the kitchen that couldn't have been Skip? Perhaps it was due to stress and anxiety? That would make sense. Like before, a long, long time ago. It's what would be said. What Glynn would say. They all would.

Truth be told, I'd endured fluctuating states of anxiety for most of my life, and so it was probably like I said – just my old bête-noir. I'd also had strange things happen before, each having a profound effect that lasted weeks, months, never completely forgotten. For example, sometimes I heard another person's thoughts. I felt I knew them, their essence, within seconds of meeting them. 'Thin-skinned' was how I'd been described. Oversensitive. Maybe one day I'd know why I attracted sudden outbursts, verbal attacks, unusual animosity and, like that day in January outside the house in Creech Cross, received direct messages from a total stranger.

No need to tell Glynn.

No need to worry him.

No need to burden him with any of this.

By the time he arrived home that evening, I'd talked myself around pretty well, and he walked in to find a log fire and supper waiting for him. I liked cooking, did my best to source natural ingredients and to understand what nutrients were needed for good health. I also found the process of chopping, stirring and mixing therapeutic. It was a nice evening. We had wine and watched a film, and for a while I almost forgot Zach's words and what he could have meant.

But that night, despite leaving the lamp on downstairs, sleep would not come. It was the strangest feeling, and I'd sensed it from day one – not exactly a prescience of impending doom, more a sense of forewarning. But back then I could not have known what was coming. At each subsequent stage there would be an explanation, a brushing-off, a dusting-down, before the next bizarre episode unfolded, one after the other.

And next was Fay's extraordinary party.

I don't know why I'd assumed it would be dinner for just the four of us, perhaps with the addition of their son, but it wasn't. The whole thing was nothing at all like I'd envisaged. For a start, she didn't have one son but two, her husband was Duncan not Aiden, and when we arrived Fay wasn't even there.

Duncan flung open the door and for a good few seconds I was completely thrown. I'd thought a man married to someone like her would be… oh, I don't know, sophisticated, maybe dry, laconic – she the colourful artistic one, he indulgent and sensible. But Duncan was the polar opposite to that pre-conceived image. He stood framed in the arched doorway, already a bit worse for wear, glass of wine in one hand, cigarette in the other.

"Greetings, fellow munchkins," he said. "Greetings! Not in Kansas anymore, eh?"

Glynn handed over the bottles of wine we'd brought – one red, one white – chatting while I gawped, grateful for a second or two to compose my face.

Duncan had very few teeth, and the wind whistled through his words on a lisp. Bird-thin legs had bowed into the shape of a wishbone. And in the light of the porch it was clear to see his bottle-green trousers were embarrassingly stained around the zipper. Terrible halitosis wafted forth long before he lunged in for a kiss, pulling me close with overly keen wiry fingers. It wasn't an air kiss, either.

"I'm afraid Fay will be late back from art class tonight, but come in, come in. The boys are here and so are Monica and Tim."

Boys? Monica and Tim?

Glynn and I looked at each other with raised eyebrows and shrugged, before following him into what was a warm, bright kitchen with a spectacular atrium, and a view of the courtyard with the spiral staircase. A multi-fuel stove dominated a generously proportioned room furnished with a couple of sofas and a TV set; and everyone turned to look as we walked in.

"This is Aiden, Fay's son," Duncan said, introducing us to a surly-looking man with jet hair and dark eyes. He wore a tight black shirt with black jeans, and sat eyeing us from one of the low sofas, a slight smirk playing around his mouth.

"Aiden, these are our new neighbours: Glynn and–"

Glynn nodded, shook his hand. "Hi!"

Stepping forward, I proffered my hand, too. "Lyddie. Lyddie Spicer."

To my chagrin, Aiden merely nodded and took another sip of wine, leaving me obliged to drop my offer of a handshake.

"Don't mind him," Duncan said, moving us on. "Bloody rude most of the time. And this is Fay's other son, Bailey."

Bailey was a much younger, thinner version of Aiden. At a guess, I'd say the elder was late twenties and the other about eighteen. Actually, very much like the young Anthony Perkins to look at – the guy who played Norman Bates – although not remotely sinister. He was just gawky and a bit nervous, wide smile, a little intense.

"Hi!"

Mercifully, Bailey was easy company and laughed at everything I said. Although, after a minute or two I had the distinct feeling he wasn't quite grasping the conversation, that I could have read out the local obituaries and had the same reaction.

"Do you have a job or go to college?" I asked.

He laughed and shook his head.

"No." His cheeks were flushed and he was shuffling from one foot to the other. "I sometimes work for Duncan."

It was just beginning to dawn on me that these boys weren't Duncan's, when a glass of white wine appeared at my elbow, along with another waft of stale garlic.

"Sorry that took so long," said Duncan, waving a cigarette around in a haphazard gesture. "Come and meet Monica and Tim. They live next door in Curfew Cottage."

I didn't start writing this diary of events until a few weeks later, after an episode with Keith Cribbs, so what I recall of the conversation with Monica is somewhat sketchy. However, I've done my best to recall it, and certain phrases stuck in my mind and most definitely stayed there.

Theirs was the low-thatched cottage between Ashe

House and The Blackthorn Brank.

"Curfew Cottage. Unusual name," I said.

"It is odd, isn't it?" Monica agreed. "We're not sure how it got its name, but they do say the abbey's curfew bell can still be heard at certain times of the year. An old wives' tale, of course, since the whole thing's in ruins. But ours is one of the few original cottages."

"The monks had a curfew?"

"Nuns. They were nuns."

"Oh, I see. How long have you lived here?"

"Eight years."

We got chatting about the history of the village, and she went on to say, "This whole valley was once a site of dark witchcraft, you know? Apparently they held esbats over where the ruins are. A long time ago, of course. We're talking centuries. But you know how superstitious and terrified everyone was back in the day?"

"How did you find out about the witchcraft?"

"We were told. Oh, and there was a bottle in our chimney. The sweep found it. You see, that's what people in the dark ages did – put bottles up chimneys." She raised her eyes to the ceiling. "Ours had a little cork stuck with pins in it and they said an evil spirit was trapped in there. There were hundreds found across the county, all stuffed high into chimneys."

I found Monica fascinating. She was tiny and wizened, bent almost double, with thinning crimson hair that barely concealed her scalp. She walked with two intricately carved ebony sticks, putting all her weight on one leg and then the other, swaying alarmingly from side to side like a pendulum, certainly requiring a lot of room; yet there was no disputing the strength of that movement. Monica was tough, a strong persona. She had clear, deep brown eyes and skin weathered to hide, like one of those old Mediterranean matriarchs dressed all in black sitting on a porch. Except Monica 'did' glitter – long, flowing skirt, poncho, all twinkling and flashing under the lights. Impossible to tell how old she was. I guessed late fifties but she could have been a decade either side. It also transpired she was employed as a criminal psychologist at a secure prison unit, and belonged to the local history society. She told me all about the alms houses and the fulling mill, and was about to say more about the Creech Abbey nuns when Tim joined us.

Tim was as vague as his wife was definite, as pale as she was vibrant, as feeble as she was robust. Apparently, he'd been in the Civil Service until a recent illness left him stripped of all confidence. Once or twice I thought he might burst into tears, and I felt dreadfully sorry for him. Pink, trembly, weepy…

Don't judge!

I brought myself up sharp. I could have everything wrong about all of them. I'd always been so quick with my intuition, usually spot-on, but after Zach's words I could no longer be sure. Really, though – did it matter? These people would hopefully become friends, or at least good neighbours, and vice-versa. That was it. But if I was to call it, I'd say I liked all of them enormously and soon relaxed, laughing along with everyone else when Fay returned halfway through dinner. She'd phoned at some point to say she'd been held up, that Duncan was to serve the casserole left in the oven. And when she finally blew in, she was all of a fluster.

"I'm so, so sorry. It's always the same – I had to clear

everything away and then drive Wendy and Sue home. Sorry, everyone, dreadfully sorry."

"Come and relax, Mummy, have a glass of wine," Duncan slurred. "We've saved you some cashrole."

Mummy?

"Just the wine. I've already eaten."

No one missed a beat. She'd already eaten…

"My wife's one of these people who picks up the can for everyone else," he explained. "WI, church fund-raisers, art class, history society, anyone who's ill and needs a lift to hospital, desserts or wine glasses providing, leaflets to hand out, raffle tickets to sell, it's always Fay."

"Probably why the house is so dirty," she said, hanging up her pashmina.

I hadn't noticed until I went to use the downstairs toilet, but it really was. Still stifling a giggle that Duncan had called his wife 'Mummy', I managed to avoid catching Glynn's eye and escaped the room. But she was right – that big, beautiful house was filthy. The doors were chipped, walls scuffed, carrier bags and shoes left everywhere, stove coated in grease, furniture powdery with dust, and a wet grey towel hung in a downstairs bathroom that had exposed plaster work and wires hanging down where a light fitting should be.

"We're doing it up," Duncan was telling Glynn when I came back. "But it's going to take another decade to get it to where it should be."

"How long have you been here?" Glynn asked.

"Eight years."

"Oh, like you!" I said to Monica.

After that, it was easy to remember the details of the evening because I've never quite been able to erase it.

Fay had taken a burnt offering out of the oven and was having to use the knife like a hacksaw to cut through the pastry. I think it was some sort of fruit flan and the syrup had welded to the base like superglue. Her face was getting redder and redder, earrings jangling madly. The two boys were smirking, wisecracks flying back and forth.

"Should we go get an axle grinder?" I said. "Might be qui… cker…"

The joke died on my lips. It was meant to be funny, to add to the hilarity.

But Fay stopped what she was doing, knife mid-air, and shot me a look that made my stomach contract. One second. That was all. She was so livid she couldn't hide it, the button eyes turned obsidian black, the sinews of her face tight.

Bailey snorted wine, had a hand over his mouth, and I didn't need to look at Glynn to know his shoulders were shaking. It was very, very hard not to laugh.

"Sorry, I didn't mean to be rude."

A mortifying silence followed while she resumed hacking off a piece of the tart, scraped a gooey mess onto a plate, then plonked it in front of me.

"Pass her the cream, Bailey."

"Thank you. Actually, it looks delicious. I'm hopeless at baking."

Thank God, I didn't add the word, 'too' at the end of that sentence because it almost slipped out. The moment passed anyway, and other people were duly served. Silently.

But it got worse.

"You've all been here for years, then?" I said. "So, you must know everyone in the village? What are they like?"

Duncan sloshed out another glass of wine, and Bailey

started to giggle. He laughed like a drain almost constantly, chuckling to himself.

"One thing you should know," said Duncan. "You have to be third generation to be accepted here. Unless you're an Ettrick, a Cribbs or a Stipple, you're an incomer and you always will be. A decade changes nothing."

"You might like Kendra, though," said Tim. "She married Mark Ettrick."

"There's a bit of a divide here," Monica explained. "You could almost draw a line down the middle of the village."

"So, apart from those of us around this table," I said, "everyone else in the village is either local, or married one?"

"No, there's Mervin and Rosamund at The Old Rectory near the abbey," said Fay, tipping a packet of macaroons onto a plate. "We've had them over a few times but they're not always here, they're dreadfully busy. That's their second home."

"He's designing us a new bridge," Monica said. "Obviously the old one's completely unsafe, and he's doing it in his own time. Isn't that fantastic?"

"We're super excited about it," said Fay.

"The old stone one after the red post? He's having it rebuilt?"

"Designing a totally new one, Lydia."

"Oh, I see."

"And there are the Cades, of course," said Duncan.

There was a collective bracing, a couple of smiles too bright, or had I imagined it? But here's where 'awkward' upped a gear. Bailey must have sensed it too, because his entire body was shaking with either mirth or nerves, maybe both. He was doing this thing of flipping a fork over and over and over.

"Stop doing that, Bailey!" Fay snapped.

He threw the fork down.

"Strange things go on in this place," he mumbled.

"Who are the Cades?" I asked. "What are they like? Whereabouts do they live?"

"We don't do gossip, dear," said Monica.

"Oh! No, of course not. I was just—"

But no one answered the question.

"Now! Who's for coffee?" said Fay. "I vote we take them into the front room. Bailey, go and give the fire a poke."

"Good idea," said Monica.

Everyone was standing up, chairs being pushed back.

"Where do the Cades live?" I asked again.

Why was that gossip? Why was no one answering? I couldn't believe it. Why were they all ignoring me? Even Glynn was walking out of the door.

The room emptied in a flash.

And then quite suddenly it was just me and Aiden.

With one arm slung over the back of a chair, he was staring directly into my eyes, a slow, confident smile twitching his lips as if he'd thoroughly enjoyed the spectacle of my humiliation.

I felt about fourteen.

"The Tollhouse," he said quietly. "The Cades live at The Tollhouse."

But here was the worst thing about that moment; not the embarrassment at being called a gossip or ignored, but the shock of electricity that passed between myself and Aiden Welch. Undeniable. Unmistakeable. And my hands shook visibly as I picked up to drink from, what I realised too late, was an empty wine glass. There was nothing I could do about it. He was not at all my type physically or personally, and I truly loved Glynn. All I can say is the more he stared at me, the more I no longer felt like myself.

The heat in the kitchen was a furnace.

"Shall we?" he said.

My face was probably red. Cheeks aflame, brain a fog.

"Shall we what?"

He smiled. "Adjourn for coffee? What did you think I meant?"

Confused, perplexed, I couldn't think what to say or how to be. Yet his eyes were fixed on me. Behind them was a flicker of movement, as fleeting as a bat melting into the night, and it was almost impossible to look away.

And so, in the absence of any coherent thought, and to my own mortification, I simply stood up, turned and fled.

***

Chapter Six

The evening became progressively more unsettling, but it wasn't until we were walking back down the lane at nearly midnight, that Glynn and I could exchange stories. For a while, we were quiet, torches in hand, heads bent against the prevailing wind. It took a lot for him to feel uneasy, but his silence and the hunch of his shoulders told me he was.

For me, it started the moment I walked into the lounge. Having bolted in from the kitchen, I'd vaguely hoped to find refuge next to Glynn on the sofa for the rest of the evening... to sit quietly, let him do what he does best – be congenial, funny, and sociable, putting everyone at ease. Instead, I walked into a time warp, and a deeply buried memory reared up and hit me in the face.

The room had the same high ceiling and small paper lightshade as the other one, from long, long ago – almost identical maroon walls, brown cotton curtains that didn't meet in the middle, and a hotch-potch array of cracked leather sofas, wooden chairs, dingy beanbags, and occasional tables. A communal place for people to sit in separate groups, like a student hall or a social club... *or for patients...*

The only difference between Fay's room and the one

my mother and I had once sat in, waiting for the doctor, was the open fire in the grate. The other room, in what had once been a Victorian residence of some splendour, had no comforting fire, just a bouquet of dried flowers on the hearth; and a children's corner with a box of battered toys, an abacus and some scuffed Penguin books.

My dismay, momentary, was a catapult straight back into the past without warning. Twice in as many days, I found myself reeling from shock and blindly dropped onto the nearest empty chair, trying to recover without anyone noticing. I was twenty-eight years old, married, happy, safe. The fire was crackling, belting out heat, and Fay was clattering around in the kitchen making coffee. The past was the past.

Fortunately, it seemed no one had noticed my alarm, everyone standing around talking. I then realised the tables and chairs had been grouped for card playing, and was relieved when Bailey and Tim joined me.

It was going to be fine, easy. I could relax, surely? And yet I couldn't. There was something about the atmosphere that felt fake, staged, and had all evening. I couldn't pinpoint quite what it was – a feeling the others were play-acting – as if they all had some secret knowledge Glynn and I weren't party to. Look, I told myself, even if there was something they all knew about the village, whether it was Keith Cribbs, as intimated by Fay, or the Cades, it had nothing to do with us.

But I was curious, always have been; couldn't leave things alone, could I?

Over the first round of whist, I said to Bailey, "Do you like living here, then?"

He had the jitters. Oh boy, did he have the jitters, one

long leg so restless it occurred to me he could be on haloperidol or something. And at my question his leg jittered faster. It hadn't been noticeable in the kitchen, but then again he'd been on the opposite side of the table.

Avoiding eye contact, he played a card, examined the rest of his hand and shrugged.

"Good, yeah."

"What was the local school like? Was it in Sherbourne? I went there the other day, it was gorgeous."

Tim was eyeing me at close range. And I sensed rather than saw his large, watery blue eyes travel down to my legs and then back up again. Next chance I had, I'd adjust the way I was sitting.

"Or Yeovil?" I said. "I suppose all the village schools have closed nowadays?"

"We didn't go to school. Mum home-schooled us."

"Wow, really? So when did you do your exams? GCSEs? I'm intrigued. I've never met anyone who didn't have to suffer school before. I hated it."

He turned the colour of a tomato.

"Stop interrogating him," said Tim.

"Oh! Was I? Sorry, Bailey. I didn't mean to. So you work for your dad? That's good."

"Duncan, yeah. He's not my dad. Sometimes."

I played a card. "Building? Is it a sort of apprenticeship? I don't know anything about the building trade. Hod-carrying? Roofing?"

It was then he looked into my eyes and I saw in them a kind of hopelessness, and it occurred to me he wasn't on a road to anywhere, that possibly he was given labouring jobs sometimes. At best.

"You live in such a beautiful place, anyway," I said.

"We heard a vixen the other night."

At this he brightened. Like a light flicking on in a dark house.

"She sounds like she's being murdered, doesn't she?"

"Yes, I wondered what on earth it was, at first."

"Mating call."

We all three then chatted about foxes, badgers, hares, owls – there were short-eared owls in Horseman's Wood, the name of the woods at the end of our garden, also barn owls and tawnies in the valley. Bailey, it turned out, was extremely knowledgeable on wildlife, and I learned a lot; that the area was rich with rare birds – redback shrikes, wrynecks, ousel and even a nightjar. He told me about wildflowers and some of the original local names – marybuds, robin hood, eltrot, gilty cup and laylock – along with those for animals and birds – nestle tripes were the smallest pigs in the litter, butsies were chicks, hummocks were cows. The evening improved, coffee was followed by brandy chasers, and the feeling I'd had earlier, of everyone knowing something except us, slowly dissolved. All too soon the evening was wrapping up, and in the end it had been easy, nice.

By then, I'd come around to reasoning that the odd atmosphere when the Cades had been mentioned could have been due to an upset or falling-out no one had wanted to discuss with newbies, and why should they? There'd also been the look Fay had given me, but then again I'd been a bit rude, and the moment replayed uncomfortably. What about Aiden? I dismissed that, too. My imagination. A moment of confusion. Got it embarrassingly wrong.

Duncan's group had thrown in the cards, and they were leaning back in their chairs, yawning. Fay and Monica were in the kitchen, and the dishwasher was whirring.

"Home time," said Tim, jumping up. "Just popping to the bathroom.

"Blimey, it's nearly midnight. We ought to be going, too," I said, shooting a look over to Glynn. "You're so lucky to live here, Bailey. It really is a beautiful village. Well, the whole area is. You ought to see where I grew up!"

But he'd stopped laughing. In a heartbeat, he was suddenly serious and still, no sign of jittery limbs or nervousness as he looked directly into my eyes. My stomach contracted a little as it had with Zach. His whole demeanour was changing. What was coming?

"I have to look after Gran," he said.

"Gran?"

Fay was coming back in, I sensed her somewhere behind and knew Bailey had, too. The room was a blur of people getting coats and standing up, when he bent closer, his voice low.

"I take care of her. I do everything."

My first thought was why no one had mentioned her existence before. My second was why a teenaged boy was left to do this... why they didn't bring in a professional carer.

Then he pretty much answered the question.

His forehead nearly touched mine as he leaned over before standing up, and his voice, when it breathed hot over my ear, was nothing like the giggling, boyish one he'd used all evening.

"She's an exorcist."

***

Chapter Seven

"Bloody hell!" Glynn said, after I'd finished telling him about Bailey.

Our footsteps were dull clomps on the wet tarmac, the first few spots of sleety rain spitting in our faces.

"I know, and no one else even mentioned her. I wonder why?"

"Does seem odd, almost like she doesn't exist."

"I'm guessing she's Fay's mother, I don't know why, but–"

"An exorcist, though?" Glynn was really shaken. "What's that all about? Don't they have to be priests?"

"Not necessarily. There are spirit release therapists and non-religious exorcists."

"I don't like that kind of stuff, Lyddie. Freaks me out."

It freaked me out, too. I was thinking both Zach and Bailey had something alarming going on, and a truckload of a million fears was rattling in.

"I know. You think I do?"

"No, of course not. I'm just wondering why that young lad has to look after the old lady. In secret."

"Me, too. Could be she prefers family to look after her."

"Fay's always out. She said so herself. Why's she left it

to the boy, though? Why just him? Aiden's built like a carthorse, so why doesn't he help? Why is only Bailey looking after her, especially a soft lad like that?"

"I don't know but it's not our business. Oh, I've just thought of something!"

Glynn was into himself again, his profile set to grim. "What?"

"No one asked me. Again. Not one person asked me a single question – where I came from, what I do, nothing. Isn't that odd?"

"How much did you tell Anna, the agent?"

Anna had shown us several houses and I'd chatted to her openly, told her loads. "Ah!"

"They already knew."

I nodded. "Makes sense."

Did it, though? Did it make sense? Why would an estate agent pass our personal information to people in the village? Even if Anna had relatives here, they wouldn't be relative newcomers like Fay and Monica. Actually, it didn't make sense at all. But we were rounding the corner to the cottage by then, it was late, and we were tired.

Skip ran up to the door to greet us. He hadn't been left alone so long since we arrived, and we made a fuss of him. Glynn then took him out for a quick spin round the garden, while I poured a couple of glasses of filtered water and took them upstairs. Inside of fifteen minutes, we were lying in bed listening to sleet spatter against the window, both of us reflecting on the evening. Glynn still hadn't told me what was on his mind. But there was definitely something.

"What did you make of Monica and Tim?"

"Really liked them," he said. "I liked all of them, even

Aiden once he got talking. Bit uncomfortable once or twice, though."

"How's that?"

"Just… Ah, it's nothing really. Couple of rough, sexist jokes, you know? It was about the pub, The Blackthorn Brank."

"Similar to what Keith Cribbs said?"

"Yeah, pushed it a bit further, though – woman shackled to the mantelpiece by the head, the um… possibilities…"

"Ugh!"

"And something else. Something about mothers… MILFs. Bit squirmy, that's all."

I hadn't been wrong about Glynn, then. Absolutely he'd been uneasy.

"I can imagine."

We were quiet for a while.

"Didn't you think it was odd that no one answered when I asked about the Cades? I was a bit embarrassed, Glynn. Even you left the room."

"Yeah, they did all go a bit quiet, come to think of it. Sorry."

"They're at The Tollhouse, anyway. Aiden told me. I think it's at the junction with Upper Creech and The Old Rectory, overlooking the abbey ruins."

"Carrie Cade's the mother," he said after a while. "The son's called Slim. And there's a daughter, Mallory. Can't remember the husband's name. Aiden was saying they've got half a dozen caravans there, and an old cottage that was supposed to have been demolished. Apparently there's tarpaulin over the roof. Slim's in there with his girlfriend."

"He told you quite a lot, then. Thought we weren't

supposed to gossip?"

"Well, Aiden did. Soon as Daddy Duncan left to do drinks or go to the bathroom for the hundredth time, Aiden gossiped like a backyard biddy pegging out the washing."

"Funny! So where did they come from? Seems all the incomers are from London."

"Dunno."

"I wonder why they went quiet about them, though?"

"A falling-out they didn't want to discuss? Just a guess. We're new here, after all. They haven't psyched us out yet."

"Yes, I thought that, too – that there'd been a falling-out or something. So, Aiden didn't say any more?"

"Not really. Duncan shut him up once or twice, now I come to think of it."

"Weird, this divide thing Monica mentioned, isn't it? I suppose it's natural for locals to be wary of newbies, but we only want to live in the country and have a peaceful life. Tim and Monica left London after his illness, apparently. He didn't say what had been wrong, just that his nerves were shattered, and he needed peace and quiet."

"Fay's first husband died when the boys were little."

"Ah, that's sad. She home-schooled them both. I didn't ask her what she'd done for a living. Do you know? I mean, was she a teacher or…?"

I felt him shrug beside me in the dark. "Don't know. You'll have to wheedle it out of her."

"Seems they were all looking for a sanctuary, doesn't it? Tim after his illness, Fay after being bereaved?"

"Could be."

"And all about the same time. What a coincidence! I enjoyed tonight in the end though, didn't you? We're ever so lucky to be here. There are short-eared owls in the woods behind us. It's called Horseman's Wood."

He put his arm around me, and we were already falling asleep, smiling to ourselves, remembering Fay's concrete-hard pastry, my stupid quip about the axle grinder, and Duncan calling Fay, 'Mummy'. But something about Fay had actually disturbed me. A niggling feeling that was to rise time and time again. There was an undercurrent. Maybe it was because of the mother upstairs? A secret to protect? And who wouldn't want to protect her family from speculation, from judgement, about something like that? They didn't know us. Couldn't trust us. And they'd been incredibly kind.

Yet for some unfathomable reason I wasn't completely convinced.

Don't judge... it's important... it isn't what it looks like round here...

There was something else behind the masks, behind the brittle shell of pretence that had cracked more than once that evening, and it wasn't about a sick old lady upstairs.

I couldn't think anymore, was submerging into sleep, seamlessly slipping away.

Only to jerk violently awake again seconds later.

Except it wasn't seconds.

It was three in the morning.

And there was a man sitting on the edge of the bed.

***

Chapter Eight

Not a living man, but a ghost! An antiquated figure with silvery hair, wearing a black coat. It was such a shock that my mind instantly shut it down. I closed my eyes. It hadn't happened. Then opened them again. He was still there. He really was.

No!

I can remember telling myself that – 'No!'

After that, I shut my eyes tightly and kept them shut, concentrating on breathing slowly, exhaling fully. Breathwork had served me well, focusing the mind, switching off rising panic. The very act of instructing the mind to count, hold, count again, to be aware of the process, stopped it wandering off along perilously dark corridors full of unknown doors, behind which there was a multitude of horrors clamouring to get out.

Eventually the panic subsided, and after a while I found the courage to open my eyes. If he was still there, despite my heart pounding ten to the dozen, and feeling sick with fright, I would ask him who he was…

But there was no one there.

Had I imagined it? A dream, or rather a nightmare? Yes, that was probably it, no doubt because of the conversation with Glynn about exorcisms?

Think of something else, for God's sake, Lyddie!

I glanced at the clock.

Three-fifteen.

The night was as still and damply cold as a church crypt, and it was then I gradually became aware of a slight pressure on my chest, making the next breath harder than it should be, as if I was underground, buried, claustrophobic. The outline around the bedroom door shone as brightly as an exit sign in a dark auditorium, and I focused on it, as the crackling horror movie of a long-buried memory slowly began to play out.

Three-fifteen.

Suddenly, I was back in the bedroom of the house I grew up in, the glow of a lamp casting shadows in the corridor outside. I was lying once more in a small single bed by the window, the smell of nicotine ingrained in the yellowing walls, the air thick and cloying with something sweet and sickly, muffled laughter coming from downstairs. Then a door opened, followed by the sound of wheezy breathing and slow, methodical footsteps thudding upstairs.

I stared hard at the light, swallowing down an age-old fear, releasing the iron breath trapped in my lungs.

It's a memory, not real, she's dead, she can't hurt me...

The memory flared and faded, flared and faded...

My dad died when I was five years old and, left alone, my mother struggled to raise me and my sister. Vivien had been ten years older than me and desperate to leave home as soon as possible, which she did at sixteen. After which it was just me and Mum. Recollecting the void after Viv had gone, the emptiness in the house with cardboard-thin walls, my stomach jolted; and in that instant the yawning, creaking lid on the box keeping all those memories at bay, threatened to lift and spill out its contents.

No!

I resumed inhaling slowly, to counting, and the next thing I knew it was morning. Glynn had pulled back the curtains, revealing the stunning view I still couldn't believe was ours. The day was sweeping with low cloud, watery sunlight scooting shadows briskly across low-lying fields; sheep bleating in the distance, wind buffeting the cottage walls. And into the drowsy state between sleeping and waking, I became aware on one level of the familiar and comforting sounds of a kettle boiling downstairs, the spring of the toaster, Skip pitter-pattering on the kitchen floor; while on another, the ghostly apparition floated back in from the night before.

I was not in fear, it being far easier to examine and analyse in the light of day, what had seemed terrifying in the endless expanse of night. Nevertheless, the instant I thought about him he was reconjured, every detail before me as if it had only just occurred.

The man had been dressed in a black, buttoned-up coat with a high collar and a pocket on the left breast. Silvery-white in essence – both hair and skin – his complexion was crepey and deeply etched, eyes mid-blue. The hair, I saw then, was swept backwards, quite long, perhaps to the shoulders. He hadn't loomed over me or tried to touch me, his expression being mild and watchful, but had simply sat on the bed. Observing.

I was deep in thought, totally within myself, as the rest, captured as if by camera to film, was subsequently projected to the now less fearful and thus more receptive mind.

Although the room had been very dark, inky black,

along with his clothing, the man himself had not been. His face had not been shadowy but clearly visible. Nor had he been one of those smoky beings with red eyes, a dark, hooded shape towering in the corner of a room, but had appeared as real as you or I. The only difference between him and a living being was the colour of his skin, which had the bloodless pallor of a corpse. But the more I thought about the apparition, the more it puzzled me. How was it possible to determine he was dressed all in black if the room was black? Yet I'd been able to determine the buttons on his coat, even a pocket. How did a person see black material against a black background?

Yet I had.

He'd been sitting on the side of the bed with the wardrobe behind him, there being only a thin glow of light around the door to the landing, just enough to see the way out. The room itself had been in complete darkness. Yet, his features had been clearly visible, even the expression in his eyes. I could barely see my own hand in that darkness! And that was when it hit me. There'd been a shimmer around him. The best way to describe it would be that he looked superimposed, stood out, like a cardboard cut-out.

Unease swept over me in a sickly wave.

It hadn't been a dream.

Not even a nightmare.

I'd been visited!

"Sleep well?"

Glynn had brought breakfast up for us and my heart went out to him. There was no way I could tell him about the ghostly visitor. It occurred to me then how much I wasn't confiding in him, painfully aware of that as I sat up and took the tray. There'd been Zach Stipple's odd change of voice and character, then Bailey's (something I'd omitted in the telling), the odd feeling on the bridge, the coloured orbs, and now the ghost. But anything to do with the supernatural disturbed him, he didn't like it, and the thing was, Glynn wasn't just my best friend but the only family I had. I didn't want to upset or alienate him, for him to think I was odd, someone he could no longer relate to. And as such he would never know certain aspects about my past, either. I wanted to protect him, you see? For him to have nothing but the best, to be happy, blissful, successful and emotionally secure.

Perhaps, I hoped it would all go away? Nothing unusual to see here! So, I told myself my intuition was way off-beam, and all would be well if only I could turn off my wild imagination, so easily whirled into a cytokine storm of self-destruction. Certainly, I didn't ever intend to be taken to another doctor's office for an analysis on my state of mind. That was my rationale for not telling him, anyway. I thought I was doing the right thing for both of us. I've often asked myself what would have happened if I had. Would he have been better prepared? Would there have been a different outcome?

I don't know, but certainly there was no way of protecting him from what happened at the abbey ruins that afternoon.

***

Chapter Nine

We'd decided, on a whim, to pack a rucksack and go exploring, much to Skip's delight. As soon as he saw the walking socks going on, the boots being laced up, he started to run around in circles, probably remembering our long hikes on the Yorkshire Moors. He'd run all day, sometimes for seven or eight hours. Skip would have been about two years old during our time at Creech Cross, and epitomised the joy of life.

There was another facet to Skip though, and why he was extra-special: if either one of us was ever a bit down, stressed, or unwell, he'd huddle close, placing his paws on one arm. No matter how much he may have wanted to go outside or get into his basket, he'd stay right there until whichever one of us it was, felt better. He'd done it since being a puppy. And the warmth of his body, the pulse of his heart, the light in his eyes... I don't know, I could be fanciful, it's what most people would say, but I felt he was a healer, a guardian. Perhaps for me in particular. We had a bond. Occasionally, I'd catch him looking at me with the most quizzical, almost yearning expression, and we didn't like to be apart. There's a reason for documenting this, by the way, but I'll come to that shortly.

"Does the floor in here feel springy to you?" Glynn asked, fastening Skip's lead.

I rocked back and forwards on the kitchen lino.

"I thought it was all new?"

"We only had a basic survey though, didn't we?"

"The extension's only a decade old."

"Yes," Glynn said. "But this bit's a hell of a lot older. The surveyor didn't pick anything up, I suppose, but—"

"So, it'll be fine. Come on, let's go!"

The plan that Sunday, was to walk up Coach Lane towards Upper Creech, then over to the abbey ruins. It was a brisk, breezy day, and we must have passed Ashe House around eleven-thirty. The upstairs curtains were still drawn, and in the drive was a bottle-green Morris Oxford, a mud-splattered white transit van, and a shiny, royal blue Subaru Impreza with what resembled an aeroplane tail on the back.

I laughed. "No prizes for guessing who drives the Subaru."

"The crumpet crate?"

"Crumpet Crate! I haven't heard that in years."

We were quiet for a while, smiling, tramping up the lane, past Curfew Cottage and The Blackthorn Brank, when he shot me a sidelong glance.

"Quite the lady killer, Aiden, isn't he?"

I kept my gaze firmly ahead, holding tightly onto Skip's lead.

"He fancied you."

I laughed. "Well, who can blame him?"

"So, you noticed?"

"No. Yes, I suppose. But he's the sort who expects all women to be attracted to him, isn't he? And I'm definitely not."

I desperately didn't want the conversation. I had the kind of looks that could cause problems – tall, willowy, auburn hair and deep green eyes. At school, I'd been waylaid in the gennel almost every day, threatened with having my head kicked in and generally ostracised. By the time I was fourteen, I'd learned not to draw attention to myself. Where I grew up it wasn't a good idea. So, automatically I sought to pour cold water on anything that might come between us. Glynn was my only real friend, I loved him, and didn't want him to have a moment of hurt or worry.

I reached for his hand. "I love you, you know?"

After a moment he said, "I love you, too."

There were several more houses on the right, a footpath signed *Dagger's Gate*, then the village green and the junction to the old stone bridge. After that there was only one more cottage, situated high on the hill before it became Upper Creech. On the left, our side, after Horseman's Wood ended, there were several large flat fields and then what looked like a campsite behind a hedge.

We wandered over.

The Tollhouse had been painted in yellow on a piece of wood balanced on the mailbox, and behind the hedge a drive wound in an S shape towards a brick-built dormer bungalow. We couldn't see much beyond an Alpine Sprite caravan and a cluster of fir trees, so took a couple of tentative steps up the drive.

"They might see us," I hissed.

Glynn gripped my hand. "Shush!"

"I feel like a naughty school kid."

We ventured in a little further. There were more evergreens, then four static caravans close to the house, one with a little plastic fence around it, and a TV set flickering inside.

"No, let's go."

"Just a minute," Glynn said, extricating his hand.

To my horror, he carried on walking further up.

I didn't like it, trailing behind at a distance. I had the distinct impression of being watched, of someone knowing we were there, and we had no right. None at all.

"Come on, let's go."

"I can smell something horrible, like rotten eggs," he said, over his shoulder.

"Glynn!"

"All right, all right," he said, just as a rather overweight bull terrier trundled down the drive towards us.

Spying Skip, the dog barked, advanced a little further, then barked again, doing his job; and so we turned and walked briskly back to the lane.

"That was so nosy," I snapped.

"I was only going to introduce us and ask for directions to the abbey. Don't worry about it."

We were marching up the lane to the crossroads. Their boundary was extensive, continuing all the way up to the junction and around the bend, where there was another driveway to the property on the corner.

Glynn hesitated.

"Oh Glynn, don't! Well, I'm not coming with you."

But he went regardless. It was impossible not to look, though. From that entrance, the dilapidated stone cottage that should have been demolished, was clearly visible. Tarpaulin covered the roof, also black plastic sheeting nailed onto some of the exposed rafters; outdoor wires hung in loops, and a badly stained mattress, along with broken furniture, had been thrown onto a tip. Several chickens ran around a yard cluttered with cars – one jacked up – a quad bike, trailers, rusty gates, corrugated iron sheets, tyres and empty oil drums. Beyond that, the large, pancake-flat fields we'd passed, lay bleakly exposed to the wind howling down the valley.

I glanced over at the road, keen to go, when the sound of voices caused me to turn back. The bull terrier was no longer alone, but accompanied by a teenage boy in trousers that bagged so low that the crotch was almost round his knees and, as was fashionable back then, the band of his Calvin Klein underpants was visible. Hair closely shaven, he wore one hooped earring, limbs long and thin.

"Can I 'elp you, mate?"

I only heard part of the conversation in the blustering wind, but Glynn had his hands in his pockets, making a friendly introduction.

"Stay! Sit!" the boy shouted to the dog, which had just spied Skip again.

It was hugely overweight, ripples of fat beneath a dull tan coat. Slumping to the ground, it remained on full alert, however, wide mouth hanging open, dripping saliva; and Skip wrapped himself around the backs of my legs.

Glynn inclined his head towards me, and the boy looked over.

I lifted a hand, waved, smiled.

Minutes later he was back and we moved swiftly off.

"What did he say?"

"Name's Slim. Knew who I was straight away. And you. Said his mother was going to invite us over sometime."

"What did you say? How did you explain being such a nosy bastard?"

He laughed. "Just that we wanted to introduce ourselves and ask the way to the abbey, but we ran into the dog and didn't know which entrance to use."

"But he bought it?"

"Shouldn't think so."

"Great. What was he like?"

"Pleasant enough. There was a girl standing in the door of that derelict place. Just watching."

"What was she like?"

"Oh, Lyds, you don't half ask a lot of questions. I don't know, difficult to tell – young, long dark hair, pale, leggings, smoking. I was slightly more concerned with being nice to the bloke holding the hammer."

"Hammer? I didn't see that."

"Said he was mending the roof."

"Bloody hell, Glynn!"

After crossing the junction, there was a fork off to the left, which crossed into a different valley, one far more secluded, a much deeper ravine and far lusher than ours. And shortly after that was the public footpath we'd been looking for. Climbing over the stile, we then set off down a narrow track which curved around the back of The Old Rectory, partly visible through the trees.

"Wow, what a pile!"

It was, too. A huge house, painted white, stood proudly overlooking both valleys, whilst being almost hidden from the road. Largely obscured by foliage, you'd have to either know it was there, or be on foot to see it. There were six long windows on both floors, three on each side of the front door. A conservatory ran the length of the far side of the house, and on the other was a garage for at least three, maybe four cars parked side by side. We could just see a swimming pool with a cover rolled over it, tennis courts, and sweeping lawns at the back. There weren't any lights on but two cars stood in the drive, both battered old Citroens held together with sticky tape by the look of it.

"So they have a house that cost at least a million, but cars that cost about eighty quid each."

I laughed. "Come on, let's find the abbey or it'll be dark before we get home."

As there was no one else around, we unclipped Skip and plodded down the path in silence, while he careered around the fields with his ears flapping wildly. And then all of a sudden, there it was. In the meadow we came to know as Briars Hay.

Creech Abbey, or what remained of it, was adjacent to a river. Much wider than the tributary running through Creech Cross, the water there streamed with velvety green fronds, pouring over glossy dark rocks, shaded by overhanging trees. The grass was luscious even at that time of year, and mesmerised, we pushed open the five-bar gate and walked towards it.

"We could have our packed lunch here," I was saying.

It was calmer there, more sheltered from the wind. And further up the valley, the outline of the mill mentioned the night before, was just visible. But as we neared, an extraordinary thing happened – the stones seemed to shimmer and the fronds of grass began to blur.

"I feel as if I've gone back in time again," I said, realising too late I hadn't told him about the bridge. "I mean, it feels so ancient. Like reliving history."

"It does feel strange."

"Is it? You feel it, too?"

"Yes, like I've been smoking weed…"

Like two kids entranced with a travelling fair, we walked under a series of broken archways, picking our way through boulders covered in moss, towards an expanse of grass in the centre. Built from soft grey-gold stone, now weathered by elements and time, the shell was that of a grand cathedral, but the foundations told a different story. Many rooms had once clustered around a large central one, with steps leading up and down to various levels. This had been a place bustling with life.

We stood in the middle of it, looking up at the dove-grey sky, envisaging how it had looked a thousand or more years ago, how it had functioned. There'd been a nine or ten-foot-wide fireplace in the great hall, another clearing beyond that which was likely the nave of a church, and a long line of arches, perhaps a corridor where the nuns had walked. How had they lived all those hundreds of years ago, I wondered? Had it been in austerity or abundance? Was the abbess kind or harsh? Who were they? And had it ended with the Dissolution?

I didn't notice at first, awareness crept in stealthily, but when I did it was as if the wind had dropped suddenly and completely, the air as still as a tomb.

And that was when I first heard it. I wasn't sure Glynn had. But then he glanced over, and there was shock in his eyes, the colour leeching from his skin.

Neither of us said a word.

A bell was tolling. An echo vibrating around walls no longer there, the sound a tuning fork in the head.

"Do you hear a bell ringing?" he said eventually.

His voice was syrupy and slow, coming from far, far away. And it seemed to me the day had darkened, that dusk was descending early. Skip was standing on the periphery with his head cocked to one side, looking in at us, as if through a pane of glass. He hadn't followed, and I knew that if I called he would not come.

It was surreal, the moment stretching out, as slowly, incrementally, a confused sound of voices reached us, the speakers not yet visible. I found I could not move. The babble grew louder, came closer. As if the abbey was about to burst into life. All around, wind flattened the fields, trees bowed and swayed, but not one blade of grass so much as quivered inside the broken walls of the ruins.

Glynn drew breath, was about to speak.

I shook my head. "Shh!"

The voices rose and fell, now whispers, now chants, as if a radio station wasn't quite tuned into the right frequency: sometimes it cleared, then it faded. It sounded like incantations, a rhyme, many whispering all at the same time, 'ess, ess, ess…' The more I strained to hear, the more elusive the words. Here and there it would surge in an overwhelming crescendo, intrusive, blocking all other thoughts. The scenery was going to change, I could feel it, another time period pulling us into its magnetic tapestry. Robed figures were emerging from the walls and my heart rate was escalating. It was difficult to breathe, and the most horrible, sickly feeling of dread was pulsing in waves.

Still I could not move, or think, or function.

A dog was barking.

Everyone in a circle… blinding light, coloured lights through a kaleidoscope on the wall… the ground rolling and swelling beneath us, and then a swirling haze of smoke…The grass was black. Screams rent the air. I broke a sweat, couldn't breathe, lungs rigid with pain. And still I couldn't move.

A dog barking. There was a dog barking.

And someone shouting, "Lyddie! Lyddie!"

I have only the vaguest recollection of walking back up the footpath, hurrying up to the lane, of being almost dragged along, boots thudding into the muddy earth. But I don't remember the bit between my heart thudding like lead, feeling as if I was being swallowed into a vortex, about to pass out, and getting home again.

And nor did Glynn.

We sat in front of the fire later that night, and glancing up sharply, I caught a haunted look in his eyes I'd never seen before. Maybe, I thought, now he'd understand if I told him. If I told him what it was like for me? But then the shutters came down, there was an almost imperceptible shake of his head, and I knew he never would. But he'd had a glimpse of something he couldn't explain, of the unknown. He'd definitely had that.

There was nothing in Glynn's demeanour that invited further discussion. He'd closed himself off and who could blame him? It was always a decision – to know or not to know. But it bugged me. I had the strongest feeling something sinister had happened in that place. Maybe the others in the village knew, and that's why there'd been a feeling they were hiding something? A coven? It was the first time that possibility occurred to me. Was there a coven there and the incomers had found out? Was that the divide Monica mentioned? Was that the reason Fay said to avoid Keith Cribbs?

This whole valley was once a site of dark witchcraft, you know? Apparently, they held esbats over where the abbey ruins are. A long, long time ago, of course...

***

Chapter Ten

"Does it worry you?"

It was the last time Glynn ever referred to the incident at the abbey.

"No," I said.

He was pleased with the answer, nodding, already dismissing the whole thing. I don't think he'd closed his mind to wanting to understand the unseen, the largely unexplained, and he wasn't likely to insist, as my mother and stepfather had, that I'd imagined everything, that I was unhinged and should 'get help'; but I didn't want to risk him pulling away from me either, to not trust my sanity if I told him what I sometimes saw.

Once, in the terraced house in Harrogate, I'd been cooking dinner when a shadow passed behind me, darkening the kitchen. On the edge of my vision, I saw it was a man with his back to me, staring out of the window. For a split second I'd thought it was Glynn and been about to speak, then understood what it was and quickly turned back, willing it to go away. When suddenly the shadow shot over and swooped round to peer in my face. Close up. Just a shadow, yet it seemed conscious, with a flash of expression in the eyes, like an image caught on a video at lightning speed. I leapt back, dropping the knife, heart hammering, just in time to see Skip's head jerk up from sleep. Not to look at me, but to follow the shadow disappearing down the hall. The dog saw that entity. I saw it. It was not my imagination.

Well, the rest of January and into February passed by in the busy blur of starting a new job, finding where to park, the location of the ward, who was who, and getting into a routine. But shortly after that the honeymoon ended. And it ended abruptly.

We didn't find out we'd been deliberately stitched-up though, until I met Kendra Ettrick at the church fête. Actually, I didn't find out a lot of things until I met Kendra. She was the most magnificent conveyor of information; and Tim was right – I did like her. I liked her a lot, albeit in a moth to a flame kind of way. Perhaps because she'd married into one of the oldest families in the area, while also allying with the incomers, those who would remain newbies no matter how many decades they lived there. It could be said she was everyone's friend, and yet she was no one's, either – rather, she was an enigma, like a cut diamond with a hundred or more facets, reflecting whatever the observer wished to see. Boy, did she enlighten me, though!

The honeymoon period ended with Glynn being correct about the springy floorboards – it turned out all of them downstairs, to varying degrees, plus joists, were crumbling with dry rot. What Kath Ettrick and her husband had done was cover them with carpet and linoleum, giving the cottage a quick, cheap makeover that looked and smelled new. We were young, had been over-keen to move, pushed by Glynn's company, pressured by buyers who kept threatening to pull out, and we'd cut costs with just a basic survey by a company which, when challenged, replied with a harsh letter peppered with legalities. At the time, we were angry, upset, and extremely worried. I was not to know, not for a long time, that the entire episode was pivotal to the fate of the valley and everyone in it. But for us, the calmness, that brief period of wonder and excitement, had certainly gone.

I met Kendra at the first and last church fête I would ever go to.

Fay had stopped me on the lane a couple of days before while I was out walking Skip. Winding down the window of the Morris Oxford, she asked how we were settling in, and during the conversation I mentioned the floorboards. Duncan or Aiden would come round and give us a quote, she said. Don't worry about it. I was a bit taken aback as we hadn't discussed what we were going to do yet, but she insisted they'd be able to help and would give us mates' rates, so I stumbled over a 'thank you', and said yes, one evening next week would be fine.

"And will you be coming to the church fête on Saturday afternoon? It's at Lower Creech Chapel."

"Oh… um… I didn't know about it."

"Two o'clock onwards, but I'd get there early or all the cakes will go. One thing the WI do superbly well here is bake."

"Well, in that case I'll definitely pop in. Is there anyone else I'll know? Apart from you?"

"I'm on Bring and Buy so I might be busy. Monica won't go, she and Tim never do. Carrie Cade might. Oh, and Kendra Ettrick. She's quite a silly girl but you might like her."

I nodded, choosing to ignore the emphasis on, 'you'. Why would she think I'd like someone silly?

"Okay, I'll pop in. Thanks."

"It would be lovely to see you there," she added, winding up the window. "Super-important to support local charity events, to show willing and so forth." She smiled. "I do my bit, anyway."

Glynn was at a work event, so I'd gone alone, quashing visions of everyone turning to stare at the stranger walking in. What was there to be nervous about? It was a common-or-garden church fund-raiser, with cake stalls, home-made gifts, preserves, a raffle, a Bring and Buy. At worst, I'd feel like a spare prick at a party. At best, I'd make a new friend or two. But I hadn't reckoned on the power of those women to intimidate.

It was held in a small room adjoining the chapel, presumably where Sunday School or children's activities were usually held, there being children's paintings on the walls, and bookcases full of children's books. Trestle tables had been set up around the perimeter, and at a rough guess about twenty or so people, mostly women, were packed elbow to elbow, some holding tea cups, chatting to each other. Fay was deep in conversation at the far end of the room, and no one stared when I walked in, thank God, although there was a shift of awareness. It was in the subtle, almost imperceptible stiffening of spines, and the slight lull in conversation, as if an unpleasant smell had just wafted in. It triggered a memory. Of my first day at school, entering a classroom full of other kids happily chatting, very friendly, enjoying themselves.

Can someone please make friends with Lydia?

"You must be 'er that's moved into Well Cottage, then?"

I looked down into the most unflinching, enormous brown eyes imaginable, the kind where the whites are visible all the way round. The woman's dark hair was cut in a severe page-boy style, her complexion heavily lined. Periodically jostled, she stood staunchly, peering upwards with owl-like attention, and I felt myself being thoroughly assessed, from my plain black boots and leggings, to my navy anorak and pony tail, then back to boring into my eyes.

Her perfume had formed a cloud and, with biscuit and coffee breath in my face, instinctively I took a step back. She was one of those people who walked right into other people's auras.

"Yes, I'm Lydia. We haven't met?"

She closed the gap again, not offering a name. "Probably a bit boring for you, things like this, I expect?" Her eyes were searching mine, left to right, right to left, left to right. "Nice you came along, anyhow."

"Oh no, not boring at all, it's my pleasure."

"Thought you'd have more exciting things to do on a Saturday afternoon?"

It was an odd line of conversation and I didn't know where she was going with it. Nor could I see how to extract myself. Who on earth was she, anyway?

"I'm here for the cakes," I said, keeping it light. "And I'd rather buy from here, you know, to contribute?"

She still hadn't taken her eyes off mine, not answering, the moment hurtling towards awkward, when a woman inching past us said, "All right, Agnus?"

"Ah, you're Agnus Stipple?" I said. "I've met your son, Zach."

"Yes, I know. Hang on a minute, let me introduce you to someone." She signalled to a young woman collecting cups on a tray, to come over, and my heart picked up a beat. Was this Kendra?

"This is one of Kathleen Ettrick's daughters," she said as the woman joined us. "The youngest, Belinda. She's at Claden Farm down the back of the lane 'ere. Your Mia started nursery yet, Bel?"

Belinda shook her head, waiting for an introduction. She was slightly built, shoulder-length dark hair tucked behind her ears, dressed in jeans, a pink bobbly sweatshirt and muddy riding boots.

"This be 'er as moved into Well Cottage."

"Hi!" I said, smiling at Belinda. "I'm Lyddie Spicer."

"Right, well I must go and circulate," Agnus said. "Nice meeting you, Lydia."

"And you."

Belinda and I were left looking at each other. Still holding the tray, she smiled faintly and briefly.

"Do you have children?"

I shook my head. "No, we've only just–"

She then turned her back on me.

There wasn't any mistaking it. A complete one hundred and eighty degree turn that could not have been quicker or slicker if performed on ice skates.

I felt a bit sick, and so embarrassed it was beyond expression. Part of me wanted to slap her across the back of the head, and another was tempted to flee immediately. Miraculously, I refrained from both, instead forcing myself to walk over to one of the cake stalls. Grab a tea loaf and get out of there, was the plan. I guess shock and humiliation must have been written all over my face.

At which point I met Kendra.

She was sitting on a small wooden chair behind a stall of cakes, elbows on her knees, a little metal tin of coins and notes on a stool beside her. Her eyes were dancing and I realised, in a heartbeat, that she'd just seen and understood exactly what had happened.

"Having fun?"

I tried to smile, although it was more likely a grimace.

"Take no notice," she said. "I'm Kendra, by the way. You're Lydia?"

I nodded. "Lyddie, yes. Hi!"

"I can recommend the fruit cake. They're all good but that's got brandy in it, and it's excellent. The best. Or you could go for the coffee sponge. Also good."

"Perfect," I said quietly. "I'll have one of each then, please."

My thoughts were purely on escape. I would never be part of anything like this. Would never be welcome. What was the point? There were happier places to be.

Kendra had stood up and was handing over the change when I found myself looking into a face that sparked with elfish mischief. She was petite, with platinum blonde hair scraped back in an elaborate, plaited chignon, too many ear piercings to count, and a circular tattoo inked on her collar bone that I tried not to stare at.

"Who've you met so far then?"

I told her – Fay's family, Monica and Tim, Zach Stipple, Keith next door. Oh, and we'd met Slim Cade outside in the drive.

She smiled. The kind that makes you smile back.

"That's what he called himself," I said.

"Real name's Jax but you can see why that's his nickname, can't you? Twin sister Mallory's just the same. Both take after their dad. Colin's about six foot four, as well. You'll not miss him, he looks like Uriah Heep."

"A character made real," I said. "Yet fictitious."

She looked at me blankly.

"You've not met Carrie yet, I take it?"

"No."

"Your lucky day then. She's on her way over!"

***

Chapter Eleven

Carrie Cade, flanked by two tall, thin youths and a man in a long dark coat, was heading towards us with the aid of a Zimmer frame; and there was no doubt she wanted to speak. Late fifties at a guess, maybe early sixties, she had frizzy, steel-wool hair, a heavy, ruddy face and sunken eyes beneath bushy brows.

"You must be Lydia? I'm Carrie, and this is my husband, Colin. My son, Slim, and daughter, Mallory. We live at The Tollhouse just up the road from you."

"Hi! Nice to meet you."

"How do you like it here?"

"We love it, yes – settling in after–"

"You'll have to come over. It's my fortieth in a couple of weeks. I'm having a party."

After that, it was a burst of information and it wasn't easy to remember everything, but, in a very short space of time I learned Mallory was in the sixth form and almost genius level in maths. She'd also been accepted by Oxford University and played hockey for the county.

Wearing baggy trousers just like Slim, her eighteen-year-old twin, Mallory stared at me, slack-jawed from beneath a baseball cap.

Slim was running his own business and would soon be a father.

The twins stood either side of their mother, Colin slightly apart, his gaze wandering around the room as we chatted. Kendra had a point about Uriah Heep. Peering at people over the top of his glasses, he appeared to be sizing them up like an undertaker for a coffin, and was indeed wringing his hands. Colin was a company director in finance, she said.

"What do you do, Lyddie?"

"I'm a nurse."

"I've been a nurse."

"Really? Where did you work?"

She'd been a senior theatre sister and then a nursing officer in London. It transpired she'd had quite a career, having been in the army prior to that, made it to officer level but chosen not to pursue because of falling in love with Colin. She'd also worked as a radio host and been offered a position as a television presenter.

"I was asked to write a book about my life," she said.

"Wow! Are you going to?"

She shrugged. "Can't be bothered. I've got too much else to do, and the family comes first."

"Of course."

She then told a story about saving someone's life, that if she hadn't been there they'd have thrown themselves onto a railway track, before going on to say she and Colin were now building up a holiday-let business. Slim was shortly to be married and her future daughter-in-law, Nylah, was expecting their first baby. She'd be a grandma soon and was very excited.

"That's sounds wonderful."

She nodded. "So, you see why I haven't got time to write a book?"

"Absolutely. Well, we've not been here long but Glynn–"

She swung round to Colin. "You ready for home, Squire?"

He nodded.

"Nice to meet you, anyway," she said. "Sorry, we've got to go. But one of my lot will drop an invitation in. For my party."

"That'd be nice, thank you."

"You will definitely come?"

"I will, yes. Thank you."

Watching them depart, Kendra said, "What do you think of the Adams family, then?"

I was in such a state of relief that Carrie had been friendly and spoken to me, I almost laughed. I don't know why I'd had such a feeling of trepidation – all the newcomers had been welcoming. Perhaps that's what Monica had meant about a divide?

"They're really nice."

"You haven't seen 'er dad yet, mind. I'd keep my distance from that one if I were you – bit of an old lech. I would never let Willow go round there."

"Your daughter?"

She nodded.

"Where's their holiday-let business? Is it on the coast? I didn't get chance to ask."

"It's just those caravans in the yard."

"Really?"

She started to laugh. "Their relatives stay there – for

weddings and christenings, of which there are surprisingly many. They always want the chapel. It's hilarious. Like the cast of Peaky Blinders tramping up the lane – blokes in shiny suits with flick knives, kids screaming, cans of lager thrown over the hedges.

"Kath's threatening to leave the church rota, because she has to do the flowers for them and clean the chapel after. Usually stinks of spliffs. They aren't even church-goers. Laughing my arse off. That's 'er by the way, glaring at us. Meet the mother-in-law."

My heart gave a little lurch. Kathleen Ettrick! We'd never met her, even though she lived in Lower Creech and had sold us the house. But what was fresh in my mind was the rotten floorboards covered up with new lino and carpet.

"The ghost of Mrs Ettrick sits and watches me," said Kendra. "Don't look round."

I looked round.

She was sitting on a wooden chair at the opposite side of the room from Kendra's stall. Her skin was deeply etched and spectral-grey, she had very short dark hair, and was dressed neatly in jeans, trainers, navy quilted jacket and a hat. I had the impression she'd once been very pretty, but Kathleen Ettrick never smiled, not once, and spoke only occasionally to one or two of the passing matrons. Even then it was with a cursory nod and minimal interaction.

"How are you liking it there, by the way? In the cottage she sold you?"

"We love it. Couldn't believe our luck."

"No one's lived there since her son went doo-lally. Did Anna tell you about that? No, I thought not. They had it kitted out for 'im. I think one of Kath's brothers lived there for a while, 'til he died of alcoholic poisoning, that is.

Anyway, then they gave it to Robin."

"Did they build the extension?"

"Yeah, her husband, that'd be my father-in-law, Tony – he's a builder, so he did it with the brother that drank himself to death. Anyway, after a bit they decided to give it to Robin, but he went mad there. Had to be sectioned."

"That's your husband's brother?"

She raised her eyes heavenwards. "Youngest. Kath had fourteen that lived. Another dozen that didn't by all accounts. One went into the Aga."

"Pardon?"

Kendra had very long fingernails, each filed to a point, painted in slate glitter with little motifs on them. She twiddled one of her many earrings with a sparkly talon.

"Stillborn, very premature, mind. Decided not to bother with another funeral so she incinerated 'im in the Aga. I shit you not. There's a grave in the garden."

I was desperate to look round at Kathleen Ettrick again.

"So, all okay for you in Well Cottage, is it?"

I barely knew her and I wasn't sure if anything I said would sweep around the matrons and be swiftly delivered to Kathleen after I'd gone.

"Yes, we're just, you know, settling in."

"They'd have put another one of her brood in there but they had a cash crisis. Had to buy a place for Robin, see, that's in a sort of sheltered complex. Got to have special psychiatric supervision." She glanced at me out of the corner of her eye, a mischievous twitch on her lips. "Bit violent. So anyway, they needed the money, which is why they sold up. The last sale fell through, did you know? After the full structural. So, when Anna, who's Kath's cousin twice-removed, by the way, heard about you two looking for—"

My stomach bounced, a descending lift juddering to an abrupt halt.

"What? Hang on a minute. A previous sale fell through after a survey?"

She nodded. "I thought you knew? That's why she snatched your hand off for the first offer."

"Oh, my good God!"

"What?"

"It's got rotten floorboards."

"Mmm, you went for the surveyor Anna recommended, didn't you?"

I was feeling hot again and more than a bit sick.

"Mark, that's my 'usband, might be able to fix it for you. He does logging but he can turn his hand to pretty much anything, so long as it's to do with wood."

"We're erm, looking into it at the moment," I said.

She nodded. "Well, let us know if you need our help. So, are you going to go to Carrie's party, then?"

I shook my head. "I don't know, I can't think."

I really couldn't. They all knew. They all bloody well knew, and so did Anna, after everything I'd told her about being stretched to the limit! No doubt the surveyor was a bloody relative, as well. The entire kitchen could cave in...

I was desperate to get home and process everything, to be alone. Shocked, shaking inside, I could feel Kathleen Ettrick's currant bun eyes boring into my back as I left. She would have known who I was. It would have been easy for her to come over and say, "Hello." But she was hardly going to do that having shafted us, was she?

Desperate for air, hurrying out to the car park, I suddenly noticed the Cade family piling into a camper van, and since my car was parked next to theirs, I stood and waited for a moment.

Kendra levelled with me, lighting up a cigarette.

"That Mallory's not right, either," she said.

I didn't think I could take much more. "How do you mean?"

"It was a few years back when she'd be about fourteen. Anyway, she shoved one of the local girls into a hedge on her way home from school. Sexually assaulted her."

I didn't know what to say.

Kendra took a drag of her cigarette and blew the smoke high into the bracing March air. Rain was spitting. "Bit of a fight about it. The girl's mother went round and practically pulled the caravan door off to get her out. Weird girl, smells like a dead badger, gawps at you with 'er mouth open."

Caravan? The girl lived in one of the caravans when she was fourteen?

Bloody hell, it was like the Jeremy Kyle Show!

That's what I was thinking. And at that stage we'd only just stepped into the weirdness that was Creech Cross, where day-to-day normality overlapped with insanity, until it was difficult to tell which was which.

Later that afternoon, I sat in the lounge gazing at the view we'd fallen for. Skip lay at my feet, eyeing me constantly in the hope of going for a long walk. But sheets of fine rain were blowing in a veil across the valley, Barrow Ridge a wash of watercolour grey. We'd extended ourselves financially to the hilt, and Kathleen Ettrick had seen us coming. Her and her second cousin twice-removed, Anna Bradley-Holt.

The wind was whipping up by then, mad March winds,

a low moan in the canopy of trees behind the cottage like pan pipes, rain sleeting against the windows. Which was the first time I became aware of the cracks, of creaking, groaning and snapping. I remember walking to the window. And noticing then, fully acknowledging for the first time, the line of trees in close proximity to the cottage. Between our cottage and Keith Cribbs' farm next door, there were several huge fields, at a guess a dozen acres or so, flat and windswept. A low stone wall separated us from the nearest field, and along that wall were trees.

In all truth, I could not even recall seeing them when we'd viewed the house, and had barely looked since. But all at once I did.

They were extremely tall. Very tall and very spindly. And in that high wind they were swaying and bending, leaning over in protracted gusts. Several branches had already fallen. Most of them, however, did appear stable. All except the closest, which, with each fresh strong blast of wind, almost levered itself out of the ground. It could, I thought with considerable alarm, easily split, uproot even, and fall onto the roof of the extension. Why the hell had trees like that been planted so close to someone's house? Why not sturdy poplars for a wind break and privacy? These weren't wind breaks so much as sails.

I began then, to feel the first flicker of fear: the expense of having the whole ground floor replaced meant taking out a loan, my job was temporary, Glynn was being stretched to the limit with his, and now there was the added worry of a tree falling onto the roof.

Well, there was nothing else for it – we'd have to go and see Keith Cribbs as soon as possible. They were on his land. It was the only way. Hopefully he'd do the decent thing?

And that night the orbs came back.

***

Chapter Twelve

This time their presence was indisputable. Not a trick of the light or an illusion caught in the corner of the eye, because I saw them and there were dozens. Suspended in the air, they were hovering around the perimeter of the bed like visitors crowding round a pram. And it seemed that in the looking, they became enlivened and emboldened, gaining in vibrancy, size, and numbers. Reacting. Most were electric blue, some orange. One in particular was huge and strangely spherical, the colour of an amber sunset.

I suppose, with the benefit of hindsight, I realise I'd gone to bed feeling anxious, my perspective very different from just a short time ago when everything had felt optimistic and exciting. Suddenly, the balance had tipped. Financial fear had opened the door to a whole host of other fears. Fears that subsequently grew. And fear makes people interpret things very differently. My mind had been churning over all the 'what-ifs', every single time bringing me back to Madeleine, the ward sister at work. There was something about her. It wasn't simply that she'd saddled me with the most unsociable shifts over Easter – that could be luck of the draw, as in it had to be someone – it was more the glacial, unconvincing half-smile. And the way, once or twice, I'd caught her staring at me intently if I happened to glance up, or see her reflection in the glass. No smile. Just a bleak, blank glare.

What if I lost my job?

The orbs were brighter than ever. Shimmering. Quivering. Alive. What were they?

A slither of fear breezed into my bones then, reminiscent of a time long ago. Were they malevolent? What did they want? Would the ghostly man in the black coat reappear? Or those tall, hooded beings with no faces, the ones that stood in the corner of the room, all black, solid black...? The lid of the box deep inside, that I kept compartmentalised and firmly shut, pushed and rattled to be opened, threatening to tip its contents into the bowl of my head... Something horribly familiar was about to surface, would materialise...

I sat up. Hot. Breathing hard.

"Lyds?" Glynn stroked the back of my arm. "Did you hear something?"

The room was velvety dark once more. Cold. No lights. No orbs. Just the wind howling and whistling outside.

"No," I said, slumping down again. "I must have drifted off. Just a weird dream. Sorry."

It was fear playing out. I'd gone to bed worried. That's what it had been. All it had been. And next day we decided to visit Keith Cribbs, face the music and get it over with. Overnight, the wind had gusted up to around fifty miles an hour and trees had fallen all over the county. Although calmer by morning, it remained gusty, and Glynn had been out and had a proper look.

"I don't know why we didn't notice before," he said.

"Blindsided, weren't we? A bit too desperate, busy with

jobs, packing, organising, working out finances. And we only saw the place once, remember?"

"Well, the trees are definitely on the old guy's land. He'll have to do the decent thing if property is at risk."

"Life, actually."

"I'd say only one of them needs to fully come down. The others are further away and look stable enough, although–"

"What if he refuses?"

"Ah, come on! If we had a tree that could fall on someone's roof, we wouldn't just leave it. Not if they might get hurt. No, it's his responsibility. He won't refuse."

"I hope you're right."

"You said he was friendly?"

I had, hadn't I? Despite the undercurrents. And certainly Keith smiled that day. In fact, he smiled pretty much all the way through the uncomfortable conversation we had.

We'd gone round about four o'clock, well after the possibility of interrupting a Sunday lunch, and hoping to catch him in. To get to his farm, we climbed over the stile where the trees were. It led to a public right of way according to the ordinance survey map, and was a simple cludge design comprised of wooden steps over the stone wall directly next to the cottage. We then crossed two large fields, heads down against the wind.

Creech Farm was a modern brick detached house with a concrete yard, and several huge barns at the back. No garden, no plants, no trees. There didn't appear to be anyone around, the windows dark, house silent, so we just knocked on the glass porch door and waited.

No answer.

"Probably out," said Glynn, ringing the bell.

"He might be in the fields?"

"Or in one of the barns?"

A door creaked inside.

"No, he's in," Glynn said.

A light had flicked on in the hall, followed by a shadow, then the sound of bolts shooting back. After opening the inner door to the house, Keith Cribbs appeared, licking an ice-cream, with the locked glass porch between us and him.

Glynn shouted above the noise of the wind, "Mr Cribbs? It's Glynn and Lyddie from next door."

Suspended from the porch ceiling was a little witch made out of felt, a poppet in a black hat and cloak sitting on a trapeze.

"Told you to use my drive!" Keith shouted through the divide. Drive was pronounced, 'droive'.

Too late, I remembered he had said that. But there was a public right of way. We hadn't trespassed.

"Sorry, Keith," I shouted back. "We forgot. But we did stick to the path."

"Told you! Use the drive. Members of the public are to use the drive!"

"We're very sorry. We forgot."

"We wondered if we could we have a word with you about the trees?" Glynn said.

"What trees?"

We were having to shout against the noise of the wind, while he stood in the hallway licking the ice-cream, making no move to enter the porch, much less open the outside door so we could speak more comfortably.

"Could you open the door so we can talk?" Glynn said. "Bit blustery out here, mate."

Keith appeared to deliberate, during which time we had no choice but to stand in the driving wind and rain, waiting for him to devour the cornet. Afterwards, he licked each finger, wiped his hands down his denim dungarees, then walked into the porch and opened the outside door.

"Nothing wrong with those trees," he said.

Glynn explained that one of them could fall on the roof.

"That's what you've got insurance for then, innet?" said Keith.

"We researched the insurance situation, Keith," I said. "It states due care should be taken to prevent an accident, so that's why we're here. To inform you that one of the trees in particular looks very unstable, and we're right underneath it. If it was on our land, we'd have it taken down, or at least the height reduced, but it's on yours so we have to ask."

"Thing is," said Keith, "your extension was built after those trees were planted, innet? Not afore."

"It's really close, Keith. Quite frightening in high gusts like we had last night."

"Thing is," he said, "who's going to pay for it, see?"

Quite suddenly, the sun broke through the scudding clouds, and for a fleeting moment his face was caught in the light, searing a lasting impression on my memory. Those rheumy eyes were absolutely cold – pale, glassy irises with pinprick pupils, behind them the quick, darting presence I'd sensed before. And I understood then, with absolute clarity and not inconsiderable horror, that he was enjoying himself.

"How about we go halves?" I suggested.

Beside me, Glynn stiffened, and I wondered if I should

have said that. Glynn had been adamant it was a last resort.

"Well, as it's your tree and your land, but we're living under it," I went on. "How about that as a solution? Then it won't be too much for either of us."

"Nothing wrong with that tree."

"Actually, it could be dangerous to life as well as property. Do you want to come and look? Do a risk assessment?"

"You get a quote then. Get three. Pick one that suits you."

"Needs to suit you, too," I said.

He laughed. "You want the tree down. You pay."

At that point he'd been about to shut the door in our faces, when a figure moved out of the shadows behind him, and we were both taken aback to see a girl emerge. Unusually short, less than five feet, she had bubbly blonde hair, close-set blue eyes, and a heavy lower jaw with sharp, jagged teeth. A piranha jaw. Had it not been for that jaw, which exposed the teeth, she might have been pretty. Instead, an unfathomable chill passed over me, like a cold breeze rippling over a pond.

"You all right, Dad?" She clutched his arm as if he was frail and vulnerable. "He's still grieving Mum," she told us. "She died seventeen years ago last week."

"This is my daughter, Cicely," Keith said. "She's an author."

We said 'hello' and that we were sorry about her mother; and then to my amazement I heard Glynn agreeing to get the quotes. He'd been adamant it was Keith's responsibility.

"We'll be in touch," he said. "Hopefully later in the week."

Keith nodded. "Let me know when you get the work done. I want to be there. It's my land."

"Sure."

But just as we turned to leave, he added, "You know the history of that cottage, do you? What went on there?" His eyes were glinting again. "Come round when you've got the quotes and I'll tell you all about it. But use the drive next time. Make sure to use the drive."

That might have been the end of it. But later that night when we were lying in bed, both of us worrying about how much the tree surgery would cost, there was an odd noise. Neither of us could work out what it was, but Skip wasn't barking and it sounded like it was outside. As it was late and pitch dark, Glynn went downstairs and checked the house was secure but didn't go out. After which it stopped.

"Doors are all locked, windows locked. Can't see anything out there."

"Maybe a wild animal?" I suggested.

We lay awake a while longer, and all was silent as before. Therefore, it was the next day, Monday, when we found out what had caused it.

Glynn had taken Skip out at six in the morning and, remembering the noise from the night before, he'd gone round to the side of the house where we thought the thudding and scratching had come from.

Keith Cribbs, we can assume it was him, had hacked the stile off the dry-stone wall, thrown the wood over into our garden, then strung a line of barbed wire along the top.

***

Chapter Thirteen

"Thought you said he was friendly?"

"I know."

"He's a slippery old git, Lyds, and we need to protect ourselves."

I closed my eyes, recalling Cicely, and the cool breeze shivering up my spine. There was something ominous about her, something, I don't know... heartless... the pleasantries a façade. And once again it felt as if Glynn and I were the only ones not party to some knowledge, some secret. I didn't say that to Glynn, I had no proof of anything, and besides, there was enough to worry about with practical matters. Every fresh gust of wind, every groan and crack of that tree, and my stomach contracted. We'd have to pay for it to be made safe as soon as possible. We both knew Keith wasn't going to.

"Perhaps that's why Fay said avoid him?" I said. "Seems like it was good advice."

"Best not to get into conversation with him again, Lyds. Don't have anything to do with him. You'll never win because he's experienced at what he does and he enjoys it. Probably gets off on it."

"Ugh! I wish you hadn't said that."

"Anyway, we'll have to bite the bullet and pay for the tree or it'll be a court order situation, and by that time the roof could have caved in." He raked his hair. "Bloody hell, we were stupid."

"Mmm. It's just annoying that people like him always get their way."

"I know, but he's not going to spoil our life or our new home. Got to feel sorry for the miserable bastard. What must it be like to be him? I wouldn't swap, would you? Anyway, we need to document everything from now on."

I agreed, and so we took photos of the tree, the damage to the stile, and logged the conversation so far. When the quotes came in, we'd photocopy the one agreed and take it round to him, signed and dated. After that, I made a concerted effort to put Keith out of my mind. Glynn was right – we had such a lot to be grateful for, and we'd soon get over this setback. I let it go the best I could, went for walks with Skip in the woods at the back of the house after work, and regained perspective. He was just one grumpy, unpleasant neighbour. We'd keep our distance.

And maybe, in a way, I can thank him, because that's when I not only started to log the situation with Keith, but events in general. My diary started that day. A busy one, as it transpired, jam-packed, a story I would never otherwise have remembered with all its complexities and detail.

Then a few days later, something else unsettling happened. I was on my own after an early shift, Glynn not yet home from seeing a client on the north Devon coast, when Aiden Welch turned up.

I'd been hand-washing clothes in the utility room at the back, having imaginary confrontations with Madeleine at work, when a feeling of being watched crawled over me and

I swung around.

How long, I thought, had he been eyeing me from behind?

Staring through the glass partition of the back door, dark eyes dancing, he let his insolent gaze finish travelling all the way up my body until it reached my face. Despite the fact it was still March and cold out of the sun, he was wearing a tight, short-sleeved white t-shirt with jeans, his broadly built body dominating the doorway. Legs like tree trunks, I thought. Thickset. Chunky. Squat. Not remotely my type. Which made what followed even more bizarre.

Skip had burst out before I could stop him and, momentarily flustered, it took me a while to get him back inside.

"I see you've got full control there," he said.

"Hi! Sorry, I wasn't expecting anyone."

"Floorboards?"

"What?"

"Ma said you needed us to give you a quote?"

"Oh yes, blimey, I'd completely forgotten. Come in."

Unprepared for the visit, I was obliged to start rolling back carpets and lino, my voice echoing self-consciously as I rabbited on about the tree, that Glynn was on his way back, and that he'd be here any moment now. I don't recall Aiden saying a word. The only thing I do remember, and it was absolutely unstoppable, was that as he stood leaning against the wall, silently watching, my head began to fill with a hot confusion of images. It was the weirdest thing. I could hear my own voice chattering away but was barely conscious of what I said, while in streamed a dozen or more scenarios – he had hold of my hair, had pushed me against the wall, his breath on my neck. We were on the bed upstairs, the marital bed… I didn't want any of it, tried to force the images out of my head, but the express train of visions still kept coming.

Eventually, he began to lever up a few boards.

"Dry rot," he said, telling me what we already knew. "Joists as well."

We stood facing each other in the darkening kitchen, his gaze burning into mine.

"Could be the air bricks," he said.

For some reason I wasn't processing anything he said. It felt as if I'd had too much wine, the scenery through the window a blur. No words, no questions, no replies would form. And still those images kept streaming into my head – him leading me upstairs, pulling me on top of him, onto white cotton sheets. I knew that his skin was silky and golden, his stomach hard as stone…

From a branch outside the open window, a blackbird's song filled the void of silence, fresh and clear and real, the heady scent of wet earth and sweet violets drifting in from the woods. We were a heartbeat away from crossing an invisible threshold, for everything I held sacred to be given away and sullied. I would be conscious of it. Would know. And still do it.

Then, thankfully, Glynn's car crunched onto the gravel outside, and the trance broke so abruptly it was like a small electric shock.

As soon as he burst in through the back door I left them to it. Turned out the extension had been done cheaply just as Kendra had said, and although there were air bricks, they were blocked with rubble on the inside. Plus, it had been empty for years and years, and no treatment had been applied to the wood. The whole of the ground floor was damp, rotten, and had to be replaced.

"I wonder where the original well was?" I said. "If it's underneath the house? It feels so cold in here sometimes."

We were sitting in the lounge with the fire lit, looking out as dusk descended.

"Can you see those?" Glynn said. "Can you see lights?"

Hovering over the low-lying fields were globes of white light, and for a moment my heart lurched, thinking of the orbs in the bedroom. So, Glynn could see them, too? I could tell him!

"Phosphorescent phenomena," he said. "Or corpse lights, if you listen to old folk tales. It's said if you see them, you'll soon die."

"Who told you that?"

He shrugged. "I was sitting next to Monica at the dinner table the other week. Think it was her."

"Will-o'-the-wisp?"

He nodded. "It's a real thing, gases over damp earth."

"Glynn, how much is it all going to cost? Can the kitchen units be rescued?"

He nodded. "Yes, thank God. And it'll be a good price from Aiden and Duncan. We'll get a loan. It'll be okay."

"At least we've both got jobs," I said, as Madeleine's face appeared in my mind's eye.

"Don't worry, Lyddie. It's just a setback."

But his voice was tight.

"We were really stupid. I hope I get another job after this one."

He stood up, went to fetch another bottle of IPA.

"One day at a time."

And that's where I left him that night, cracking open another bottle, a fourth, a fifth, watching television, some inane, mind-numbing show about people we didn't know and never would.

And then a week later Aiden Welch came back.

Once again finding me alone.

One of the tree surgeons we'd asked for a quote had only just left. I'd rushed upstairs for a shower, then, remembering the door wasn't locked, bounded downstairs.

He was at the back door again, staring in through the glass. There'd been no sound. No crunch of gravel. No bark from Skip. And I physically jumped in shock.

Opening the door a few inches, the thought resounded in my head, that if I hadn't remembered it still being unlocked I'd have been in the shower. And why the hell didn't he use the front door like everyone else?

"You nearly gave me a heart attack. I didn't know anyone was there. Glynn will be home in a minute."

He thrust a piece of paper at me. "Ma's done you a quote. It'll probably be June, but we'll let you know."

"Thanks. Glynn will be home soon."

He held my gaze.

"Yeah, you said. You're a nurse, right?"

"Yes."

"Bailey told you about Letitia?"

"Who?"

"Ma wasn't keen at first, but it's getting more difficult for Bailey to look after Gran, so we wondered if you'd be interested in some part-time work? Unofficial. Just to give my brother a break..." He was staring at me intensely, unnervingly so. "Sitting with her, mostly."

The visions were back, as if this invisible, imaginary affair had picked up where it left off, and was careering into the next instalment – Aiden leading me by the hand, along a gloomy, oak-panelled corridor. I could sense the stillness of Ashe House, the echoing walls, feel the power of the charge between us, all pretence now stripped away as the bedroom door closed behind us. Dark red curtains billowing in the breeze... the painting of a woman on the opposite wall...

His eyes bored into mine. "We'd pay you. Whatever you want."

That night, I am sorry to say I lay there thinking about him. While Glynn slept beside me, my head was full of Aiden Welch, his dark hair stark against the white of a pillow, in a bedroom dimmed by red curtains pulled against the glare of the afternoon sun. In the corner there was a single white wardrobe with a door not properly shut, and the painting on the wall was now clear; it was of a woman lying on a beach, foaming waves caressing tanned skin, long auburn hair splayed behind. And as his hands traced every curve of my body, into my senses came the scent of violets, the song of a blackbird from the courtyard below, and the illicit electric thrill of crossing a threshold into forbidden realms.

Working in their house, it would be possible. Empty days. Empty rooms...

Fay's son!

And then into the darkness came the orbs, dancing their cosmic dance, and it seemed to me they were brighter than stars, spirited and conscious.

***

Chapter Fourteen

Mary Letitia Killen was the old lady's name. She was ninety-five.

I was not to meet her for a while yet, though. First, there were a couple of incidents. Taken independently they may have been nothing, barely worth mentioning, but a true picture requires thousands of different brushstrokes, each one integral to the whole, and back then I was a long way from seeing truth.

The first occurred while I was driving to work. It would have been about ten past seven when I set off that morning, later than planned, but, traffic permitting, I should have been able to get to work on time. Coach Lane was empty. So far, so good. Then, turning right at the junction towards the old stone bridge, I saw the road was clear and I was pleased. I should make it! But no sooner had I driven over the bridge when I spotted the tail end of a car ahead, and quickly closed the gap.

It was an old silver Citroen, the cracked rear lights held together with sticky tape, and instantly recognisable as one of the cars belonging to Professor Yates or his wife at The Old Rectory. A quick glance at the speedometer showed they were trundling along at around twenty-five miles an hour, and with no way to get past I was forced to drop back. Periodically, the driver braked, on the slightest of bends, or for no discernible reason at all, and changing down to second gear, I took a deep breath. It wasn't far to the main road. Maybe the professor and his wife were very old? Or hadn't twigged anyone was behind?

At that moment, though, the driver checked the rear-view mirror. Ah, so they did know. Well, maybe they were nervous? Eventually, we reached the junction at the red signpost, at which point they sat for quite a while. In fact, they sat so long I thought they'd parked. Not one car passed on the main road from either direction, and for a minute, slightly confused, I waited. The road was absolutely clear. Why didn't they move off? Bird song could be heard. I tried not to look at the clock on the dash, but my stomach was beginning to tie itself into knots. I'd be late! And Madeleine wasn't exactly forgiving.

I've mentioned my anxiety around her before. Madeleine. Not to be abbreviated. Petite, with dark hair styled in a similar way to an old-fashioned Marcel wave, she had a permanent, almost saintly half-smile on her face. Madeleine, however, was not saintly. Madeleine was merciless. She had the power to allocate life-ruining shifts, repeatedly assign the most violent and incontinent of patients, and to write performance reports bearing almost no resemblance to reality – reports that were damning enough to cancel all plans a person might have harboured for a future career.

Having observed the Citroen's taped-up rear light at close range for what seemed like an eternity, my heart began to hammer ever faster, one hand hovering over the horn... should I, shouldn't I? When all at once the driver shot off like a bullet from a gun. Great! I followed briskly. Now there was a chance to make up time. However, they appeared to have settled at around forty mph, so, with the road clear and a straight stretch coming up, I indicated to overtake. But just as I pulled out and accelerated, the Citroen gravitated towards the centre of the road and blocked me. Then braked. So hard I nearly ran in the back of it.

"What the fuck?"

Immediately, I pulled back in.

So did the Citroen.

There was still about half a mile of straight road ahead. After that, it would snake with twists and turns, and be far too dangerous to overtake. The driver must have drifted out without realising, I thought. It couldn't possibly have been deliberate. So, I tried again. Indicated and pulled out. There was plenty of space, plenty of time, and no reason the driver could not allow the person behind to get past. After all, they'd now slowed to less than forty miles an hour.

Within a couple of seconds, I drew level and, curious, glanced sidelong at the driver on passing – male, bespectacled, light brown hair, pale face – when incredibly, horrifyingly, he began to speed up, accelerating rapidly to seventy, then eighty. My car didn't have enough power, it had a much smaller engine, and in the interests of safety I was forced once again to drop back. After which there was no choice but to sit behind him all the way along the winding, bending road into town. On bends, he braked abruptly, leaning over as if on a yacht, speed down to twenty. I was nearly crying with frustration and rage by the time I got to work, ten minutes late and yet to park.

As I hurried up the steps to the hospital, something about him was bothering me hugely, nagging, insistent and disconcerting, but there wasn't time to think that day; and thus it was weeks, months even, before it was to resurface. A piece of the painting that didn't yet make any sense.

The other incident was to do with the tree surgeon. We'd contacted three independent firms, none of them local, and the quotes came in between seven and twelve hundred pounds, far higher than anticipated. We'd thought, based on work Glynn had paid for the previous year, that it would be around three hundred. Obviously, we took the cheapest, after which we photocopied the estimate and dropped it through Keith's letterbox together with the date booked. No way, we decided, were we calling on him personally. We'd bitten the bullet on paying, informed him, that was it.

On Saturday morning, two blokes in a truck arrived, Glynn went out to meet them, and shortly afterwards Keith Cribbs ambled over. The job took two hours. They worked quickly with ropes and chainsaws, and were pleasant enough. However, it turned out the price did not include chopping or stacking the wood for us. The price was solely for the job of taking the tree down. As such, the options were to either leave the fallen wood where it was, or take it away for an additional fee. Keith told Glynn he was okay with it being left where it was, and relieved, he thanked him. Maybe between them they could sort it out later.

I never went out and so didn't know, at that point, what had been said. But I did know what happened next because I was watching from the bathroom window between the slats of the Venetian blinds. Something, call it instinct, kept me there.

Glynn handed over our seven hundred pounds in cash, obtained a handwritten receipt, and then walked back towards the house. It had all looked and sounded very congenial, with a few laughs, all four of them smoking. But as soon as Glynn closed the front door behind him, the one who'd taken the money peeled off a wad of notes and handed them to Keith Cribbs, who proceeded to count them out. And I distinctly heard the other one say, as he clicked the rear guard of the truck into place, that they'd see him later at 'The Brank.' That it was 'his round'.

The Brank? I was puzzled. Hadn't the inn been closed for decades?

I didn't tell Glynn straight away what I'd seen, but the felled tree plus all of the branches, vanished from the field while we were both at work a few days later. And so on impulse, after noticing Keith's Mitsubishi pick-up truck trundle past one morning, I drove up to his farm on the pretext of dropping in a copy of the receipt, because I had this hunch. I didn't bother leaving the receipt, of course, it was just in case he or Cicely appeared. What I wanted to know was if my hunch was correct. And it was. At the back of his farm, piled behind in the yard, was a load of freshly cut logs. Chopped and stacked.

I knew our money had included sawing them. That we'd been fitted up. But that company hadn't even been local. How had it happened? Did Keith know every tree-logger inside two counties?

Driving home from Keith's farm deep in thought, a bit despondent, I let myself in with the intention of taking Skip out for a walk, when I noticed a leaflet on the mat.

Handwritten, it was an invitation to Carrie Cade's birthday party. I remember standing with it in my hand.

Thank God, there were nice people in the world. All these undercurrents I sensed were getting out of hand again, because it was pretty simple, really; Keith had stitched us up for money, just as Kath had. They didn't care about us because we were new here, strangers to them. The professor's driving was shit. And Fay was protecting her mother. That's all there was to it. My imagination had run away with me completely. Of course, the old boys would give themselves backhanders. Of course, some people took advantage, were rude, or changed personality behind the wheel; but most were straightforward and kind.

Like Glynn said, we were not going to let anyone spoil our lives. We loved it there. Worked hard to be there. And really, all was well. I'd never seen so many daffodils in all my life. There were thousands of them, brilliant golden trumpets heralding the advent of Spring. There'd been a hare on the lawn that morning, blossom buds were on the verge of emerging, irises rising up around the wild pond, marsh marigolds a splash of yellow around the edges. The earth was sweet, sun warmer, days longer, as the wheel turned and clicked into Ostara, the season of abundance and fertility. Besides, here was someone who had kept her word and invited us into her home. Kendra would probably be there, too.

Really, we couldn't let someone like Keith Cribbs bring us down, because there was so much to look forward to. A statement that now reads back like dramatic irony...

***

Chapter Fifteen

As the equinox approached and the winds blew warmer, I took Skip for longer and longer walks, usually into the woodland via the gate at the end of the garden. It was such a pleasure. There were no formal paths, the grass untrodden except for us. Violets clustered in shaded dells, and primroses, lemon and rose, appeared on the banks with the dandelions. It was an enchanted place, a cathedral of birdsong, drilling woodpeckers, and humming bees, with the ever-present trickle of Horseshoe Brook in the background.

About halfway in, there was a huge boulder etched with an arrow and the words, *1.5 miles*, although it didn't say where to, and I wondered if that was the original track up to The Tollhouse and Upper Creech. Certainly the wood ran adjacent to Coach Lane, ending only with the large expanse of fields now belonging to the Cade family. One morning, I'd been about to loop around as usual and return to the cottage, when I noticed a recently trodden track, a fox-run perhaps, shooting off at right angles, and on impulse decided to see if there was an exit to Coach Lane. I was going to offer to sit with Fay's elderly mother for a few hours a week if it helped the family, and we could certainly do with the extra income. It couldn't be in a professional capacity, but might work well for all parties.

By then, Glynn was working a lot more hours, taking on weekend and evening work others didn't want. He was also drinking more. But if I questioned him, the barriers went up. We each had our way of dealing with stress, I suppose, and that was his. Mine was to go on ever longer walks. I found solace and peace in nature, and the more I went out with Skip, the stronger the bond. I loved that dog more than I can say. We walked everywhere together – up to Barrow Ridge, down into the valley, skirting the abbey ruins, then back up through the woods. We must have been a well-known sight.

Well, that day Fay's Morris Oxford was the only car in the drive. I'd already decided that if the Subaru was there, I'd leave it and come back another time. So, I tied Skip to the fence, then bounded up the steps to the front door.

Fay seemed flustered. "Oh! I'm just off out!"

"Sorry. No problem, I can come back another time. It's just that Aiden said you'd appreciate someone sitting with your mum, and asked if I'd call in sometime."

She stared at me askance. She was wearing a turban and hoop earrings, reds and blacks, something floaty, maybe a kaftan.

"Honestly, don't worry. I can come back," I repeated. "I was just out with Skip and happened to be passing."

"No, no, it's all right. Come in. As a matter of fact, the boys will be back soon. I was waiting for them so I could go out. I'll take you up to Mum." He hands were flapping around, cheeks pink, as she ushered me inside. "But I'll have to leave you alone with her for a minute. I've got the cakes to pack up yet. For the history society meeting."

We were standing in the cool shade of the hallway, beneath a paper moon lightshade. Rucksacks and trainers were strewn across the bare floor, coat pegs weighted with layers of anoraks, coats and fleeces, and I found myself staring into the lounge we'd sat and played cards in. It seemed gloomier than before, more reminiscent than ever of a disused social club or an empty waiting room.

Fay glanced at her watch and headed for the staircase.

"Come on up. Be warned, though – she has dreadful dementia."

"I didn't realise she had dementia, Fay. Don't worry, I'm used to it. That's what I work with at the moment."

She glanced over her shoulder.

"It won't be like Letitia's. She talks gobbledygook like you've never heard in your life, utter nonsense, so take no notice. None of it is remotely true, either. She'll fabricate the most outrageous lies. Just for fun, probably."

A portrait of a man with dark eyes faced us on the first-floor landing. He wore a wig in the style of a judge, a red coat, and had several dogs at his feet. I felt as though I'd seen him before somewhere, but Fay swept past in a hurry, leading the way down another dark oak corridor, until we came to a door at the far end, and a bedroom overlooking the front garden with Barrow Ridge beyond.

Mary Letitia Killen was Irish, had brilliant azure eyes and a shock of long white hair.

"Mum, this is Lyddie. She's our new neighbour, and a nurse."

The old lady's voice was weak, croaky and cross as she gazed around wildly and said, "What is it? What are you saying? I don't understand! Why do you keep making me go to work?"

Fay raised her eyes to the heavens. "Good luck. Anyway, I'll be back in a jiffy."

After she'd gone, I took hold of the fragile-looking hand reaching out for mine.

"What beautiful eyes," said Letitia, her grip surprisingly strong.

It took a moment. I think my eyebrows must have reached my hairline. The old lady's voice wasn't weak and croaky at all now, but lilting and powerful, her eyes as bright and sharp as silver glinting in the sun.

"Thank you." This must be a rare lucid moment, I thought. "You're very kind. How are you feeling today?"

"Well done, Bailey. He got Aiden to bring you, did he? He's cleverer than you think, you know? Now, I've something to tell you and it's important. You will listen to me, won't you?"

She'd spoken all in a rush, and lapsed for a moment, catching her breath, staring out of the window at Barrow Ridge, at the dance of sunlight on the canopy of trees below, and the granite grey clouds rolling heavily across the sky.

"Sit down next to me, Lydia."

"Oh, please call me Lyddie. Lyddie Spicer. I only just moved to the village with my husband, Glynn."

"Yes, I know who you are. There's a message for you."

She then repeated, pretty much verbatim, what Zach Stipple had said.

"You've to be careful. It's not what you think here. Don't be too quick to judge, to take sides."

My face must have registered shock, because her voice then softened. "And consider stepping away from your own perspective. It's holding you back, Lyddie, keeping you a prisoner. You've been through such a lot."

For a while, I couldn't think what to say. Fay's advice was still ringing in my ears, that Letitia spoke nonsense and to take no notice. But she wasn't like any patient with dementia I'd ever come across. And her grip on my hand was as strong as iron. Bemused, I stared into sapphire crystal eyes, wide and honest and piercing.

Eventually, I said, "Someone else said a very similar thing to me not so long ago. Couple of months–"

"You've to be very careful who you trust."

I nodded. "Well, we've had a few incidents here, but–"

"They'll not be coincidences. They're trying to find your boundaries, get your measure. But this is the important thing – you've got something they want but they don't know you've got it yet. It was never found. When the time comes, you've to keep it to yourself though, do you understand?"

Fay's footsteps were pounding up the stairs. There was a slam of a door.

"Two minutes," she called.

The papery hand drew mine closer towards her by the wrist. "You have the most unusual aura I've ever seen, child. Do you not know? Do you not know?"

"Know what?

By then, Fay's shadow was darkening the corridor outside, and I could only shake my head, puzzled.

"Everything all right?" Fay asked.

I muttered something about being happy to come back if Letitia would like me to. I really, badly wanted to go back.

"We were talking about the wild flowers in the woods this time of year," Letitia said, lapsing into the feeble, croaky voice she'd used before. "She's seen violets already, Fay. Now how about that? And isn't it wonderful to hear the blackbirds sing?"

Were we? Had I? Was it?

Of violets and blackbirds, there'd been no mention. We hadn't discussed wildflowers or anything like that. In fact, both images in the same sentence set my heart racing.

My heels clattered after Fay's down the corridor and, perhaps because I wasn't thinking clearly, the next part is also vague. But as we walked back to the staircase, one of the doors that had previously been shut was now ajar, and without forethought, I glanced in. Less than a second. Enough, however, to notice the crimson curtains drawn against the afternoon light, a single white wardrobe, and a painting on the opposite wall to the bed – of a woman on a seashore, reclining in the waves with her head back, face to the sun, long auburn hair flowing behind her... Exactly the same scene, the same room, the same painting that had been in my dreams the evening Aiden called, along with the song of a blackbird, and the scent of violets.

At some point, Fay and I had stood in the kitchen and agreed thirty pounds cash for a couple of hours each week, so Bailey could 'get out more'. I would sit and talk with Letitia, perhaps help her with things Bailey couldn't manage, personal matters. And a few minutes later I was outside again, bending to unfasten Skip's lead.

His concerned brown eyes met mine.

"It's okay," I reassured him. "Just a bit of an odd conversation."

Shortly after that, however, things were to take an even stranger turn, this time in the form of Carrie Cade's party. I'd never seen anyone slapped across the face in front of all their neighbours before, and haven't since. But that's what happened. Not a sharp slap of pique, either, but a serious crack with full weight behind it. Twice. The backhander even harder. It was a wonder the man's head was still on.

***

Chapter Sixteen

The night after seeing Letitia, I lay next to Glynn, once more wide-eyed and sleepless. Judgement, again! And what was it I had that they wanted? Who were 'they'?

Consider stepping away from your own perspective. It's holding you back, Lyddie, keeping you a prisoner. What on earth was she talking about? But most of all, what disturbed me beyond anything else was how she'd known about the dreams, the visions that had wormed their way into my mind with Aiden. Because I had the feeling that when she'd spoken to Fay as I was leaving, those words had been meant for me.

Glynn had come home late that night, wanting only to eat before slumping in front of the television with a few bottles of IPA. But before he did, I told him I'd agreed to help with Letitia, and somehow ended up mentioning the incident with Professor Yates.

"See it all the time, Lyds. Lots of people like to police others when they get a chance."

"I know, but it was like something out of that movie, what was it… *Duel*? It seemed, I dunno, nasty, personal. Like he knew who I was. To be honest, it upset me."

"Guessing it was meant to."

"Why, though?"

He shrugged. "People, innit?"

"There's something else, too."

I then told him about the cut the tree surgeons had given to Keith Cribbs and the pile of logs he'd had at our expense."

"Fuckers."

"Yes. There wasn't anything else we could have done though, was there?"

"No. Look, don't piss me off any more, Lyds. Tell me something nice."

"Sorry."

I talked instead about the walk in the woods, the fallow deer in the glade, and the screech owl that evening. But not being able to talk to him about all the things I needed to, meant being alone with my thoughts, and at times I questioned my own sanity. Was I seeing and hearing things, perceiving things, that weren't there? For a while I thought that.

My eyes bored into the darkness of the bedroom, focusing on the strip of light around the border of the door, anticipating the strange, dancing orbs. There was an echoing coldness in the cottage, and I became convinced there was a well underneath the house. I could even picture it – a deep, circular stone construction, marsh water oozing through mossy cracks, dripping steadily into a blackened pool at the bottom.

Eventually, dozens of bright blue orbs began to appear around the bed, lanterns suspended in the velvet black night. But despite the stirring of fear inside, increasingly I found I could gaze at them curiously, more accepting of their presence. Perhaps there was an earthly explanation?

Could it be related to the phosphorescence over the fields? For a while I thought that, too.

But during the night, in the hypnagogic state between sleeping and waking, a man spoke into my ear, as clearly, precisely and deliberately as if he were sitting right next to me. It was the voice of an old man, the accent strong Dorset.

"*All of the old paths interweave and interlock, criss-crossing into the mizmaze!*"

I jumped awake. The only sound was the rise and fall of Glynn's breathing.

My heart was hammering hard. I had to get a hold of myself, inhale to the count of ten, release it slowly, concentrate solely on that, and not on the possibility, the horrible and very real possibility, that the ghostly man in black was going to reappear. That he'd been real, after all. Was the voice his? Was it him? Had he been sitting on the side of the bed all this time, watching me?

I was plunged into terror in a heartbeat. All the fears came back. One after the other. Culminating with Madeleine again. I didn't want to worry him because we needed every penny. And so I hadn't told him about her. Madeleine with the Marcel wave hair, almost all of it clumped on one side of her head, the mad, staring left eye, the permanent half-smile on her lips, 'Could you step into my office for a moment, Nurse Spicer?'

Again?

What if I lost my job?

I could not sleep... had to think of something nice. The night, though, seemed interminable. I kept staring into the corners, half expecting to see the hooded creatures with no faces, and it wasn't until a faint grey thread of light appeared through the curtains, that I finally relaxed enough to sleep. It would be all right, everything would be all right. I reassured myself repeatedly... everything all right... everything perfectly fine... Before finding myself back in the room with the picture of the woman on the beach.

Aiden's room.

That's where I was. No doubt about it. In a lucid dream, lying on a bed of crumpled sheets, red curtains drawn against the sun. I could smell, touch and taste his warm, musky skin, feel the pulsing waves of pleasure within me. Someone was clattering crockery downstairs in the kitchen like it was an easy Sunday morning, wind rustling the ash trees outside, and we were looking deeply into each other's eyes. I will not describe what felt like drugged, drunken treachery. I just pray that on some level it wasn't real, that because it was in my mind it did not make it so. I honestly cannot say. Except it felt deeply unsettling, like the illusional trick of a devil.

When I awoke, it was to an empty bed. Glynn had already left for work, sunlight was streaming through the windows, clouds were scooting across Barrow Ridge. It felt closer to the seasons there in Creech Cross, to the earth, to the old ways and the turn of the wheel. I had a strong sense, could picture, that there'd once been a maypole on the village green, that the people here had celebrated Ostara, Beltane, the Solstices, Lammas, Samhain... but also that something had happened in our cottage, an event that was traumatic and somehow pivotal. But I had no idea how I knew those things.

Which brings me to Carrie Cade's birthday, because it was on the equinox, the beginning of Ostara, or Easter.

I was looking forward to it. Something nice, I thought,

a celebration. Glynn was working so it meant going alone, but I didn't mind. Dressing to cover all bases, I chose a knee-length denim skirt with low-heeled tan boots, a white fitted shirt with three-quarter-length sleeves, and a navy woollen jacket in case it was cold in the house. I ate a sandwich before I went, in case there wasn't any food, then wrapped a bottle of decent white wine plus the box of hand creams made with essential oils that I'd bought.

Carrie answered the door.

"Ooh, lovely. Thanks!"

Plonking the gifts on the kitchen table, she then led the way to a room at the back, where there was, she said, a buffet.

"Plenty to eat. Dig in and then we'll start. I think everyone's here now. We're in the lounge. Just come through when you've loaded up."

Start?

I will describe the buffet only because it became relevant. A bag of apples and oranges had been emptied onto a tray. On another were whole, floury white bread buns, not sliced or buttered, and a huge slab of cheddar still in its waxy casing, was on another. There was also a joint of ham and several boxes of Aldi sausage rolls stacked one on top of the other. A couple of carving knives and a packet of serviettes completed the buffet, along with half a dozen Easter eggs, also still in boxes. Nothing had been touched.

I picked up an apple, gradually becoming aware of others in what had at first appeared to be an empty room. Mallory and Slim, both wearing baseball caps as before, stood like bouncers with arms folded by the entrance to the lounge. 'Starting' must be in there, I thought, gravitating towards it, which was when I noticed the man in the lilac woollen sweater. Pale brown hair, pale face, and glasses. Next to him was someone wearing trousers held up by red braces, a checked shirt and a flat cap, also wearing glasses but squinting through jam-jar-bottom thickness. The last time I'd seen anyone dressed like that, it was my old grandad, a coalminer from Wakefield, and I think I must have gawped a second too long, because the man in the lilac sweater was smirking, and with an uncomfortable lurch I recognised who he was.

We were the only people in the room apart from the bull terrier, who was panting hotly, and wetly, by the table, strands of saliva hanging from his mouth as he focused with absolute intent on the ham joint.

"Um, is your dog all right left there?" I called after Carrie.

She paused and, still clutching the Zimmer frame, glanced over her shoulder. "Yes, of course," she laughed. "He's vegetarian."

I laughed too, wondering if she was going to introduce me to Professor Yates.

"Anyway, come on in, we're ready," she said. "Is that all you want to eat?"

In the absence of any drinks, I nodded. "Yes, thanks. Sorry, I'm holding you all up."

She turned back towards the lounge. "Come on through."

And it was only then, as I made to follow her in, that I noticed the altar on the sideboard behind the professor.

***

Chapter Seventeen

I had to walk past them. So, I smiled and nodded, at the same time trying to surreptitiously eye the altar behind.

"Hello!" I said. "Hello!"

The altar was, to put it mildly, different. There was a candle at either side, and in the middle a vase of dandelions, nettles, primroses and violets, a branch with early sprigs on it, and several painted eggs. So far, so good. There were also model creatures, either knitted or made out of felt, mostly rabbits, hares and chickens. However, the major jarring difference, between that altar and anything else I'd ever seen, was the picture above it. 'Jarring difference' being an understatement.

I walked into the lounge with my eyes wide. Had I just seen what I thought I'd seen? A lewd depiction of a horned deity? Was it really doing what I thought it was doing?

The lounge looked perfectly mundane, and I struggled for a moment to process the incongruity – on the one hand, the explicit erotica of a dark being with burning red eyes clearly raping a naked cherubic girl in a wooded dell, and on the other, here was a room full of people ready for a family party. I was clutching the apple, still reeling, attempting to make sense of a layout I'd just begun to realise was odd. In the centre was a large table, behind it a row of people, rather like an interview panel. Everyone else was seated as if in a cinema, the atmosphere one of expectation.

"Drink, Lyddie?"

I swung round to find, with relief, that it was Kendra.

"Oh, hi! Sorry, I didn't see you there."

She handed over a glass of wine laced with herbs, and I heard her say to the people behind, "Here you go, Mervin. And Rosamund. How are you?"

Noticing a chair by the door to the dining room, I quickly sat down and scanned the room. Part of me was wondering how soon I could leave, but another part was curious to see how this panned out. Monica, easily identifiable by the scarlet hair and glittery headband, was sitting with Tim on the front row, and Fay was chatting to one of several people I didn't know. In fact, there was no one else in the room I knew. Perhaps the rest were locals? It was possible. Maybe the Cade family rubbed along well with them?

Or had I got that wrong and the other guests were family? Kendra said they came for weddings and christenings, so probably birthdays, too? Yes, of course! And the more I looked around, the more I thought that would be the case, because most of them looked pretty smart. Many of the women wore neat shift dresses, and apart from an old man with wild white hair and a roving eye, the men were in suits.

Alas, I could not have been more wrong.

Carrie was now at the head of the table, clearing her throat to speak, and Mallory and Slim slinked inside. But just before the door closed behind them, I noticed the bull terrier grab his chance and lunge for the ham joint on the table, his enormous paws dragging the tablecloth off along with the plate.

I called out. "Mallory, the dog's got the ham!"

"I told you, he's vegetarian," Carrie shouted. "He won't touch it. Come on in, Mallory. We're waiting."

Mallory closed the door as if nothing had happened and the scene of the dog hunkering down on the carpet, slavering victoriously over the joint, vanished from view.

Kendra slipped onto the seat next to me, stifling a giggle.

"Thank you all for coming today," Carrie said.

I was trying so hard not to laugh, but the giggle was infectious. It was like being back in school and Kendra's influence was only making it worse. She was openly snorting, and to avoid drawing attention to myself, I took a sip of wine and tried to think of something serious. It certainly took my mind off the dog, anyway, immediately hitting the back of the throat. Syrupy, like the homemade gooseberry wine my grandad specialised in, the alcohol crossed the blood-brain barrier almost instantaneously. Another couple of gulps and I didn't think I'd be able to spell my own name. It had the bitter sweetness of herbs, but also a rooty, earthy ingredient that remained elusive, a concoction that tasted like weed, valerian and methylated spirit. It fogged the brain, glazed the eyes and furred the tongue and in minutes, the room and everyone in it were swimming in and out of focus.

"Happy Birthday, Carrie!" someone said, raising a toast.

"Happy Birthday," I muttered, trying to hold onto my seat.

"Do you want another one?" Kendra whispered.

"Although, I'd advise going easy on it. This stuff could anaesthetise a bull."

"God, no. I mean, thank you but…"

"Chucked mine in the pot plant and I think it just died."

Afternoon sun had broken through the clouds, streaming through the French doors, the heating was on full and I took off my navy jacket, slinging it drunkenly over the back of a chair I hoped was my own. The room had gone quiet all of a sudden, the hush almost reverential, as everyone waited for Carrie's speech. Mallory and Slim were behind her, backs to the wall, observing us like a couple of special agents, and the girl on a chair next to Slim, with hair hanging either side of her face in long black curtains, I guessed was his wife-to-be. She had the look of someone on drugs; she seemed vague, not really present.

"That's Nylah Trask," Kendra whispered. "She was the cleaner but Slim knocked her up. She's about five months gone, I think."

Someone turned round to glare at us, and Kendra smiled.

"So," Carrie said. "First of all, thank you for the pressies. I'll enjoy opening those later. And I hope you've all had your fill to eat and drink?"

Everyone murmured appreciatively and I started to giggle again, thinking the only one to have had his fill was the dog.

"And let us all welcome in Ostara. Here's to fertility, love, rebirth and regeneration." She lifted her glass to Nylah. "To new life!"

"Hear, hear!"

"We'll have our true celebration later tonight as always,

and–"

Several people laughed.

"Yes. And I hope everyone will join in the fun. We also have a new member, who accepted our invitation today, and that's Lyddie Spicer. Welcome, Lyddie!"

I know I coloured up, a hot colour infused by the wine.

"Welcome, Lyddie!"

"Welcome!"

One by one they turned to look at me and raise a glass. There was something strange about the whole thing, but I couldn't put my finger on what it was. It felt… and maybe this is only with the benefit of hindsight, but… ritualistic.

"However, before we can move onto the fun and games, there's business to attend to. As you know, Professor Yates has designed a new bridge to replace the old stone one, and is trying to raise funds. He's a professor of architecture and has brought the design for everyone to see. Slim, will you pass it round?"

There was a bit of commotion as the drawing was duly handed from one to the other, and everyone nodded and smiled. So, these people can't be her relatives then, I was thinking, or they wouldn't be asked to look at a picture of the new bridge, surely? I was one of the last to see it, along with Kendra. Not sure what to expect, I remember staring at it, and rapidly sobering up. Totally out of keeping with the old village, here was a design more suited to an inner-city docklands. Of stainless steel predominantly, it had four rails and in between were Perspex panels, interlocked with oversized bolts. Very urban. Very futuristic. I didn't know whether, as a new person to the village, I should voice my thoughts, because that design would undoubtedly spoil the aesthetics and obliterate its history. Or to stay quiet. Would my feelings even hold any sway, because everyone else seemed so enthusiastic?

"And don't worry, all the costings have been done," Carrie went on, now sporting spectacles and holding up a piece of paper. "It works out at five hundred and eighty-four pounds each, seeing as local people won't be chipping in. And not including Professor Yates, of course, since he did the design for free."

The shock was a punch to the gut.

"They've got to be kidding," I said under my breath.

But several people had started to clap, hands pointed in the direction of the man in the lilac sweater. One or two of them had even stood up, giving him an ovation.

I broke a sweat. Glynn and I really didn't have any more money. We were skint for the foreseeable. We couldn't even rob Peter to pay Paul, with overdrafts and loans already maxed out. I wanted to leave, and leave at once. Run out, in fact. But into my rapidly clearing brain, came comprehension – she'd said the locals wouldn't pay. That meant the people here weren't locals, either. So, they must be relatives. In which case, what the hell did this have to do with them? It didn't make sense.

"Are you all right, Lyddie?"

Carrie addressed me directly and everyone turned round. Monica's silver headband was glinting in the sunlight, Tim's watery eyes set in a shiny pink face, Fay's turquoise pashmina, the man with the wild white hair and bulbous eyes. They were all looking at me quizzically. Eyes from every angle. And words of panic just flew out of my mouth.

"We can't afford that. We only just moved here. We don't have the money."

There were a few sighs, mutterings, people turning away again.

"Where've I heard that before?"

"So much for community spirit."

"Exactly."

"Well, we've done our best to keep the cost reasonable," said Monica. She looked at the professor. "I suppose we could look at suppliers again and see if more savings could be made?"

We?

There was a slight, almost imperceptible nod from Mervin Yates, before, fortunately, Carrie moved on to talk about a charity she'd set up, that was designed for local improvement, the planting of trees lining the roads and ideas for the village green. They began to discuss an upcoming summer fair and ideas for stalls. The traditional event could be used to garner more funds, she said, which were badly needed. So far, they'd gone door to door and raised four hundred pounds, but eighty had already been spent, so there was a long way to go.

"That was obviously for today's buffet."

My eyes widened for the second time in less than ten minutes.

"So, along with fundraising, we need ideas on how to make our village more beautiful," Colin added. "How do we spend the money?"

They were talking across one another when suddenly I heard my name.

"Lyddie?"

Carrie had me pinned for the second time.

"Would you be interested in selling raffle tickets door to door?"

I had no answer prepared.

But as it turned out, there was no need. Because a woman had stood up. And she appeared to be waiting for people to notice her, which, one by one, they did. The room fell quiet. I recognised her instantly as Agnus Stipple, who that day was dressed in a poncho, baggy jeans and pink plimsolls. With a fixed look on her face, large brown eyes unblinking, she'd started to walk towards Mervin Yates.

"What the fuck?" Kendra hissed.

Methodically, it could be said ceremonially, she was making her way across the room to where he was leaning against the far wall with his arms folded. On reaching him, for a second or two they stood as opponents. And then she drew back her hand as if to hit an Ace serve, and walloped him across the face.

Kendra gasped.

No one in the room said a word.

And then the backhander came, belting him so hard on the other side it was a miracle his skull didn't dislocate from the spine. It was so violent, you could hear the air whistle before impact. His glasses were thrown across the carpet, and he staggered slightly.

Still no one spoke.

Nor did Agnus.

And then someone took hold of her elbow and led her quietly from the room.

"Fuck me!" Kendra hissed.

"That was assault," I whispered.

"Wouldn't think she had it in 'er, would you? She nearly took his frickin' head off."

A woman had her arm around Agnus in the dining room, we could see through the gap. She was stone still, not one word, not a whimper, the scene reminiscent of a mind control agent who'd carried out an assassination – no emotion, totally detached. I really wanted to leave so badly. The atmosphere was extremely odd and I was very uncomfortable. It's hard to explain, but I felt that staying was somehow consenting to it being acceptable. And here's the thing; it was a slow dawning, if you like, a gradual realisation, but the reaction in the room wasn't like mine. The others didn't seem shocked. And Mervin, who had a fuchsia handprint on both cheeks, was retrieving his glasses as if nothing particularly untoward had happened. And something even weirder – as he put them back on, he glanced up and caught my eye. Why would he look at me? Why me? And what was it with that smirk? Not laughing exactly, but highly self-satisfied. In fact, the atmosphere in the whole room was electric. It occurred to me then, that they weren't upset at all, they were excited!

"I think I'll go in a bit," I said to Kendra.

"I'll come with you."

We went up to her cottage, which was the one high on the hill overlooking the village, and that afternoon she filled me in on what Monica may condemn as gossip, but I considered survival information.

My instincts hadn't been wrong, at all – it was indeed a very strange village. Not just in the way Keith Cribbs had portrayed, with macabre tales from the distant past of hangings, wife torture and murder. But with far more recent incidents.

'All of the old paths interweave and interlock, criss-crossing into the mizmaze.'

***

125

Chapter Eighteen

"I can't believe what she did," I said. "I mean, she really whacked him."

I was seriously shocked. There'd been plenty of spats and brawls where I grew up, but never in someone's front room. Or without a build-up, a warning. There hadn't even been an argument.

Kendra was fizzing with laughter as she made tea. "His head wobbled like a punchball. Striker Stipple had to reach up! It was hilarious!"

Her kitchen was small and modern, yet homely, with bunches of dried flowers hanging from hooks along with copper pans.

"There you go, lovely," she said, plonking a plate of chocolate cake in front of me. "Help yourself to cream. How do you like your tea?"

"Today? Strong. Very. No sugar, thanks."

"It was a bit of a shock, wasn't it? Maybe I shouldn't have given Striker Stipple a second glass of Nylah's nettle wine."

"What had he done?"

She sat down, shrugged.

"God knows. I'll give you the recipe for this cake if you

like?"

"It's divine. Thanks, I was starving."

"What? After that eighty-pound buffet they laid on?"

"The dog enjoyed it, anyway."

We started to laugh again.

"You've got a lovely place here. Fantastic view."

Indicating the binoculars on the window sill, she smiled. "It's not called Watch Cottage for nothing. You'd be amazed at what I can see from up here."

"Really?"

"Listen, I'll tell you something, right? When the Cade family first came here, they told us Colin was a financial advisor."

"Oh, that's what Carrie told me. I thought he still was."

She shook her head. "First thing he did was go door to door asking for money. So nothing changes, does it – door to door for money? Back then, it was him wanting to set up as a loan shark. Honest to God, I shit you not. Came here and said did we want to invest in his loan shark business?"

I was picturing little business cards with sharks on. "What did you say?"

"Mark isn't a man of many words, Lyddie. He just waited 'til he'd finished the spiel, then said, 'No' and shut the door.'"

"Good for him. Actually, I'm a bit worried about the bridge money. Glynn's going to be really upset."

"Well, think about that one though, because we do need a new bridge. It's not far off collapsing."

"Isn't it down to the council?"

"Not a public highway, is it? Believe it or not, it's an unowned road, and neither of the councils will adopt it. Bit of an odd one legally. It could give way, though."

"But there are a few hundred people in these three villages, why is it down to just us?"

"You tried asking Keith Cribbs for money, lately?"

It was obvious by the glint in her eyes that she knew we had.

"I'm guessing you heard about the trees?"

"Of course we did. Drinks on him at The Brank, thanks to you two, although I don't think he bought more than one round, tight old git."

I'd wanted to ask more about The Brank but Kendra was quizzing me on when we'd gone over to see Keith, and the moment was lost. I do remember her frowning when I mentioned Cicely, like a cloud passing behind her eyes, but again I only thought about that in retrospect. I guess I was too busy divulging everything I hadn't been able to tell Glynn. Kendra was a confidante, a best friend, I suppose. Funny and kind, she understood without lengthy explanations and I found I could tell her anything.

"I've been asked to sit with Fay's elderly mother," I said. "We need the extra money and she's very sweet." Kendra was making another pot of tea and I spoke to her back. "Fay said she had dementia, but she's actually lucid most of the time. I find her really interesting. Anyway, I'm looking forward to seeing her again."

"Really? I've not seen her for years," she said vaguely.

But when she turned around, her demeanour had changed and become more serious. "So, what do you know about the history of this village?"

"How do you mean?"

"It's a very strange place."

"Monica said there'd once been witchcraft here. Oh, and when I met Keith, he gave a pretty gruesome account of murders and hangings–"

"She was right about the witchcraft. Did she tell you a bottle was found in their chimney?"

"Monica? Yes."

"Used to be the custom at one time to exorcise an evil spirit from someone, then trap it in a bottle, similar to the 'jinn' in middle eastern countries, genie of the lamp."

"Oh yes, of course!"

"What they did round here was to cork it, then stick pins in, confining the demon to the bottle for all eternity lest it go back into the person. Then it'd be hidden up the chimney, or sometimes buried. Anyway, what did Monica go and do when the sweep found it, but pull out the pins and the cork!"

"And did anything happen?"

"You tell me. Listen to this. Tim was up in London at the time, and whilst you might think he's a bit of a tosser, he was actually quite high up in the civil service, some said the secret service. Anyway, he knew Fay's first husband, did you know?"

"No. Really?"

She was scrambling around in her bag. "Mind if I smoke?"

"Of course, not. Your kitchen."

"Yeah, Curfew Cottage was their second home. So, shortly after finding that bottle, Fay's husband dropped stone dead and Tim went down sick. No one knew what was wrong with him but he lost the use of his legs, crumpled to the floor, which wouldn't be difficult to picture, and had a nervous breakdown. After that, Monica found a job at the prison and they moved here permanently. Might be the genie in the bottle." She lit up a cigarette. "Then again, it might not!"

"Probably just a nervous breakdown. Stressful job."

"Could be. Anyway, on the subject of tragedies – Fay's place. Long before they showed up, story was a girl drowned in what was once a wild pond at the back of the house. Then after that, her sister jumped to her death from the top floor."

"That's terrible!"

"It belonged to the Stipples. They go way back, one of the oldest families, and that used to be the grandest house for miles around, really classy. But after the girls' deaths, the wife went into depression and had to be admitted to a psychiatric unit. They said she was… what's the word when you can't move?"

"Catatonic?"

"That's it. Like a statue, she was. Never came out of it, neither. Died a horrible death. So, the place was just abandoned for years. No one who inherited it wanted to move in. And none of the locals would so much as cross the threshold, said it was haunted." She paused for a few seconds, took a long inhalation and blew out a plume of smoke. "After that, more and more of the land was parcelled off and sold, but in the end the house was left derelict. Until Fay and Duncan turned up. Good thing he's a builder, innet?"

I nodded.

"Mark says yours was another one of the original cottages. Six or seven hundred years old, probably. Apparently, it was burnt to the ground centuries ago, just a shell left, a forgotten hovel, until it was rebuilt in the early nineteen hundreds. It belonged to the Cribbs family originally, but a dispute ended with it being torched, and after that it belonged to the Ettricks."

"Torched?"

"Revenge for something, apparently. I'd love to know more."

I felt a bit sick. So, that's what Keith had no doubt wanted to tell us.

Eyeing me, she stubbed out her cigarette and abruptly changed the subject.

"So, what do you think – Aiden Welch is a bit of a looker, right?"

"Eh?"

She was looking right into my eyes.

"Fit as fook, admit it!"

"God, no. Not my type, at all."

She grinned. "I wouldn't go anywhere near him if I were you."

"I wasn't going to."

"Had an affair with one of Kath Ettrick's daughters. She was married with kids, and when the husband found out he shot himself. That was only last year. At one of the farms in Lower Creech. And in that same village, a matter of weeks before you moved here, one of the farmers strung himself up in Buckholt Woods. That's why it's ringed off. Never used to be."

"Oh, I heard about that but I didn't realise—"

"They said it was after government officials told him to destroy half his livestock based on some tests, that he became depressed and then the Inland Revenue was on his back, as well. But word had it he'd also had an altercation with Fay Welch. We're not sure what it was about exactly, but it's known his daughter had been seeing Aiden and he wasn't happy about it. He'd gone a bit mad, they said.

Something had got to him, into his mind, but me and Mark never heard no more."

"Poor man."

"So you see, every single dwelling in this village, Lyddie! All 'ad tragedies. I've only scraped the surface. There've been divorces, suicides, stillbirths, miscarriages, accidents, you name it. Oh, and then there's The Old Rectory. Before the professors moved in, there was an incident with the previous owners. That's how it came to be sold to outsiders. No one local wanted it. Superstitious lot, see? They'll not live in a place where something bad's happened, that be why so many houses are burnt out and a new build goes up."

"What happened at The Old Rectory? A murder?"

"Not exactly. But the husband, another member of the ill-fated Stipple family, this one in his late seventies, tripped down the stairs and broke his neck. But here's the thing – the day after the funeral, the wife looked in the mirror and noticed her eye-whites were the colour of mustard. Turned out she'd got stage four pancreatic cancer and didn't know. No symptoms before then. Hadn't been a drinker, not even on prescription drugs. But within a fortnight she was dead."

"Oh, blimey!"

"I'm telling you, every single house in this village! Weird, innet? I mean, there was a time, see, when this place was thriving and full of very wealthy families. Ashe House belonged to one of the richest farmers in the county. There was a stagecoach route running through the village, and The Blackthorn Brank was a busy inn with rooms above it and stables at the back. And then there was the abbey and the mill afore that, and lots of local businesses. They had women here winding string all day long, sitting in circles, singing rhymes, winding string... imagine. Anyway, it was a thriving place. But..."

She drained her tea.

"Something changed here. Turned it from light to dark. Just not sure when."

I shook my head.

"I'd love to know what happened," she said. "Wouldn't you?"

***

Chapter Nineteen

I'd badly wanted to tell her then, to confide in someone who might understand, about the coloured orbs and the apparition. They seemed so relevant to the ancient history haunting the village, and I'd been on the verge of blurting it out when a little tug inside reined me in. She'd think I was suggestible, unhinged – this savvy, worldly-wise woman with her quick wit and long, pointed fingernails, that day painted magenta with glittery flecks that caught the light.

Her hair was platinum blonde, arranged in plaits threaded with tiny beads into a high pony tail that cascaded to her shoulders. Every finger had at least one silver ring on it, her make-up artful, eyelids emerald green with black liner, lashes false. But my attention was once again drawn to the tattoo on her collar bone. A circle within a circle, hieroglyphs, a flower, a central star… I tried not to stare. What did she know? I should be more precise. What did she know spiritually?

I was also tempered by her quick glance at the clock on the wall. Mark and Willow would be home soon and she'd to get a meal on.

"I have to get back, too," I said, pushing back my chair. "Got to walk Skip. Thanks ever so much for the tea and cake, anyway. And the chat."

We walked to the front door.

"I wonder how the party's going at The Tollhouse? If Fay and Monica stayed after what happened?"

She winked. "I'll find out. And I'm sure we'll hear the party once her rels turn up. Her old dad gets down on the dance floor, apparently."

"Would he be the one with a shock of white hair, and one eye that's a bit—?"

"Roving? One focusing on your legs, the other doing a stock-take of the drinks cabinet? Yeah, that'd be him. Mitch Cade. I'd stay well clear if I were you."

I hurried back down the lane, puzzling over who all those people had been. If they weren't locals and the relatives hadn't turned up yet, then who? Kendra hadn't said why Agnus slapped the professor, either. In fact, she'd evaded the question. None of my business, I suppose. Yet... oh, I don't know, I had the feeling she knew. It seemed everyone knew something we didn't. Maybe that accounted for all those sly, secret smirks? Well, they could keep their weirdness to themselves, I thought, still of the belief we could live there independently and not be drawn in.

Glynn's car was in the drive when I rounded the corner. A company car, it was a smart red Audi and my heart lurched at the sight of it, remembering the money they wanted for the bridge. His stress levels were already through the roof, but it was hardly something I could keep from him. Sooner or later he'd be approached and it would look mighty odd if he didn't know.

He was stretched out on the sofa in front of the television.

"Good time?"

"Interesting. What about you?"

"Knackered."

"I'll give Skip a quick walk, then get dinner on. Won't be long."

After we'd eaten, I turned the game show off and asked if we could talk for a while.

"What about?"

I told him then about Carrie's party, thinking he'd laugh about the vegetarian bull terrier, but he didn't. Instead, he was pan-faced. Like he knew I was working up to something. To be fair to him, he was working extremely long days and had little sleep, his eyes were bleary and his skin pinched. But even though I could see he was waiting for the punch in the gut, the reason for the serious talk, I went all around the houses first, telling him about the slap, the demons in the bottles, the tragedies in almost every house, and the history of our cottage.

"It's such a peculiar place," I said. "And there's something interesting here, too. You know what Monica said about witchcraft and–"

"Is this going anywhere, Lyds? Only I really am seriously tired."

"Sorry, I wasn't thinking. You're right anyway, it's probably nothing."

"It is nothing. There are tragedies, affairs, illnesses and coincidences everywhere; and right up to pretty recent times there were public hangings and local bullies with mobs and pitchforks getting rid of people they didn't like. Not that long ago. The only thing that would be interesting is the one thing Kendra, gob on a stick, didn't actually tell you."

"The bridge? Because actually, I was about to–"

"Well, um, partly that–"

"Hang on, hang on… You already know they want money?"

He'd completely thrown me. How did he know? So, why hadn't he said? I'd looked an idiot that afternoon.

"Mervin got himself onto the parish council, didn't she tell you? The pair of them, him and his wife, Rosamund, aren't liked."

"What are we going to do about it, though? Apparently, they're not asking the locals for money, just us."

"I'll sort it," he said, turning back to the television set.

It only came to me later, a lot later – the following day, in fact – that the bridge was not what he meant, or only 'partly'. The 'one thing' she hadn't told me, hadn't been that.

Perhaps it was around that time, pinpointed to the equinox on account of it being Carrie Cade's birthday, that I felt the bond between Glynn and I slipping loose. Almost overnight, I felt less sure of him, yet couldn't quite say how or why it happened. All I know is that I slept alone that night. And when I woke up it was to an empty bed, curtains still closed.

That would have been a Sunday. He'd driven off, muttering about getting some stuff from the supermarket and, feeling bewildered, I took Skip out for a walk. What had I done to upset him? The more I walked, the more I thought it probably wasn't my fault at all. He was stressed and tired, and likely needed some alone time. It would blow over. It could take a year to get back on our feet, and that took some coming to terms with. I guess it just hurt that he'd shut me out.

Skip and I trekked up Stonebarrow Hill behind Keith Cribbs' farm, towards Barrow Ridge. It was a far longer route than necessary, but taking the bridleways cutting through his land was not an option, especially on my own. In the end, it didn't really matter, though. I craved time, peace, solitude. A couple of buzzards circled overhead, screeching, riding the air currents, the grassland high on the hill bleak and windswept, perfect for how I felt that day.

Nothing grew on the burial mound. But the notion of hundreds, possibly thousands of skeletons in a giant tomb beneath the ground, felt in harmony with the soughing of the wind in the trees, and the eternal feeling of ever-circling lives. And the climb to the top was well worth it. There was a panoramic view up there, with the mellow downs of Dorset to the east, a glint of the English Channel to the south, and verdant forest behind. I sat with my back to one of the ancient ash trees said to have once served as gallows, and fancied I could hear whistling, humming, a rhythmic beat, the vibrations of the land. But it was more likely the strange acoustics of the valley, the wind howling through the abbey ruins, and the way sound carried on the air.

Certainly it was the perfect spot to observe the length of Creech Cross, to view the criss-crossing of tracks, and the layout of farms and fields. Halfway down Coach Lane, the chimney stacks of Ashe House were easy to pick out, as was Horseman's Wood and the roof of our cottage in the crook of the bend; the flat fields opposite, and Buckholt Wood where I met Keith Cribbs that first day. My gaze then swept back up the lane to the top, to the crossroads with Upper Creech. The Old Rectory, white and stately, stood proudly at the helm of the valley. The Stipples had probably been the local gentry, I thought. Hadn't Kendra said the family owned both Ashe House and The Old Rectory? Agnus had married into the family... My train of thought then circled back to the slap, and the nagging question – why had no one present been shocked except me? There was something I was missing. And who the hell were the others? Where had they come from?

I became lost in time, turning questions over in my mind that had no answer. Who had Glynn been talking to about the bridge? He'd hardly been here, he'd been away working all hours, often leaving and coming home after dark. So who? And when? And why hadn't he told me what he knew? By then, the clouds were heavier and threatening rain. I should have set back long ago, but had become transfixed by the ruins of Creech Abbey. From up there, it was clear to see what a stunning location it was in. It must have been the most peaceful, not to mention abundant, place to have lived and worked, the valley so sylvan, the river wider there, probably full of fish, sheep grazing in the fields. The nuns would have had a walled kitchen garden, an orchard, and woodland...

On a line, it had been built on a spirit line, an ancient magical place alive with earth energy, a connection...

I don't know how I knew, but I just did. And in that moment, as the words came into my head in a stream of consciousness, I caught a glimpse of how it had once been. Only not an abbey. I didn't see an abbey. Instead, there were elaborate domes, spiralled turrets, and copper spikes flashing in sunlight. The scene caught and snatched at my heart, a split second of partial sight into another realm, another time, another reality...

It was so brief, so fleeting, that hand on heart I could

not attest to the vision ever having happened, and in one blink it vanished, the view once more of ruined arches and fallen boulders. But it was then I saw a faint haze, a shimmer, as I had when Glynn and I visited that first time. Followed by a mirage. At first, I couldn't quite believe it. I blinked several times and looked again. Surely not? No, there was nothing.

But in that second of surprise, I thought there were figures there, in long white gowns, holding hands in a circle, chanting like children amid the ruins. Girls, they were girls… not nuns, but girls with ribbons in hair so long it streamed to the waist. I closed my eyes and tried to recall the image. They'd been dancing in the middle of the ruins, in the same area Glynn and I had sat in that day. Three. I think three girls…

It was an energetic imprint, of course, that's what it was. I'd read people had seen something similar at Versailles, reporting the atmosphere had turned electric, static had been felt, and several people had seen the same hazy blue scene at exactly the same time, of those from another time in history, another era, milling around the lawns.

Frowning, I stood up. The first vision, if it had been one and not the memory of a book I'd once read, for example, had been one of inspirational, fantastical beauty; the second of young girls in white dresses. So, why had Glynn and I both experienced such a sickly, oppressive atmosphere there? One of madness, burning and screaming? Even Skip hadn't wanted to cross the boundary.

Something changed here. Turned it from light to dark…

The images were hard to shake off, setting off another trail of thoughts. And it wasn't until I was pulling my rucksack back on, that Glynn came to mind again. I hadn't thought about him for hours, and reality punched hard.

The only thing that would be interesting… is the one thing Kendra, gob on a stick, didn't actually tell you.

He hadn't meant the bridge.

So, what the hell had he meant?

I resolved to ask him when I got back, and set off at a brisk pace. By then, the wind had whipped up and, with the sky darkening, I hurried down Stonebarrow Lane, hoping Glynn would be home. The journey back seemed a lot longer and I was out of breath by the time Well Cottage finally came into view. With Skip on the lead, pulling me up the lane, we rounded the bend past Keith Cribbs' driveway, and relief washed through me at the sight of the Audi. He must be feeling better after a good night's sleep, I thought; re-stocking with things he wanted, getting his car cleaned too, by the look of it. Rested and back to being himself. How could I have thought this was all about me and my hurt feelings? How could I have been so self-centred? The man was exhausted.

And then I saw her.

She was leaning over the garden wall chatting to Glynn. Painted-on jeans, riding boots, dark hair tucked behind her ears, holding the reins of a chestnut mare.

And he was sparky, had come alive, chest puffed out, hands in his pockets. I could hear them, the rise in her voice as she told him some tale or other, the roar of his laugh. Flirting, his eyes all aglitter, with the woman who'd turned her back on me. Belinda Ettrick.

***

Chapter Twenty

I had more of a moment to prepare than Glynn did. By the time she glanced over her shoulder and saw me, my face was already arranged in a congenial expression. I could, I reasoned, be imagining a problem where there wasn't one. We'd not been together very long, had married for love. This was probably nothing. Completely innocent.

Like it was with Aiden Welch for me?

There was my conscience, you see, and that was likely another reason I didn't ask what they'd been talking about, or if it was she who'd told him about the bridge. If he wanted to tell me, he would. Wouldn't he? One thing was for sure, however. As the days grew longer and the seasonal wheel turned, the chasm that had opened between us, widened.

In aching contrast, the valley's beauty increased by the day, burgeoning into spring. And by April it was an impressionist's dream of bluebells in the woodland behind the cottage. A place of immense peace and tranquil timelessness, it was utterly sacred. It was like walking through a door into eons past, to a slower age when our ancestors had walked in the same long, lush grass, heard the same birdsong, and delighted in the same ethereal beauty.

One morning we came across a deer and her calf, soaking up early rays of sun in a dappled glade. Skip stopped as I did, all of us quite still, and then we walked softly past, the scene magical, in harmony; and it could just as easily have been a thousand years before. It would not have been too far-fetched to re-conjure the hunting grounds of old, the battle grounds of King Arthur's men, or local women gathering herbs, wild garlic or nettles. Those times felt but a heartbeat away. And the reason I describe the woods as magical, healing even, has a purpose. Because it felt as if Glynn had been cut adrift, and when the accident happened, that place became a sanctuary. A refuge.

But before that there was a sequence of events, which I've tried to recall as accurately as possible, trying to make sense of it, to find a connection. And in the midst of everything, there was Letitia. Perhaps Letitia was the lynchpin in the story. I don't know. Certainly the outcome might have been very different without her.

I'd been keen to go back and see her. She was one of those unique individuals who hold a special kind of magic; a keeper of wisdom, of deep secrets and hidden knowledge. On my part, this knowing was as instinctive as it was a certainty, and I was drawn to her as surely as a tightly-pulled thread of fate.

I'd been seeing her once a week for a while, as agreed, with the occasional drop-in if Bailey or Fay were the only ones home. It would be fair to say I became very fond of Letitia, always anticipating she might be as lucid as she was the first time; that she'd expand on the tantalising things she'd said. Alas, since then she'd become noticeably drowsier, and when she did talk, it was rambling and nostalgic. Mostly our chats were restricted to her younger life: she liked to reminisce about dance halls, days collecting shells on a deserted beach, laughing with schoolfriends, going to a travelling fair with a boy she'd liked. But more and more frequently she'd nod off mid-sentence, slumbering in a cloud of lily-of-the-valley talcum powder, eyelids heavy, breathing slow and slightly rattling. I would ask Bailey to help me prop her up higher, encourage her to drink the lemon-infused spring water she liked, change her nightgown, brush her hair, but mostly sit and hold her hand. And talk. She asked me to. A smile playing around her lips.

"Crystal child," she murmured once, so faintly I almost didn't catch it.

"What do you mean, Letitia?"

"Crystal aura," she said. "You're a rare being."

I didn't know what she meant, and it didn't seem to me to be important, so at the time it passed me by. I had a million and one other things that were far more concerning, and one of them was her declining health. It was not my business to ask about her in a professional capacity – Fay explained that the local medical centre was aware, that repeat prescriptions were collected – I was simply asked to be with her, to tend to the little things Bailey wouldn't know to do. And so, in the hush of that sun-drenched bedroom with the white curtains adorned with little sprigs of cornflower, I told her everything. I confided as if to a guardian angel, from the day of my father's death to the coloured orbs in the cottage bedroom. I told her about the long walks, the odd sensation at the abbey ruins, and even about the apparition of the man in the black coat.

The only thing I never told Letitia about was her

grandson, Aiden. I didn't want to upset her, but to colour in a life she could no longer see, to be guided by the squeeze of her hand, the occasional flicker of a glance, murmur of advice. And afterwards, walking away down the lane, I'd always feel as if a layer of cloud had been lifted, the way ahead had become clearer. I truly looked forward to going. And I know she enjoyed my visits.

During that time, I walked through Horseman's Wood almost every day, and Skip and I always had it to ourselves. There'd never been any evidence of anyone else using it, not so much as a footprint. Then one morning, just after climbing over the stile and dropping onto the lane to go and check on Letitia, I ran into Kendra, out walking her golden retriever.

"Oh, I wondered where you walked Skip," she said. "Beautiful day, innet?"

"I know. The woods are stunning. I've never seen so many bluebells – it's a shimmering haze."

"I'm just surprised Keith hasn't put a stop to it."

"How do you mean? I thought it was common ground, like most woods…"

She was shaking her head. "No, he owns it, right up to the Cades' fields."

"I didn't know that. There's never been anyone in there except me, not another soul. And we have a gate at the bottom of the garden leading right into it."

She shook her head. "I'd stay quiet then."

"Yes, I will. So, how are you? How's Willow?"

"Good, yes. And you?"

I wanted to confide. I felt she'd be the one understand about Belinda. In fact, she'd probably have information to make me feel better, because ever since the day I'd come home to find Glynn flirting with Belinda, it had gnawed away at me. I'd be the last to know, wouldn't I? My heart lurched at the thought. Was he seeing her? Seriously? I couldn't ask him, you see. Either he'd be livid and push me away even more, or he'd colour up and I'd find out what I wasn't ready to know. God, I needed a friend.

"Few issues at work, otherwise all's well, thanks."

"Well, we'd best crack on, stuff to do. Listen anyway, come over if you ever need to talk? Best time for me would be early afternoon, about two."

"Thanks, I might do that."

"You don't have to ring first. Just come up."

We did become friends. Although I never told her about Glynn and Belinda, and I don't know why. But it was after the accident. And after I bumped into Cicely Cribbs in the woods next day.

It happened before an early shift, so it would have been shortly after six in the morning. A low mist hovered in the bluebell haze of the woodland, pine and sweet earth scenting the air. Skip was on the lead because of nesting birds and little creatures in the foliage and undergrowth, but he was pulsing with delight, alive and alert, our footfalls gentle, soundless almost. At one with nature, seamless, at peace.

When we heard a sound. Both of us at the same time. And we slowed.

Someone was walking towards us.

The path, such as it was, had been trodden only by us, a flattening of grass, a meandering way through trees, bracken and brambles. We were level with an ancient oak when we stopped and waited, prepared to move aside for whoever was coming. At around the four-foot mark, the tree branched into several directions, forming a seat, a perfect tree house, its various hollows providing shelter for owls, foxes, squirrels and hares. And I was looking at this, noticing it properly for the first time, as the thud of footsteps rapidly approached, not sure who it would be at such a pace. I remember a huge wave of unease passing over me. And seconds later, through the mist, at the point when she was almost upon us, Cicely Cribbs emerged.

For a moment, her appearance was so incongruous, so absurdly imprinted on the ancient scene, as to seem unreal. Cicely had on tracksuit bottoms, stark white trainers with neon stripes, and a luminescent pink t-shirt. As recalled from the only other time I'd seen her, she had bubbles of bright yellow hair, and an unusual mouth. I'd been unkind likening her to a piranha fish, but she truly did resemble one. And that morning, I found myself looking once more into a face with small, doll-blue eyes, and a mouth stretching into a smile that revealed only the bottom row of teeth. Sharp, jagged teeth. The jaw was square, the chest barrelled, the legs very short and thin.

"Who are you?" she said.

As we'd already met, I was taken aback for a second or two.

"Hi! Um…we met a few weeks ago when my husband and I came to talk to you about the tree. Lyddie and Glynn from Well Cottage?"

She kept the jagged smile in place. "No, I've never met you before. I wasn't expecting to see a member of the public in here. Anyway, I'll tell Dad I've seen you."

Then next day, when I got home from work, there were *Private! Keep Out!* boards nailed right across the trees facing our house.

I was upset, can't deny it. But I decided to ignore the signs and take our usual walk. Not because I wanted to trespass on someone else's land, but because according to the ordnance survey map there was definitely a right of way there, and I did no harm. Besides, it cut ten minutes off the trip to see Letitia, and call it a hunch, but I had to see her. There was something bothering me that was getting stronger, and on that day, the day of the accident, it should have become clear to me what it was. But, as I said, there was an accident.

After work, so around five o'clock, tamping down my upset about the *Keep Out!* signs, I put Skip on the lead and unlatched the garden gate. It was a warm, balmy evening, and somewhere deep within the woods a woodpecker was drilling away on a tree trunk. Significantly more alert than usual, I set off walking through the long, sweet grass, the trip fortunately without incident, then climbed over the stile to the lane and over to Ashe House. I then tied Skip to the post and rail fence by the paddock where he'd be in the shade and could lie on the grass in safety. Ten or fifteen minutes tops, I told him, noting with relief there were no cars in the drive. Hopefully, only Bailey was home.

He took me straight up and I walked in, expecting to see Letitia's startling blue eyes flick open, for a smile to curve her lips.

"She's sleeping," he said.

"Let's prop her up a bit, Bailey. Her chest's ever so rattly."

"Lyddie's here, Gran."

We couldn't rouse her, but she was murmuring, as if lucidly walking through a dream, and I stroked her hair back from her forehead.

"I've just popped in to see if you're all right, Letitia. But I'll be back later in the week. It'll be May the first. May Day. So beautiful out there just now. And the cherry blossom will be out soon, right outside your window."

Her eyelids flickered.

"She can hear you," Bailey said. "I'm not sure why she's asleep all the time. Her meds haven't changed."

"Tired," Letitia said. "So tired."

"I'll leave you to sleep," I said, rooting around in my bag. "But I've brought some more CDs, the ones you wanted."

I'd bought her Faure's *Requiem*, Debussy, Nat King Cole, Otis Reading and Matt Munro.

"Bailey will put them on for you.

"*Days Like These*," she said. "Matt Munro. *Days Like These*."

He put the music on and I was about to leave when she took hold of my wrist and said, "Tell him no more injections."

Bailey and I stared at each other. He seemed as surprised as I was.

He looked from her to me and back to his grandma again. "What injections?"

I waited but no more was said, and Letitia had sunk once more into sleep.

We walked together towards the stairs, then paused on the landing. Fay was now clomping around in the kitchen, the narrow, winding steps up to the top floor gloomy overhead.

"She doesn't have any," he whispered.

"What did she mean, then?"

"I don't know."

"Does a doctor or nurse come in from the Practice?"

"No. No one comes. She takes what I fetch for her. To keep her comfortable. But Lyddie, she doesn't have any injections."

"It's okay, I believe you. Maybe she's a little confused?"

He nodded but looked disturbed, puzzled.

As we plodded downstairs we were both deep in thought. Was someone going in and sedating her? But who? Why? Yet, it would sure as hell make sense. Why hadn't I realised? I was berating myself, had assumed it was side effects from her tablets, and a natural deterioration... But then again, surely not? Surely no one was injecting sedatives without Bailey or Fay knowing?

It bugged me. Bugged me a lot. And was most definitely on my mind. It therefore took a moment to register when I left Ashe House and walked over to the fence, that Skip wasn't there.

Where he should have been, there was now an empty space.

And not only was he not there, but his lead had been hung over the rail, neatly folded. I stared at the lead. And the kick to my heart was that of a horse. I cannot tell you, cannot begin to describe, the shock or the panic. He hadn't broken free, it was deliberate.

Hot blood pounded in my ears.

"What the fuck?"

Lunging for his lead, I ran onto the lane, scanning both ways. Just as a dark grey Citroen went by. I had a glimpse, a brief one, of a person in a flat cap and checked shirt at the wheel. Rosamund, I thought, as the blur of a smiling white face in glasses passed by.

I wanted to flag her down, to say please let me know if you see my spaniel running around. But she didn't see me waving my arms and calling out. I was running after her car by then, feet pounding on the tarmac, each impact banging into the joints. Shouting for him, calling at the top of my voice, not giving a damn what anyone thought. There are no words to convey my distress and there never will be. I'd brought him up from six weeks old, he would come and put his paws on my lap when he knew I was upset. I adored him.

And when I saw the heap of fur lying on the road, I knew it was him. I'd just rounded the corner to Well Cottage when I heard what I thought was a dull thud. I didn't need to guess or to actually see what had happened. I just knew. That car had clipped him. Just. It had only just happened and it was her. In my mind's eye I saw his body roll. And as I ran around the horseshoe bend, I already knew the bundle of tan and white fur on the side of the road would be his.

The expletives regarding Rosamund came later. All I knew at that moment was that my beautiful, loving, gorgeous dog was, I thought at the time, dead. Except he wasn't. Thank God, he wasn't. And I wouldn't even have shared any of this if it wasn't significant. Glynn was home by then and I thanked God for that, too. We lifted him onto the back seat of my car and got Skip into emergency surgery within the hour. The vets were excellent, used to farm accidents, to emergency ops. And Skip was saved. Not in distress for long and home a couple of days later. But for several nights I'd lain awake and sobbed myself hoarse.

Someone had untied him from the fence. Some bastard had let him loose and on instinct he'd run for home.

And that woman, that damn woman in the flat cap, would have seen me running down the lane, would surely have noticed me waving frantically in the rearview mirror, yet made the choice not to stop. That she'd been the one to hit him was without doubt. She'd been peering over the steering wheel, driving at a snail's pace. How could she not have seen me? How could she not have seen Skip and braked in time? She wasn't exactly speeding.

Then the following day, which I'd taken off work because I couldn't keep it together to be honest, calling in sick with a sudden head cold, we had a visitor.

Fay Welch.

She said she'd heard about the accident and was terribly sorry. Glynn did the talking. I was red-eyed and kept bursting into tears. It just kept welling up how much it must have shocked and hurt my dog, that his hip had been broken, the femur fractured.

But then she glanced over at me and said, "Still, it was no one's fault, was it?"

I didn't know what to say.

"I know Rosamund's been crying her eyes out. She's terribly upset, so you won't be angry with her, will you?"

The air, after she'd gone, was blue. I couldn't speak to her at all, and was thankful Glynn stepped in. Afterwards, I strode up Stonebarrow Hill to the Ridge and raged and raged.

"That was no fucking accident!"

And when we went to collect him two days later, I vowed never to leave him vulnerable like that again. Next time I went to see Letitia, he would stay home. Some will say he's only a spaniel and others will totally understand. But love is love. And the incident changed the way I felt about the place. There was a mind-switch, if you like, a sudden awareness. Nothing definitive, no one particular person. But rather, a dark energy swirling, a myriad of spiteful spirits, a malice stirred.

And the knowledge that had previously eluded me, was also beginning to surface. It would come to me in dreams, on waking, on drifting into exhausted sleep. All at once I'd see their smiles. Sly, secretive smiles. Fay, on telling me not to be angry with Rosamund, had turned away and I'd just caught it. There'd been Madeleine at work, Rosamund as she drove past Ashe House, and Mervin after he'd been slapped. And then Cicely, when she'd turned to go after saying she'd 'tell Dad'.

The only person I could talk to about anything spiritual, about intuition and undercurrents, who might understand, was Letitia. And so later that week, on May Day, the day I was due to sit with her, I prayed she would be lucid.

Alas, it was the very last time I saw her.

After which matters unfolded very quickly.

***

153

Chapter Twenty-One

The difference from just a few days before was stark and I did a double-take. Letitia was sitting up, her eyes the same glittering sapphire blue as when I first saw her. Nor did she doze off mid-sentence or gaze unseeingly through the window. In fact, she was almost sparking with all she had to say.

I'd brought up tea and scones. Bailey was the only one home and had been agitated. I wanted to talk to him but he'd ushered me upstairs, instead.

"She's having a good day and wants to talk to you before Mum gets back. Go on. She loves my scones and she needs to eat."

"I've two daughters and a son," she said. "Not just Fay."

"Two other children? I didn't realise."

"James and Isobel."

Her piercing blue eyes searched mine.

"Are they still in Ireland?"

"Fay. She never could make anything of herself, and after, you know, with having taken her on, she'd never felt good enough. I suppose that's how it felt to her, that the others were mine and she adopted. But she never took to anything, Lydia. I told you, she never took to anything."

Had she? Had she told me that? I'd no idea Fay was

adopted or that there were other children. I tried not to show my surprise, didn't press her, and certainly never asked about exorcism – a topic which seemed too dark to broach – even though I was bursting to know. There was something so innocent about Letitia. I can't explain. She was like a wondrous, slightly bemused fairy who'd accidentally landed on the wrong planet.

She'd been born and raised on the west coast of Ireland, had her children there, then moved to London to be near Fay. She talked a lot about the village she grew up in, and once touched on what she termed the disgrace of a local priest. I'd assumed she was of the Catholic religion, but there were no rosary beads, no pictures of Mother Mary on the wall. Nothing to support that.

For a while, she sat eating her scone, looking out at what was a heart-achingly beautiful afternoon. Letitia was adamant she'd never go to a hospital; that when she left the earthly plane, she wanted the last thing she saw to be clouds whipping across the sky and sunshine dappling the fields; the last thing she heard to be the cries of buzzards, the song of a blackbird or the ethereal call of an owl. Letitia loved the scent of lavender in her room, for the bedclothes to smell of fresh air, and her skin of rose or lily of the valley. 'Divine' was her word. All that was beautiful, natural, and given freely to us, was divine.

"There's only one thing I'd like more," she said. "The sound of the ocean crashing onto the beach, and the cries of gulls on the wind... Do you understand what I mean, Lyddie? About human dignity? Dignity and grace."

I nodded, thinking about some of the patients on the ward, how they'd lost the ability to recognise those they loved, to communicate, to feed or wash themselves; who died surrounded by strangers in uniforms – these human beings who had loved, been loved, had jobs, hopes and dreams.

"I followed her," she said, startling me out of my reverie. "I followed Fay to London, you know? It was not what I wanted to do, not at all."

"Oh?"

"She'd met a fellow in Dublin. She could never take to anything, did I tell you? First it was a haberdashery store, then a gentleman's outfitters. Well, that's what she told me but it was an out-and-out lie. To be sure, she was working in a common public house, where folk stand up on the table and sing of an afternoon. And it was there she met Malcom, the handsome devil that blew across the Irish Sea on an ill wind. Mark my words, never was there a term more apt for a man such as he."

"Was he English?"

"London banker. She thought she'd be rich. Upped and went before I'd even chance to meet him, or I could have told her what I saw in his heart. But…" She reached over and gripped my hand, searching my eyes in that way she had, as if reading the blueprint of my soul. "But I had to help her, Lydia. She needed me in a way the others did not. I'd no money, of course, just a widow's pension, but I found a place not too far from where they were living, and soon found out what he was. I'd not been wrong about that blackened heart."

Downstairs, there were footsteps clomping around, and one or two doors slammed. Was Fay back already? I was beginning to realise, though, that she avoided too much contact with her mother, and probably wouldn't come up. Letitia and I were in a bubble, a cocoon, and I knew then that the story would be told.

"He was in a cult," she said, leaning back against the pillows. "I've to tell you this. Him and the other man, the one she stayed friends with. They're here now, in the village, in one of the cottages up the lane, and there's–"

"Tim? Tim and Monica? A cult?"

"That would be him."

"But Malcom died," I whispered.

"Yes, his tongue was cut out. And then his heart."

"He was murdered? Oh, my God!"

Suddenly, it made sense that Tim had suffered a nervous breakdown. And why Fay, traumatised, had fled here… out of the way, off the map…

"And so I helped her. I'd known I'd be needed and don't ask me how," Letitia said. "But I could feel the darkness rolling in. After his death, Fay was told Malcom owed most of his wealth to creditors, and when all was sold there was precious little left. She fell to pieces, you know? Went back to working in a bar for a while. But when the dust settled it turned out she'd inherited Ashe House, the only problem being it wasn't fit to live in. The place was derelict, a fallen palace without a roof. And shortly after that she met Duncan, a builder."

"Well, it's very beautiful," I said.

"She doesn't love him. The man. Duncan. The more she despises him, the uglier he gets. She can't love, you know? She doesn't know how."

I squeezed her hand.

"I called her after the fae because that's how I thought of her, a tiny pixie baby just a few days old, left on the church steps with a note to say it was up to the priest to take care of his own. And since an unknown girl was found drowned in the bay that same morning, we can imagine what happened there, can we not?"

I simply held her hand and watched her fluttering eyelashes as she floated into REM sleep for a few minutes, this gentle old lady with talc-white hair and skin, lying back against goose-down pillows, not a sound in the room other than the sigh and fall of her breath.

After a while I said, "I never knew my grandma. I've got a vague memory of my grandad, on Dad's side – he was a coalman – but after that there was only Mum. How lucky Bailey is to have you."

I recognised I never mentioned Aiden. That I never uttered his name. That he was not someone I felt remotely comfortable around. But Bailey, I did. He was also the one who attended to most of Letitia's needs. He brought her meals, little things she fancied eating like a slice of cake or her favourite, cucumber sliced onto hot, buttered toast; and he'd bring her a bowl of soapy water to wash in, or help her to the bathroom and wait outside until she'd finished. She ought to have had proper regular help, but wouldn't hear of it. It was the only time I ever heard her raise her voice, and she could be fierce, could pierce the heart with one arrow. But I felt it wouldn't be long before there'd be no choice. Alas, it never came to that. Like I said, it was the last day I saw her.

"To be loved," I said quietly. "To love and be loved. Even if you lose them, no one can ever take away the love you once had, still have, and always will. I'm not feeling sorry for myself, Letitia. But I never had that."

Her eyes flashed open so suddenly I jumped back. I honestly didn't think she'd heard, although I should have known better.

"Oh, but you do know love, Lydia."

We stared into each other's eyes, and I saw then that she knew about Glynn and she knew about Skip. She knew how my heart ached for both.

"And that love you must keep in your heart, my crystal one. Don't let the world harden and embitter your soul. Because it will try."

I told her then, as matter-of-factly as I could, about how Skip's lead had been unclipped and draped over the fence, how he'd been knocked over by a car, and that the person had never apologised. I could not, however, disclose that her daughter, the one she'd done her best to save, had smiled while telling me it was no one's fault.

"I know he's only a dog, that's what people will say, that I was lucky it wasn't a child. But he means a lot to me."

"Love is love," she muttered. "Would the world not just understand that? Love is what you are, where you come from. Love is why you're here for me over and above what they asked you to do. Love can be a kind word, a holding of the hand... and sometimes the facing-down of evil..."

And then I asked her. It just came out. "Letitia, Bailey told me. He said you'd been an exorcist."

"Ah, I wondered when you'd get around to asking that!"

"You don't have to tell me. Only if you want to. But you said so much on our first meeting, and I'm curious."

"Of course you are, and it's important to question everything and think for yourself. This is your soul journey. Seek always to understand as you navigate the path of earthly life, child. But beware, too. There are devils on it, and none so dangerous as those of the false light. You must know yourself and rid yourself of those preconceptions, of those limitations. Can you not see?"

I nodded. But who was she talking about? Who was a devil, a false light? What were my preconceptions? But I knew the answer to the last question because I saw them rise in the recess of my mind, felt them emerge from the darkness; hooded, smoky figures standing faceless and silent in the corner of my childhood bedroom.

"Don't be in fear, Lydia. Or it will imprison you."

My God, I was thinking, she reads my mind!

"But to answer your question. I would have been a lot younger than you, about eighteen or so, when I had what could be termed an epiphany. I was sitting on the beach back home, gazing out at the waves, thinking how America was just across the water. It was known the local priest was abusing some of the children, but not one person in that village had the courage to do a thing about it. And all at once it came to me. I saw how evil works, how it hides in the human vessel, deceives and lies, preying on weaknesses, lurking behind the sweetest of smiles and the most respectable of positions. But oh, how it hides, Lydia, and how outraged and cowardly it is when confronted."

"I've read a lot about that, the priests–"

"It's everywhere, Lydia."

"In people?"

"Of course, it's in people. They make choices, every day they make choices. But the really clever ones will pretend to serve the light. You'll only suspect if you pay close attention to how they make you feel, and you'll only know for sure, if they're cornered. Lies have many versions Lydia, but the truth has only one. They don't like to be exposed."

"And that's what you can exorcise?"

"Not like you'd see in the film," she said, pronouncing film as 'fillem'. "The soul must acknowledge what's going on. And then they must want to do something about it. Not all of them want to, you understand, which is when innocents around them get hurt. Children. Teenagers. The hapless and unguarded." Her eyes fixed on mine. "And now I must say something to you and to you alone."

She had a tight hold of my hand.

"I thought we'd left it all behind, but I see now they came with us."

"Who?"

She shook her head.

"I am to tell you – know yourself so you will not be deceived. And keep a hold of what is yours. It is hidden but you are the one who will find it. Do not give it to those who seek. For the love of God, be careful who you trust." She pointed to her own heart. "Listen to this. Listen to this."

"Who? Don't give them what?"

It had cost her a great deal to say so much and, with her renewed vigour spent, she lay limp as a rag doll on the bed, fragile, like an aged silk curtain that could, should a window be opened, fragment to dust in the breeze.

Her lips parted slightly. "I can't do it anymore... I have to watch them, see the shadows attached... to... Fay..."

"Them? Attached?"

I felt so ignorant for not understanding, but I didn't. Not then. Nor what was at stake.

"They are such fools, not knowing what they do, lusting after glitter. And Aiden... Be aware, all the time, be aware... you see the trick... and the magician will fail..."

***

161

Chapter Twenty-Two

Before I left Letitia, I kissed her gently on the forehead over the third eye, which I'd read somewhere was a gift of love, not realising I'd never see her again. The conversation had left me spiralling. It wasn't Fay, I realised, who kept her distance from her mother, but the other way round. Letitia didn't want Fay anywhere near her, and I had the feeling Bailey was her constant bodyguard.

I couldn't go straight home. I felt agitated. Not only had I not recovered from the shock of Skip's accident, but the difference in Letitia's lucidity was marked. It was not until I'd closed her door behind me, however, that the implication struck me with force.

No more injections…

Someone had definitely been giving her sedatives, and that person had since stopped. Was it Fay? Seriously? But why, and how had she got hold of them? Maybe Bailey had found out?

I wanted to have a word with him if I could, but on heading to the stairwell I noticed one of the bedroom doors was open and even before levelling with it, I knew whose it was. Aiden had come home early. And I made a mistake. I glanced in.

The moment stretched into aeons, reality merging with recurring dreams I wished I didn't have. On another level, my infinitely wiser self whispered that behind this man's seductive façade lay a hedonistic, self-centred ego with a trail of emotional debris in his wake. But my wiser self was a long way off that day, and her voice went unheard.

The first of May. Beltane. Dark red curtains had been drawn against the late afternoon sun, and on the wall above the Edwardian mantelpiece, the woman in the painting lay on the beach in the swell of the gilt-crested waves, head back, abandoned and inviting...

His voice, deep and syrupy, resonated around the chambers of my heart.

"Come in, Lydia!"

I saw him then, in the reflection of the mirror on the dresser, reclining on the bed, the unmade bed, on a disarray of crumpled white sheets. His hair, black and gleaming, was damp. He and Duncan had finished for the day, he'd just showered. And that was why he was half naked. He didn't know I was there. This I told myself as, transfixed, I stared back through the mirror.

"I need to talk to you."

The images came rapidly and happened the second our eyes locked in the glass. He had my hair pulled back in one hand, the other pushing up my top... It could be that quick, the line crossed in a heartbeat. But those thoughts... those images... were not mine. They were not my wish, my fantasy or my will. I already knew what he was. Yet, the effect was powerful and, unable to break the contact, I found I couldn't move. I have no idea what I must have looked like, what was written on my face or showing in my eyes, except that I was mesmerised – entranced, for want of a better word. Had he walked towards me in that moment, taken my hands, led me into the room and kicked shut the door, there was nothing I would have done to stop him. And I think that, in hindsight, was what appalled me the most. My free will had been overridden.

But there was a sudden crash downstairs, a loud one followed by a shout and a round of expletives, and in an instant the trance had broken. The effect was like a jug of freezing water thrown in the face.

"Sorry," I called out. "I didn't realise you were in there. It was my day to see Letitia. Got to go!"

Not waiting for an answer, I flew downstairs; and it wasn't until I'd reached the top of Barrow Ridge that I could recount the incident with any degree of clarity, to rewind and go through what happened. And to be mortified.

Speaking to Bailey in the kitchen had passed in a daze of barely registered information. It seemed Aiden really had needed to talk to me. Bailey said they were ready to start work on the floorboards, and Aiden had wanted to discuss dates because it could be as early as the following week.

I sat staring across the valley. Whilst it was true Glynn and I had drifted away from each other, I'd succumbed to the charms of someone I didn't even like, someone swaggeringly repellent. Yet those fantasies had materialised against my will. How could that happen? Was this the part of me I didn't know well enough – a weakness, a need, a chink in the armour? Looking for love but finding something fake, grasping at anything to soothe the pain of the child. Because somehow Aiden was worming into my mind.

Oh, God. Glynn and I would stay together… wouldn't

we?

Up on the ridge it was peaceful, dusk settling over the valley in the most heavenly lilac glow, a lone thrush singing its last melody of the day. Soon it would be dark and the walk home would be long, yet there was no impetus to move. I really ought to go home. I'd had nothing to eat since lunchtime, my bones were cold, muscles stiff. I thought then of creature comforts, a hot bath, buttered toast, and tried to imagine standing up and setting back but could not.

Instead, for the second time that day I was hypnotised. Because down in the basin of the valley, among the ruins of Creech Abbey, a ball of black mist was rising into the air.

Déja-vu skittered across my heart. The last time I'd seen phantom images down there had been at the equinox. Today was the first of May, Beltane. They kept the traditions alive here and I wondered if what I'd seen before had not, in fact, been a ghostly vision but a celebration, a heralding of Spring? I liked the idea. Of course! And this was the same. A Beltane ceremony. And the reason the image was distorted was because it was dusk, and the dying embers of the day were clouded with shadows.

But my eyes did not deceive me, even if my rational mind could.

Apparently they held esbats over where the abbey ruins are...

Something changed here. Turned it from light to dark. Just not sure when...

The black mist was not a ball so much as a swirling, circling mass, that now rose like a swarm of locusts; and as my eyes focused and I leaned forwards to get a closer, clearer look, I fancied, although could not be sure, that I could hear drums, and a low hum rising in crescendo.

The black cloud became a spinning vortex.

Then a horrible, piercing scream rent the velvet air of the night.

***

Chapter Twenty-Three

With the vixen's cry, the scene dissipated, fragmenting to nothing more than a few scraps of charred paper floating in the air, the valley calm and silent once more.

Squinting into the gloom, I checked and checked again. There was smoke, I could smell smoke. No, I was wrong. I was wrong as a child, had been wrong at the equinox. And I was wrong again now. The imagination was a powerful thing. The child psychiatrist had said as much, dismissing all I'd confessed. I was an impressionable, suggestible individual who'd made incendiary and hurtful accusations against her mother.

Darkness fell quickly and I stood up, grateful for the full moon lighting the way. It was an easy walk going home, the path down Stonebarrow Hill a long, silvery ribbon. All was well. Nothing had happened. Soon be home. The thought of dark witchcraft and demonic summoning, however, was ever-present. Was that what was going on down there? But even if there was a coven, realistically what could they do? They couldn't hurt us. Couldn't harm us. And probably it didn't exist at all. Whatever made me think it did? Where had the idea come from? Because Monica said it had, centuries ago? There was no evidence for that. My fears were my own from long, long ago – perhaps the preconceptions Letitia referred to, because all of that had turned out to be imagination, my own bad dreams.

We were safe here. Over and over I told myself that. I mean, it was ridiculous! There was absolutely nothing to support the notion of a dark arts coven. The altar at the Cades' house had been purely traditional, a centuries-old custom to celebrate nature, the turn of the wheel. And besides, they were incomers, not the locals, the ones who might carry on some kind of ancient sacrificial rite.

Sacrificial rite! Would I listen to myself?

My footsteps thudded dully on the lane as I neared the village, the air cool, sky a dazzle of a million stars. By then, I'd almost convinced myself there was no substance to my theory of a modern-day coven. I'd read far too much into things others had said. What had happened in the past had not bled into the present day. Those things had died out and no longer existed. But I was arguing with myself when the truth was, I didn't know for sure. And if others were practising dark arts, then maybe it was naïve, foolish even, to try and persuade myself otherwise. The knowledge and manipulation of the unseen had been used for thousands of years, not hundreds. Christ had cast out demons. So, who was I to say it was nonsense? I'd seen those things with my own eyes... those horrible, menacing shapes...

More than once, I glanced over my shoulder, convinced someone was close behind, thoroughly spooked as my thoughts chattered on, out of control. If there was a coven here, was it the continuation of a tradition? Were the tales of hangings and stabbings actually cover stories for human sacrifices? What about the suicides and tragic accidents?

There'd been an awful lot in one very small village!

I managed to talk myself into a frenzy of fear, increasingly convinced there were thudding footsteps behind me on the lane. I could hear them, and the realisation was a shock. Speeding up, out of breath, I didn't relax again until the lights of Well Cottage appeared ahead, and the last few hundred yards were a near sprint. On reaching the garden gate, I lunged for it and swung quickly around. Who was there? Some follower so close my skin prickled all over.

The pine trees above Keith Cribbs' house spiked the starlit sky, black and still, and a lone barn owl hooted into the echoes of the night. The valley was magical, it pulsed with hidden life, overlaid with imprints from centuries past; and in a rush it occurred to me I knew nothing about its history. Or its people. The ones who turned their backs and closed off their expressions and their doors, barring gates and fencing off pathways. I knew nothing about any of it. This was fear of the unknown, pure and simple – the most disempowering emotion of all. And that was the point at which I vowed to change that.

I need to find out what I'm frightened of. Both here in the village, and inside myself.

Letitia's words had finally made sense. The old lady was not afraid. But nor was she in blissful ignorance. She knew all about the darkness. And still she was not afraid. Which meant she had mastered her experience here on earth, where I had not.

And after that, we found the casket.

***

Chapter Twenty-Four

The casket was discovered during the first week in June, a couple of weeks after Letitia's funeral. Oddly, the news of her death wasn't a shock. Perhaps, on some level, I already knew. And so did she. In retrospect, it was in her last words: 'I can't do it anymore… I have to watch them, see the shadows attached…to…Fay…'

Duncan had been the one to phone. He and the boys had intended to start work on our floorboards that week, but Bailey was utterly distraught, and Fay's brother and sister were coming over from Ireland. Apparently, there was a lot to sort out.

It was a church service, held in Upper Creech, to which Glynn and I were invited. I was grateful for that, because I wanted to say goodbye respectfully, and to hear her life acknowledged. It had been a privilege to know such a beautiful soul, a higher being who generously bestowed grace, wisdom and compassion on all those she met. I wrote down as much as I could remember, trusting that one day it would make sense. At the time, though, it seemed she'd talked in riddles. It was only as the years passed and the complex tapestry of characters, timelines and events emerged, that it struck me how clairvoyant, how visionary, she actually was.

Glynn and I sat at the back of a packed congregation, and my heart lurched at the sight of Bailey among the pallbearers. His eyes were red-raw, his young face ashen with grief and fatigue. He was sobbing so hard when they walked past with the coffin, that his pain tore at me like a claw, my eyes filling with tears that I rapidly blinked away. I'd never told Glynn how much I loved the old lady, or related the depth of our conversations. She'd known me without words, saw the damaged child within, and her heart had connected to mine.

The hymn chosen was *The Day Thou Gavest, Lord Is Ended*, the tune the old one, the heartbreaking one, and my throat constricted. I couldn't sing. Instead, I looked around at the rest of the congregation. An aisle separated three sections of pews in what was a small, compact chapel. Fay, a stiff-backed figure in a purple coat, sat on the front row of the middle section between her two sons. Monica and Tim were behind. And I was idly working out who was who, when a small, blonde-haired woman glanced over her shoulder and shot me a look. Brilliant azure eyes met mine, the effect utterly unnerving. It was like looking at a younger version of Letitia.

She had to be Isobel.

After the hymn, the vicar spoke in a dull monotone for a while, and then Fay went up to the pulpit and read Letitia's favourite poem, *The Song of Wandering Aengus* by William Butler Yeats. The delivery was that of one auditioning for a role in a Westend play, projecting the voice, periodically pausing for dramatic effect, focusing on one side of the church, then the other. And afterwards, spilling out into the warm May sunshine, people shook her hand, said how difficult that must have been for her, how composed she'd been, how admirable.

I must be missing something, I thought, observing from the sidelines, because for me at least, the meaning and poignancy of the words had become lost in what had been a thespian masquerade. The reading had not been about Letitia, at all. It had been about Fay.

Something a tad spooky happened then. At the exact moment the thought hit me, she glanced up as suddenly and sharply as she had at the dinner party. Hazel button eyes fastened onto mine, and for a second I felt pinned like an insect to a board. Guilty as charged.

Don't judge... you've not to judge...

"See the real family turned up, then?" Kendra said.

I jumped round. "Oh hi, Kendra! I didn't see you in the church."

Instinctively, we drifted away from the throng. At the top of the graveyard, a hole had been dug, and a couple of men in black suits were waiting.

"I want to be cremated when my time comes," I said.

"I don't. Or how will I keep coming back?"

"Eh?"

She laughed.

"That must be Isobel," I said, indicating the small blonde lady in the black trouser suit. "She's got the same eyes as Letitia. Gave me quite a turn."

"Yes. And the brother's the one with grey hair next to her – blue cravat, tall with a beard."

Fay's siblings had moved away to sit on a bench, both older than her, both visibly upset, the woman's face tear-stained and blotchy.

"She was a truly sweet lady, you know? I was with her

quite a lot at the end."

"So I heard."

"Bailey's taken it hard."

"Poor sod. Makes you wonder if he'll ever escape."

"Escape?"

"Well, what's he gonna do? Think about it! Poor lad's backward, isn't he? Tied to Fay's broom for the rest of his natural. Doing all her housework. It's like Norman Bates in *Psycho*. When she pops off she'll still be telling him what to do." She then did a hissing impression in my ear: "You haven't got a girl in there, have you, Norman?"

"Surely Aiden will look out for him? And Duncan?"

"They use him for manual work, bung him a few quid. Anyway, talking of Aiden – look, that's his latest fancy piece! Imagine rocking up to a funeral dressed like that."

I glanced over. A woman was running a hand up and down Aiden's back. Late forties at a guess, she had waist-length, curtain-straight black hair and an enormous pneumatic chest, much revealed and deeply tanned.

"Dusted with glitter," said Kendra. "She's dusted them."

I only had a brief impression, however, of bare legs, stiletto heels, and flashing white teeth, because someone was watching us. I could feel the heat, laser rays scorching into the side of my face. And glancing over, it was a shock to find Duncan not just staring, but glaring at me. He appeared to be beside himself with rage, fuming, indignant, and I hurriedly looked away, embarrassed and confused. What was the matter with him? Why was he so angry? And why just me? Others were looking at Aiden's girlfriend, too. In fact, nearly everyone was.

"Um… are these people local or relatives?"

"Neither," said Kendra, as the crowd began to gravitate towards the grave. "Most are here to support Fay. So, that'd be amateur dramatics, art class, history society..."

I began to feel then, as if I was in freefall, a little unhinged, as once again everything felt curiously staged, like rent-a-crowd or something. All I can say is my own feelings were real enough, and I found the day unbearably sad. I'd miss Letitia dearly, but nowhere near as much as Bailey would, and my heart went out to him.

As soon as the burial was over, he wandered off with Zach Stipple, the two of them loping over the fields towards Barrow Ridge.

"Pair of no-hopers," said Kendra. "Barely a brain cell between them. Sad, innet?"

I watched them vanish into the shadows of the hill, wishing I could have gone with them, pondering on their friendship, the kind that was almost telepathic, so quiet, so respectful and close. Surely, the most healing thing to do was to immerse oneself in nature, to process the grief, to say goodbye in the quiet of the mind? I was glad he had a friendship like that, and felt less concerned about him because of it. I was also relieved Aiden had a girlfriend. It simplified matters, drew a clear line. Whatever had I been thinking? What a fool, eh? At least that particular illusion, or delusion, was over, along with any misunderstandings.

Shortly after that, a couple of weeks later, Duncan rang with a date to start work on the floorboards. First week in June. Apparently, James and Isobel had ended up staying for nearly three weeks and were contesting the Will. It had been extremely acrimonious, it seemed, with legal action ensuing. But finally, they'd gone back to Ireland.

"It's been very upsetting for Fay," he said, when the

three of them arrived that first day. "And for me. I threw my lot into that house, my life's savings, to provide a good home for Fay and the boys. It was derelict. No roof. No one would live there, and Malcom had been selling off more and more land to service his debts. He didn't want to live there, either."

"I see."

Duncan shrugged. "I sold up everything in London, started again here. Renovated the house. Massive job." He shrugged. "Then found I couldn't get jobs because the locals have rigged up business far and wide. It's like the Mafia. So, we're broke. Might not look like it but that house swallowed everything I'd got. Anyway, the row's been about Letitia's savings and a cottage in County Clare she'd rented out. Those two said it was theirs, but the Will was changed last year. We sold the lot. We needed it."

I pulled a face. "I'm sure it can be settled. These situations can be terrible for everyone."

Duncan was not an attractive man. In fact, he was hard to look at close range. But I had the feeling there was a whole lot going on behind the scenes he wasn't comfortable with. More than that. He was incensed, livid, and it was eating away at him. That was not my business though, and besides, on some level he'd consented. I didn't trust him. Not because he was a dishonest man, far from it, but because he was weak. And because of that strangely hostile look he'd shot my way at the funeral. It was often in those unguarded moments that masks fell away.

"How's Bailey doing?"

He nodded.

"Yeah, okay. It's better for him to work, takes his mind off things."

The following couple of weeks weren't easy, it has to be said. The rooms being worked on were partitioned off with plastic sheeting, and the noise and mess began. I was just thankful the weather was fine and we could be outside. But I longed for the work to be over. It seemed interminable. Not only that but there was a peculiarly strained atmosphere between the three men, an enforced jollity – play-acting again, each putting on a front, truths unspoken, gaps too wide. They wanted to rub along, but could not.

To some extent there was a similar situation between myself and Glynn, pretending everything was perfectly normal. But it wasn't. Both of us now harboured secrets. Neither wanting to hear the other's.

Nevertheless, the first week was relatively easy going, a lull, before the kitchen units had to be dismantled. It took three of them a full day to take it apart, and after making a start on prising up the rotten boards, Aiden and Duncan went outside for a smoke before packing up for the day. The place was a mess, the kitchen a gaping dark hole that reeked like a dredged river bed, with pretty much everything except the plumbed-in sink now stacked in the garage. I stood on the perimeter looking in. It wouldn't be for long. Not long. Another week. No more. Hopefully.

Bailey had gone underground to do a recce with the torch.

"Really ancient under here," he called up.

I peered down.

"The original cottage foundations?"

His voice echoed around the dank pit.

"Yeah, but there's like, I dunno, it looks like an old well at the far end."

My heart did a little flip. So it was there!

"Just… thing is… you might wanna come down here, Lyddie? Come and have a look at this."

I didn't want to go down at all, but, unable to contain my curiosity, I dropped through the gap between the joists and into the cool, dripping darkness. The distant bob of the torch was hovering around the point where the old stone foundations petered out and, crouching low, I made my way over to Bailey and peered into a dark puddle far below.

"I thought there was a well under the house," I said, as the torchlight flashed around the cobbled interior.

"Should have been sealed off properly," he said. "But that's Tony for you. I don't know how he gets so much work, the corners he cuts."

Something caught in the light then, lodged far below in a crack in the wall.

We both saw it at the same time. He flicked the torch back. A flash of metal.

"What's that?"

"Dunno."

"How do we get it out?"

"I'll have to go down. Here, hold the torch."

It is hidden but you are the one who will find it…

Automatically, I glanced back towards the dim light of the kitchen. The other two mustn't know, that's all I could think; they mustn't catch us. But Bailey had already gone over the side. Occasional rocks stuck out of the sides, no doubt so the well could be maintained; and quickly and agilely, as if he did that kind of thing all the time, Bailey went down as if on a ladder and was back up before I'd had chance to worry.

It was a lead casket, grimy with age and coated green.

Handing it over, he said, "Bit of a struggle to get it out,

it was really wedged in."

"This is going to sound weird," I said, springing the catch, "but your grandma told me there was something hidden here. I didn't know what she meant."

He nodded. "It's not weird. She didn't get chance to tell you half of what she needed to—"

An outside door slammed upstairs and we both started.

"Bailey? You under there, bro?"

He shouted back. "Yeah. Just having a root round. I'll walk home."

"Right. Well, we're off now. Tell the lady of the manor we'll see her in the morning, wherever she is."

"Will do!"

I had the torch shining on a leatherbound prayerbook and an old manuscript.

Dated 1669, inked in spidery, almost illegible writing, it had been signed by Randall Cribbs.

***

Chapter Twenty-Five

Glynn was due home any moment, and after Bailey left, on instinct I hid it. I didn't trust Glynn. Partly because of Belinda, but also because, without relating what Letitia had said, which he'd probably dismiss as nonsense, he might tell someone else about its existence.

In addition to that, the minute script, penned in old English, would take time and patience to decipher: *Bee not only scandalous… she come whome to I wun night… how bist thine, ses he…*

For the time being, I concealed it in a suitcase in the attic, after which there were precious few opportunities to read it in private – half an hour here, half an hour there at most. I was desperate to understand its significance, why it was so important, and how Letitia knew it was there. Who the people were who wanted it. Why the secrecy? It was frustrating not having the time to read it properly. The opportunity, however, was to come in a most unexpected, not to mention painful, way.

Summer solstice was fast approaching. June was a warm and fragrant month, the valley rich, verdant, lush. Hart's tongue and campion sprang up in the garden, along with ox-eye daisies, buttercups and wild honeysuckle. I yearned to be outdoors, instead of inside the hospital in regulation shoes with the heating on. I remember standing in the sluice room staring out of the window at the downs. How could I get time off?

Then shortly afterwards the following happened: I'd gone to change a nasogastric feed for an angry old man, who no longer knew where he was or who he was. And that morning he was extraordinarily aggressive, far more so than usual. Madeleine was in her office again with the consultant, Dr Christian, and I'd been rushing from task to task, when the man, who was doubly incontinent and had soiled the bed, suddenly whipped round and grabbed my arm. Fetid breath hit me full in the face as he scrambled to get out of bed, bony limbs flailing wildly, yelling at the top of his lungs.

In the confusion that followed, with myself and an auxiliary wrestling to stop him from falling, Madeleine walked in – clean, brisk and crisp, face set in a half-smile.

"What on earth is going on, Nurse?"

The man's faeces-encrusted nails were digging into my forearm. He was calling me a witch, a demon, sour breath spitting out the remains of a porridge breakfast. Sweat had beaded on his face, his thrashing limbs were long sticks of bone, as lethal as hockey sticks in a vitriolic match. I had glanced over at Madeleine for less than a second when suddenly, there was a sickening crack of bone upon bone. His other arm, which I thought the auxiliary had hold of, smashed into my temple, the fist balled into a punch. After which everything went black.

I don't know how long I was down for, but when I regained consciousness, the auxiliary had pulled up the protective bar of the bed and someone was shouting for the junior doctor. Vaguely, I wondered why the man had been so violent. Hadn't he had his medication? He was a big man, a retired builder. Unfortunately, the dementia had progressed rapidly, leaving him both physically and verbally aggressive; and we were half his size.

A male voice permeated the ensuing fog, asking if I was all right, but I couldn't answer. The nausea was overwhelming, my sight blurred. I remember being helped onto a plastic chair.

"That's odd. Meds have been signed for, but I've never seen him like this before. We increased the risperidone, as well," said the same male voice.

His white coat wafted around the room. Aftershave, something fresh, with lime and coconut in it, and an overtone of chemicals.

Madeleine hadn't sedated this violent, confused man, that's all I could think. She hadn't given him his meds, had she? I knew, while at the same time couldn't know, not for sure. Signed for but not given?

"Let's give you something to calm you down, Albert," said the man – not Doctor Christian, the one with the soft brown eyes who told Madeleine she had a beautiful complexion, but a younger one, the SHO.

There was a struggle, tense instructions to hold him so the injection could go into the thigh.

"There, that's better. You'll be more peaceful now. You've hurt one of our nurses, and we can't have that, can we?"

The SHO had a hold of my upper arm and was pulling me to my feet. I think I was crying.

"Put her in my office for a bit," Madeleine said. "She'll be fine."

"No…"

We were in the corridor.

"No," I said. "I'm going for a break. It's been three hours. I feel sick."

"I'll walk with you."

We sat for a while, he and I, at a table by the window, a couple of paper cups of hot, sweet tea between us, and a ropy cheese sandwich on white.

"Are you going to be okay?"

I nodded. "Yes. I'll call the nursing officer, though. I think I've got mild concussion."

"You can't go back to work."

"No, I know."

And that's what happened that day. I was kept under observation for a few hours but managed to persuade them to let me go home, that it was just a nasty headache and a shock, that the punch hadn't been as hard as it had. I know I cried on the drive back, howled actually. It wasn't the man's fault, not at all. It was just the being hit when I'd been trying to help him, and then Madeleine's smile when she wafted into the room. She didn't care that I saw her smile, either. He'd been prescribed nitrazepam at night and risperidone in the morning. The drugs prevented him from being violent, and becoming agitated and upset. I'd never had any problems with him before.

She hadn't given his meds, had she? Then she'd allocated his care to me. And not only that, she'd also sent one of her acolytes to work with me that day, a woman who'd stood there and watched, done little to help until Madeleine came in.

The incident was to haunt me later, and for a long time afterwards. A situation that would become horrifically clear.

But there was an upside to that day, as if a game of spiritual chess was being played, because I subsequently found myself home alone, lying in bed that afternoon, as the solstice drew nearer, and the Welch boys worked downstairs on the last of the kitchen boards.

Sunlight was dappling through the breeze of the curtains, dancing on the ceiling in a kaleidoscope of flickering leaves. I'd slipped in quietly, having stopped only to make tea in the utility room and check on Skip in the garden pen Glynn had rigged up, before going back outside again, in through the front door and up to bed. Downstairs, plastic sheeting separated the sawdust-sprayed kitchen from the stairwell, and so I'd only seen Aiden's blurry face staring through the dividing veil.

"I'm upstairs with a headache," I called, not waiting for a reply.

Glynn was away on a course all week, and had left that morning for Hove on the south coast. It was, therefore, a perfect opportunity to get the casket down and read more of the manuscript. How fortuitous, I thought, was that? To date, I'd only managed to scan it, picking out names and dates, forming a rough impression of what appeared to be a confession, as it ended with the words… *to depart this earth with dignity, and may God rest my eternal soul. Amen. Randall Cribbs.*

Problem was, I had the opportunity that afternoon, but not the will. Drifting in and out of consciousness, the recent trauma of bone hitting bone was still reverberating around the cage of my skull, and from time to time, grief overwhelmed me in a rush of tears.

Madeleine had done it on purpose.

But why? Why did she hate me so much?

She didn't appear to hate the others, and there were younger, far prettier girls than me working in that hospital. Nor did she make life difficult for the confident, glamorous female house officer either, or the ward sisters she sat with at coffee breaks. Seemingly very popular, she'd regularly describe dinner parties she went to, how friends and family would be coming to her that weekend, the holidays and nights out they had together. All told with that saintly, slightly dreamy smile. Which was when it hit me, an arrow to the heart.

My eyes sprang wide open.

Of course!

At first, I couldn't quite believe it. And even then it didn't completely make sense. That would come later, much later. Nevertheless, the notion resonated as true. I just couldn't prove it because it was so crazy, so off-the-wall.

Although the manuscript was written in old English, names and dates needed no interpretation, and they peppered the document, had been pretty much all I could understand. And along with Cribbs, Ettrick and Stipple, one of the other names mentioned had been Parcet. There'd been a Loveday Parcet, referred to as 'daughter of Jack'. Right at the beginning of the manuscript, or confession as I'd come to think of it.

Madeleine's surname was Parcet. Sister Parcet.

Maybe it wasn't significant. After all, loads of people had the same surname round there. But there'd been another line that stood out, one of the few that didn't need much deciphering, and which suddenly stuck in the craw.

He'd written, *She of the sly, secret smile.*

Those secretive smiles...

My God, was there a connection? Could there be?

And it was at that moment, just as the dawn of awakening began to spread through me like a hot rash, when Aiden Welch pushed open the bedroom door and walked straight in.

***

Chapter Twenty-Six

There were no niceties or apologies; not even a word of introduction. He simply strode into the hush of the sun-dappled bedroom, and sat on my white cotton bedding.

Aiden, I realised, got in with his eyes. There was no doubting the man's physical beauty, but it was not that which arrested the senses, instead it was the power of intent. Time, as before when I'd stood in the doorway to his room, seemed to stop. And as such, the whole thing played out in slow motion, when in reality it must have happened in an instant.

Part of me, the observer, watched in fascination, another part on high alert. In the distance, a truck had started up. Duncan and Bailey were going home for the day. They'd finished, were leaving. Did they know Aiden had come upstairs? That I was alone with him? I opened my mouth to speak but my head was still throbbing, my thoughts muddied, and no words formed. He was leaning forwards, arms either side of my body, as slowly, oh-so-slowly, he bent his head to mine.

The summer breeze fluttered at the curtains and the trance deepened. I was floating in warm sea mist, lulled by the rhythm of the ocean, caressed by the sun, the sea and salty air. His lips had curved into a knowing smile; that he would get what he came for, that it was a given, his head tilting just slightly to one side, brushing the corner of my lips. And as before, it was as if we were already in the act, sheets pulled down…

My inner voice was shouting, yelling, horrified, aware of being swept into ever deeper waters, yet powerless against the tide. Afterwards, I thought locked-in syndrome must be like that, or deep hypnosis. His mouth had locked onto mine, velvety soft, insistent, and part of me wanted him to do it, to go further. He had me hooked. Had won. He almost laughed. I felt it. At which point he abruptly drew back, so swiftly there was a draught of cool air between us, and reached into his pocket for a cigarette.

It was a shock to the senses.

"So, we've pretty much finished work," he said. "We'll put the units back in tomorrow, then Bailey will be down to clear up." He was eyeing me steadily, objectively, through narrow eyes. "Me and Dunc start a new job day after, Yeovil way."

Once again, I felt utterly foolish, left floundering, wondering what the hell just happened. The image of the glamorous woman he'd been with at Letitia's funeral, flashed into my muzzy, concussed mind. He was playing me, wasn't he? Just for kicks?

His eyes settled on my lips, moving down to my throat.

"You're very beautiful, you know? Kind of like one of those ancient Irish goddesses – the Tuatha Dé Danann – tall and slender, fiery hair, alabaster skin, emerald green eyes."

I should have told him to go. Everything about it was wrong. Yet, I couldn't. Like having a third glass of wine when you know you should stop. But you don't. You've already drunk from the vine, had a taste. You want another. And with each glass your willpower dissipates further.

"I'll be off then?" he said.

"Yes."

"You want me to?"

His eyes held mine, and I saw in them the glint of challenge, the excitement. What would it be like, I thought? If we did…?

The moment was the single most excruciatingly intense one I've ever experienced. Time ceased to exist, until there was nothing at all… nothing except that decision… yes or no. A blackbird sang from the wire outside the window, and sweet, heady violets scented the room… Yes or no?

"Yes," I said.

His eyebrows lifted.

"Yes, I want you to go."

He vanished as quickly and silently as Dracula into the night.

"See you on the solstice, then."

I admit he got into my head. What intrigued me though, and concerned me greatly, was not so much his ability to do it, as my inability to stop it. He was also correct that we'd meet again soon, and that it would be on the solstice.

Before then, however, there were more opportunities to read the manuscript, to parallel a time four hundred years ago, with what was rapidly building up in the present day. It wasn't that afternoon, because after he'd gone I went downstairs, brought Skip inside, then locked the back door and promptly fell asleep. Not an easy sleep, but fitful, with repeated and concerted efforts to kick Aiden Welch out of my dreams. In the end I took paracetamol, which isn't advisable following a head injury, but I took the risk and oblivion followed. Much needed. And the following sick-days merging with off-duty, meant the rest of the week was sublimely free. No Glynn. No work. No disturbances.

Making sense of it, however, wasn't an easy task, as the writing was not only spidery and faded, but miniscule, as difficult to decipher as Shakespeare, and full of colloquialisms. What I decided to do was tackle it sentence by sentence and work through the text like a translator. It might have been an idea to find someone who specialised in that kind of thing, and perhaps I would have done if Letitia hadn't been so adamant I keep it to myself. But the very fact she'd known this was hidden and that I'd find it, convinced me of the need for secrecy. How had she known? There had to be something highly significant about this document, a reason for reading it, and understanding its content. That reason, however, was still elusive.

I began work.

'Randall Cribbs
13th May, 1669
Creech Cross Cottage'

And as I worked, a picture gradually began to emerge, the words spoken into my dream replaying like an old song.

'*All of the old paths interweave and interlock, criss-crossing into the mizmaze.*'

I became lost in Randall's world, transported back in time, and was quite disorientated when a couple of days later a knock came at the door, and Bailey turned up.

He'd come to fix the tiles and clear up the mess, he said, after Aiden and Duncan had put the kitchen units back in. He took his time, methodical and careful, making a neat job of everything, and I didn't mind. Later, we sat outside on the lawn with a cold cider each.

"Did she tell you about the maze?" he said.

"Maze?"

"I've been getting Skip to roll over. Watch!"

"What maze?"

His question was a jolt, because of the voice in my dream, and the words replaying in my head.

"She didn't get time, did she? She would have done if she could. They stopped her. But you know that. Anyway, I've got to tell you while I can. It's up at the abbey."

"Stopped her? No, I don't know anything about it. Tell me! I think it might be important."

"Do you mind if I smoke?"

"Of course not."

He lit up a cigarette and stretched out his legs.

"It was a highly unusual maze, said to pre-date medieval times, even the abbey itself, cut into the earth thousands of years ago. Letitia said it's from another age, one you can't even begin to imagine. She could see it in her mind's eye."

Instantly, an image flashed into my head. It had been on the week of the equinox... a fleeting vision I'd immediately disregarded as fantasy, of elaborate domes, spiralled turrets, and copper spikes...

"When we first came here, she went up there, said she could feel it through the soles of her bare feet, could picture what it looked like. A carved wheel within a wheel, within it sixteen petals of a flower divided into three, so forty-eight sections, each scored with intricate narrow channels that twist and coil into the far corners. An incredible maze, she said, the corridors as convoluted as knotted string. And at the centre there's a star. Inside that a tesseract."

"Tesseract?"

"A four-dimensional cube. It's supposed to represent the journey of the soul, through all its dark, blind challenges of life, before returning to the solar heart. However, only one section of one of the petals will allow the seeker into the centre. Impossible to find without guidance. Without instruction. Unless the traveller is clear-sighted and spiritually ready. The soul will be as lost as it is in life, careering down a thousand dark alleys, coiling into a mass of dead-ends, until he or she realises they're in a maze, a game, and finally begins to seek the light again."

"Wow!"

Bailey had, once again, stunned me. Fluent and articulate, animated and incredibly knowledgeable. Had he got all this from Letitia?

"But here's the main thing: Letitia said it's a stargate, or a portal, and when at certain junctures in time, the fixed stars are in perfect alignment with zodiacal signs, those in the tesseract will receive higher consciousness and be gifted with psychic abilities such as telekinesis, telepathy, astral projection and clairvoyance, even teleportation. The entire location is on a crystalline energy grid. The St Michael and Mary ley lines cross at that point, but also it's a nucleus, a kind of hub, where spirit lines from across the earth converge. She was shocked at its power. Stunned at what was lying underneath the ground."

"You know, Glynn and I both had a really strange experience up there. We were within the walls of the great hall. We must have been sitting right on top of it."

"You were. It's at the front beneath what was a huge circular window."

My heart did a little flip. The vision of coloured lights

through a kaleidoscope on the wall… Had there once been a circular stained-glass window there?

"But, and we're not sure when this happened because we haven't got the full story, the energy was corrupted."

My heart was racing along.

Something changed here. Turned it from light to dark…

"You all right, Lyddie? Only you keep looking at me as if I'm talking in Greek or something."

"No, I mean, yes. I'm fine. It's just, I don't know, what do you call it…? Synchronicity, that's it. I can't explain."

He nodded.

"Whoever corrupted it, couldn't use the maze to get what they wanted, though. They couldn't get to the centre without guidance or instruction. And the only person who allegedly had a map showing how to navigate it, with diagrams of when the stars are in alignment, was a local witch. Story goes they murdered her and ransacked her cottage, but never found them. It was suspected she'd given them to the nuns, but even after they'd been invaded and burned out, they were still never found. So that's the question: do those maps exist somewhere, or not?"

I felt a shiver pass over my back.

You've got something they want.

Present tense?

"The grid's powerful in its own right though, with or without knowledge of the maze. So, the power was inverted, used for self-gain, with sacrifices and summoning at every turn of the wheel, bringing in dark entities from the lower astral planes. You'll have heard about the tragedies in this village, I suppose? That'd be the price the rest of the people paid for their personal appetites to be indulged. What they didn't realise, though, or probably thought they could control, was that evil has to be evil. Demons aren't going to do what they're told for long. Sooner or later they want dominance, will possess a less evil vessel, and humans, even the worst, have some light in them. But these things don't. It then becomes a fight, with them demanding more and more blood, more fear, more destruction. And if they don't get it, they will grind down the host until it's possessed. After that, the only way to take the demon out is with fire. Burn the host. Leave not one drop of blood behind."

I think my mouth had dropped open.

Burn the host…

"You've got that look again, Lyddie."

There was no way I could explain what those last two sentences meant to me, largely because, if it was true, it would explain something monumental. There was more, though. He kept saying, 'they'.

"No. God, no. I was thinking of what your grandma said to me the last time I saw her. About having something 'they' want. Who are 'they'? She was talking in the present tense. But what you're saying doesn't sound like anything new—"

"It isn't! And it's still going on. Lyddie, this is really important and I've got to ask. What does it say in that manuscript we found? And was there a map of the maze? Something like that? It was the most important thing Letitia had to tell you. Us."

I was about to answer when a shadow fell over us.

"Everything all right, mate?"

We'd been utterly absorbed and, caught out, neither of us had noticed Aiden's approach. Bailey scrambled to his feet, red-faced and nervous in an instant.

"Only, I left the circular saw behind," Aiden said.

Aiden had heard us talking. Of that I was absolutely certain. And I could see by Bailey's face that he was, too. He'd been chatting away, confidently, a grown man with power and self-knowledge.

I honestly don't think Aiden had ever seen or heard him like that. It was written in the slackness of his expression, in the shock behind the eyes.

"I'll help you finish up," he said. "Then you can come back in the van with me to Yeovil."

***

Chapter Twenty-Seven

The next time I saw Aiden, it was exactly as he'd said, at the summer solstice.

There was a fête on the village green that weekend, the afternoon sunny and breezy, with a slight chill in the air. I remember I'd gone to a great deal of trouble with the way I looked. Instead of paring it down as usual, I wore white jeans, a white shirt, and a navy sweater. My hair was in a high pony tail and I'd put on eye make-up, as well as lip gloss. Glynn, who'd been away all week, kept looking at me as if he'd never seen me before, and for the first time in a very long time, I realised I wanted to be looked at. I was not honest with myself, however, about who by.

Try as I might, I could not get the image of Aiden Welch out of my head, and found myself pathetically scanning the crowds like a lovesick teen, knowing we'd meet again because he'd told me so... had stated the fact most emphatically, while his eyes burned into mine.

It looked like an ordinary day in the English countryside, with bunting and balloons blowing in the wind, stalls selling cakes and jam, plants, a raffle, cream teas, and various competitions. But as Glynn paid the entrance fee and I was looking around, an otherworldly atmosphere crept over the scene. The hum of conversation became a burring drone, the atmosphere was charged with static. Not for the first time, it struck me there was a strange magic there, as if time had looped around so many times that the overlays had merged. From medieval to Edwardian, voices fading in and out…

I came to with a slight lurch, suddenly aware Glynn had disappeared, having murmured something about an ice-cream. I barely heard him, busy scanning faces as I wandered from stall to stall. At one point my eyes met with Kathleen Ettrick's. She had, even on a summer's day, the greyish pallor of a ghost, as if she might at any given moment blend with the scenery and return to a bygone age. Monica was drinking tea with someone, scarlet hair and sequinned caftan twinkling in the sunlight. She really loved her glitter. And leaning against a fence, baseball caps pulled low, Slim and Mallory Cade smoked, cigarettes held between forefinger and thumb, silently observing.

"I see Colin's on the cadge again," said a familiar voice.

"Oh hi, Kendra!"

I was thrilled to see her.

"Have you seen that?"

"What?"

We were looking at a stall manned by Colin Cade. Next to him, Carrie, wearing a voluminous flowery dress that ballooned in the wind, stood clutching her Zimmer frame, wild grey hair floating in ribbons around her face. Pinned to the front of the stall was a banner proclaiming: *Let's make our villages pretty again! Donations needed.*

"Caused a right old stink, that has," Kendra said. "Insinuating our villages weren't pretty in the first place. And they've had hundreds off the oldies in Upper Creech, telling them they'd be planting apple blossoms. Not so much as a daffodil's been planted, my lovely. But what they have had are two more parties. Big funeral last weekend from their place, did you see it?"

"No, I've been a bit preoccupied."

"No, well they have to go past our place, see? And I've got a bird's-eye view, particularly with my binoculars. Usual mob turned up, anyhow – shiny suits, peaky blinders, long coats and flat caps."

"Who died?"

"She had a still birth."

"Who? Carrie?"

"Mallory. Don't know how that happened with 'er being gay."

"Blimey."

"Yeah, don't ask. I reckon it was the grandad, Mitch Cade. Lives in the caravan at the back, the one with the picket fence."

"Oh, my God! Serious?"

Kendra nodded.

"Actually, I know it for a fact because Mallory told Willow."

"I haven't seen them since the slap. I ought to go over. Did you ever find out what that was about, by the way?"

She hesitated, then shook her head. "To do with the bridge, I think."

"What happened about the money for that?"

"Not enough at the moment. Just the club so far. So, you enjoying yourself? How's it going down there at Swamp Manor?"

"You mean the floorboards? Finished, thank God. All we've got to do now is pay the bank back for the next decade."

"Well, at least you won't fall through the floor. Oh look, Aiden's fancy piece is back."

She wasn't looking at Aiden's girlfriend, though. She was looking at me. Gauging my reaction. But why? There was absolutely nothing to know. Yet her questioning eyes burned into the side of my face as, involuntarily, reluctantly, I glanced over.

This time 'Fancy Piece' was wearing extremely scanty shorts, and again rubbing her palm up and down his spine while he chatted to someone.

"Beautiful, isn't she?"

"Oh yes, absolutely."

"I wish I had legs like that."

"Yes."

"Don't you think she's incredible looking? Like a model?"

"I suppose so, yes."

"You've got eyes. You can see!"

But my eyes and being able to see with them had actually focused on someone else by then. My husband. Glynn was chatting, so closely their foreheads were almost touching as they sat eating ice-cream, with Belinda Ettrick.

Kendra's attention switched.

"That's one I'd want to watch," she said. "Belinda Ettrick's had more men in this village than I've had hot pasties, and that's a lot."

My spirits plunged. A cloud of darkness instantly descended. I could barely function. This was right in front of my face. In public.

"You all right?" Kendra said. She put a hand on my upper arm. "Don't worry, she's a terrible flirt but you knock spots off her. Go and sit on his knee or something. You're his wife. Piss her off."

I smiled faintly, choking back an eruption of chaotic emotions. Glynn and I had drifted apart and I didn't even know why. As if a cord had been cut, I was floating backwards into outer space. To confound matters, Mervin and Rosamund had just arrived, and in two days' time I had go back to work and face Madeleine again. Suddenly, everything was too much.

"No, but I think I'll go home. I've left Skip."

"How is he? Recovering?"

My voice came from far away, sounding tight, forced.

"Yes thanks, almost back to normal. But to be honest, it's a bit difficult to be around Rosamund and Mervin. They never even said sorry."

"No, well, it was an accident."

"They should have apologised."

"Yes, you're right."

I was fuming and beginning to steam over.

"Carrie's waving. I think she wants to talk to you."

"Yes. Anyway, good to see you."

"And you. See you again soon. Come up anytime for a coffee. Or give me a ring!"

After that, it was autopilot. Carrie had wanted to apologise for the slapping incident and to say how embarrassed they all were. My replies made as if someone else was speaking.

"No worries," floated on the air.

I was introduced properly to Nylah, who was heavily pregnant, and then had a completely unmemorable chat with Monica. Something about supporting local charities and that she would see me again soon.

See you again soon... see you soon... we'll meet again soon...

I know I went home with a few cakes in a bag, walked down the lane alone, that my footsteps echoed on the tarmac, and that I'd hurried. I must have changed my clothing, got Skip onto a lead and walked up Stonebarrow Hill to the top of the Ridge in a daze. Because my next clear shard of memory was sitting on top of Barrow Ridge with my back against one of the old trees, Skip lying next to me in the long grass. It was one of my favourite places in the world.

From far below, voices carried on the air, the smell of a barbecue drifting up, music thumping. I don't think, not since being a child of ten, that I'd ever felt so lost, so completely thrown off course as being unable to see ahead even to the next day. Words swirled around inside the dark bowl of my head. There was a pattern. I should know what it was. Yet did not.

Dusk was descending on the valley and I did not want to go home. Only to sit there for a very long time, with no end to it.

Maybe I dozed, or floated away on a tide of thoughts and dreams? But it was there, maybe hours later, when I saw again what I'd seen at Beltane after leaving Letitia for the last time. Smoke. There was definitely smoke down there at the abbey ruins. It would have been quite dark by then, and cold had stolen into my bones. The summer fête had long since been packed up, crowds dispersed, and there wasn't a sound except for a swarm of bees. No, not bees. Humming. At first I thought there was something wrong with my ears, actually shook my head, but as I concentrated on the smoke, I accepted that it was humming, and it was getting louder, permeating the air, getting inside my head. And a whirling black plume was rising from the earth below, from within the arches as it had before, spreading out across the whole valley.

That time I knew it was real. No doubt at all. A group was down there and it could not be coincidence it was happening again. There was a coven here. My God, there really was!

Certain lines and phrases from Randall Cribbs' manuscript then jumped into my mind.

Thirteen of them in number…

It is my belief that my daughter danced with the devil…

It was still going on. Whatever they did, they were still doing it.

It was then I became aware of how dark it was. Skip had sat quietly for hours, patiently waiting as if for someone in a coma.

"Sorry, old boy," I said, reaching for his lead. "Let's go!"

Which was when we both heard it.

He leapt around, ears pricked, eyes wide. Staring into the umbra of the shadow from where the sound had emanated.

The sigh of a long-held breath had been a matter of feet away.

***

Chapter Twenty-Eight

Not a figment of my imagination that time. But absolutely real.

I broke into a flat-out run, with nothing but roaring in my ears, careering over slippery boulders, tearing through ferns, hurtling over the plateau of the ridge towards the lane. They'd be local, I was thinking; would know shortcuts, be familiar with the landscape. And they were gaining ground, rapidly closing the gap, footsteps fast and light. An image burned onto my mind of two men in dark clothing, stealthy predators either side. I could not run any faster. My chest was on fire, legs screaming towards the pain barrier. I couldn't keep that kind of speed up for long. They'd catch me.

Scree slipped beneath my feet as I hared onto the downhill path, moonlight washing the plain below as Keith's farm came into view. I hurled myself over the stile into his fields. With breath nearly spent and cramp setting in, I almost fell down the hill, convinced the men would pounce any moment. Their breath was on my neck, hands about to clutch at my clothing, shadows overwhelming mine. But the lights of Keith's house were looming up rapidly, and I tore down to the back yard, not caring how annoyed he might be, at which point all the sensor lights came on, lighting it up like a football pitch. I was nearly passing out with pain, couldn't draw another breath, when I grabbed a spade in the full glare of the lights, and with my back to the barn, whipped round.

There was a clear view all the way up the fields to the post and rail fence bordering Stonebarrow Lane at the top.

No one there.

Keith, however, was standing outside. For some reason, all I could see was the little swinging witch in the glow of his glass porch.

"You're on my property, miss."

"There was a man up there," I gasped. "Maybe two."

"Shouldn't be out alone then, should you? Not at night."

I wanted to say, 'Oh, piss off,' but didn't want to engage with him. Instead, I apologised for the disturbance and hurried away, hobbling and light-headed, clutching the stitch in my side.

That there was a coven, or some sort of cult in the village, I was then certain. Perhaps they had guards or lookouts? All groups of that nature were secret. Not everyone was in it, but there'd be those who knew, who were aware and stayed silent out of fear or weakness, like my mother's neighbours, colleagues and family had. And then there were those who watched yet did not see, believing there was nothing else in the universe beyond their world. Leaving those who had experienced otherwise, so very much alone.

So, who the hell had chased me?

As I hastened away down Keith's drive, with him watching all the way, the image of Slim and Mallory Cade kept coming to mind. Both were tall, reed-thin, and the fields bordering their house were adjacent to the marsh track leading up to the hill. It could easily have been them.

Perhaps I should talk to Kendra, brave it and ask what was going on? I was beginning to feel unsafe, could no longer write events off as fanciful. I really needed to know who was who. I felt... targeted... watched. How adept was this coven? Could they do what my mother's had done – project those horrible things, cause accidents? Was it happening all over again?

Don't think about this too much, I told myself. *Kick them out of your head. Look into the abyss too long and it will look back at you. Think of something else. For God's sake, think of something else.*

Finally, the lights of Well Cottage were in sight and I hurried up the lane, relieved to see Skip standing in the drive, panting, waiting. Even with a damaged leg he'd been well ahead of me.

What about talking to Glynn, I thought, putting my key into the lock. Glynn, who'd spent the afternoon flirting with Belinda Ettrick. The sadness of that washed over me in a wave as I let myself into the silent house.

A lamp was on downstairs. He'd obviously gone to bed.

Oh, no. Oh, God. I was going to lose him, wasn't I? My best friend, my only friend, didn't even care I wasn't home.

Panic was surfacing. It had been threatening for a while, but now there was no stopping it. And after ushering Skip into his room, topping up his water and shutting the door, the enormity of what had just happened finally hit home. I stood in the middle of the unlit kitchen and realised I was shaking violently. It was quite a phenomenon. I'd seen many people in shock, but experiencing it myself was altogether different. The last time it happened I'd been ten years old. My whole body went into an uncontrollable tremor, teeth chattering, and wouldn't stop. Deep within, a cold, empty terror began to spread its tentacles, a helpless loneliness, a feeling of abandonment and loss, like being dropped into a bottomless black ocean. But the freezing cold, the inability to move, was the absolute worst. I couldn't help it. There was no one. I had no one.

Which was where Glynn found me, standing looking out at Barrow Ridge, shaking like I had a rigor, icy cold and rooted to the floor. The box lid that had been so firmly closed all those years, had opened, its contents bursting out: what my mother had been doing, who the people were downstairs.

Burn the host…

I'd never told the child psychiatrist it was her, because my mother had been with me, and I knew what she could do if I betrayed her. So, they prescribed medication and said it was all my imagination. Not one single person had believed me, let alone said they understood, or put an arm around me. Not one. Not a single doctor, not a single teacher, not one neighbour, not one friend. But it had been me and me alone who'd crept downstairs, creaked open the door, and seen what my mother and those other people were doing. And I had seen those smoky beings with red eyes standing around my bed.

There'd been a nurse there that day in the doctor's office, looking at me with such pity. And it was then I'd vowed to become one too, that I would be the one person who stood by the lost and helpless soul who needed someone to believe them, no matter what their story, because there was nothing worse than not being believed when you told the truth.

But it's not real, Lydia. It's not real. We know you believe it, but it's not real. It's not possible.

"Lyddie?"

Glynn was standing in the doorway, face set to annoyance and confusion.

Could I trust him?

"Where the hell have you been? What's going on?"

Still, I couldn't move or speak.

He was furious and there was nothing I could do. One of my hands was trying to grab hold of a kitchen chair.

"It's fucking eleven o'clock at night, Lydia."

"I know, but—"

"Right! I'm not doing this now. We'll talk in the morning. I need my sleep." He pointed a finger. "You need to fucking well sort yourself out."

Somehow, I managed to treat my own shock, to boil the kettle, pour hot water on two tablespoons of honey, to sip it slowly until the jittering stopped, then climb the stairs to bed. But just before sweet oblivion came, like familiar old friends, the orbs appeared. Orange, bright blue, some round, some spherical... and they were everywhere. The room was full of them. Would the ghostly man appear too, I vaguely wondered. Perhaps he came to sit with me anyway? Perhaps he was part of the coven? Perhaps he was the devil himself?

"No," I murmured. "No... I don't want to go to the dark..."

There were no dreams that night. Only unconscious oblivion. And the following morning, Glynn had pulled back the curtains and a mug of coffee was on the bedside table. Next time I woke it was to the sound of football on the television drifting up the stairs and I got up, showered and washed my hair, grateful, relieved, he was there. Then afterwards, we sat in the kitchen over a late breakfast, bacon and tomato sandwiches, more toast, more coffee.

Eventually he said, "So, what happened last night?"

I remembered a line from somewhere, about evil needing truth to be suppressed at all costs. To succeed it needed cowards, weakness, fear. And so, whether or not he thought I was loopy-loo, I was going to tell him.

"All right. Cards on the table. But both of us, right?"

Raising an eyebrow, he said, "Of course."

"Okay, well you've been away a lot recently and we've not seen much of each other. So, yesterday should have been a nice day for us. Instead, you spent it with Belinda Ettrick. Rude Belinda. The madam who turned her back on me."

"She's not like that. She's a really nice woman, Lyddie."

"No. She's only a really nice woman to you. She was bloody horrible to me."

He shrugged. "Well, you can be a bit aloof sometimes."

"What? You're defending her and attacking me?"

"Don't be stupid."

"Oh, I see. I'm stupid and aloof while she's really nice. I saw you both, you know? I do have eyes."

"Eyes that misinterpret."

"Really?"

"Yes, really. We were talking about the bridge money. There's no way I could find another five hundred quid after all we've had to spend on this place, thanks to her family and that Cribbs twat next door. So, that day you came back from a walk and found me talking to her at the gate–"

"Flirting and laughing?"

"You saw it that way. It was probably just a joke at that particular moment."

"Don't try to make out I'm deluded."

"I'm not. I'm telling you how it is. And yes, I've spoken to her a few times since she rides her horse up and down the lane. Anyway, that day I was hedge-cutting, and found out a lot more. She said the locals don't want the bridge disturbing on account of the witches' skulls and bones buried underneath it. The stones are engraved with symbols so the witches' spirits can connect with the earth and protect them. The local people won't pay for it to be re-built, and she said not to hand over any money because it definitely won't happen and we'd never get it back, either. They've given money to the Cades, though – well, everyone except Keith Cribbs, because trees were going to be planted and they didn't disagree. She said there's no argument with the Cades. Just with the bridge idea."

"They've given money to the Cades?"

"Seems so. But there's a stand-off regarding the bridge. Anyway, Fay had already asked me for 'my share' of the money for the bridge, since apparently I use it every day. But I said I couldn't afford it, so if they want money from me they'll have to hire you out as a prostitute on the town hall steps. I think that's when we laughed, when you caught us."

"I see."

My face was aflame. He was telling the truth about Belinda. Although, Belinda was no innocent. She knew exactly what she was doing. And maybe those protecting the bridge, and the witches' old bones, were the ones in the coven?

"So, let me get this right, Lyds? I'm working all the hours God gives to pay for our home, I'm knackered every weekend, and you thought I was risking all that to have an affair? So, instead of talking to me you throw a massive strop and disappear 'til gone midnight to try and stress me a bit more? Or do you just like drama?"

That put it in a different light. "No, no, of course not. It wasn't like that. I've got enough drama at work, if you remember – getting hit across the head by a patient, the ward sister being a psychopath: 'Just come into my office a moment, Lydia. We've had another complaint, Lydia… I'm afraid I won't be able to give you a very good reference, Lydia…' And that's on the back of Skip being knocked down and almost killed, and all the floorboards up. Anyway, I'm sorry. I did get the wrong end of the stick, then."

"Yes."

"I was hurt, I admit it. So, I left the fête and took Skip out for a long walk instead. It was nice up there on the ridge, calming. But then, I don't know, I must have nodded off because suddenly it was dark. And I thought I saw something."

I told him then, about the vision on the first of May, and that I'd seen it again.

"In the end, it doesn't matter what you or I believe though, does it? It's what they believe, and what they act out, that we have to be aware of. Practising dark arts never went away. People still do this stuff, and you've got to ask yourself why. We can't say it's rubbish if they're sacrificing living things or causing accidents. And on a practical earthly level, there really was someone up there last night who didn't want me there. Got to ask yourself why, if what they're doing is harmless. Skip heard them at the same time I did, and we both ran like hell. I cut through Keith Cribbs' place because I was scared to death. Anyway, whoever it was chased me, Glynn. So, why would they do that?"

He frowned.

"Look, I know what I saw. And why would someone be up there watching me?"

"Are you sure it wasn't a wild animal?"

I started then, to doubt my own mind again. To doubt my own senses. But there had been a tall thin figure, a shadow dividing into two.

"No. I definitely saw two tall figures. I can't be certain who they were, though."

We were quiet for a while.

"Beltane," I said. "Beltane and now the solstice. Lammas next, I'm guessing."

"What's that?"

"August, when the wheel turns again."

"Pagan stuff, it's harmless. People want to protect their ways of doing things. Then you've got newbies who want to make what they see as improvements, to impress themselves on the place. Causes division. Simple, really."

It sounded simple and I could easily see his point of view. Monica had also spoken of a divide, but I was beginning to think it was not between the newcomers and the locals. There was something else. And the spat about the bridge was very telling.

"To be honest, I'm relieved about the bridge situation, but I've got a feeling the divide here isn't clear cut, at all. And I know what I saw down there at the abbey. It wasn't a bonfire after a few bottles of wine. It was a whirling black vortex, like a tornado, that's the best I can describe it. And the whole valley was, I don't know, it was like a tuning fork – a high-pitched hum vibrating through the skull."

He looked at me as if I was insane.

"It's okay. Don't believe me if you don't want. But you experienced something for yourself when we went there in broad daylight. And Skip wouldn't go anywhere near it."

"True. I suppose there are places like that. The Bermuda Triangle, for example."

"There's a history here that could help explain things. Beneath the abbey, there's an ancient maze on an energy grid. It's apparently thousands of years old, possibly from another age, and at certain astrological points in time it was said those who navigated to the centre could gain psychic powers. Only it was corrupted. Used for dark instead of light. Something happened. And since then, the whole valley has been beset with tragedy."

He pulled a face. "Who's told you all that?"

"Quite a few people."

I was a bit deflated, feeling like I'd been mauled in a battle, that I couldn't get him on side or even to meet half way.

"Don't be cross, Lyddie. You know I'm a realist, that I stick to known facts. But something you just said did actually make sense."

"Gee, thanks."

"That it's not what we believe, but what others believe. And there are a lot of nutters in the world. It worries me as well, that you went up to the ridge alone, and I want you to promise me you won't do that again."

"Of course. I mean, I'm stupid, obviously. But not that stupid."

"I've had an idea, though."

"Oh?"

"Why don't you and I go up to the Ridge together at this next point on the wheel as you call it, then if anything happens I'll see for myself?"

"All right. That's a good idea. I'll go with that. Thank you."

He looked into my eyes. "So what else haven't you told me?"

"How do you know there's something else?"

"Because you never breathed a word about an ancient maze and astrological points in time before. Come on, I'm intrigued."

Should I tell him about the manuscript in the casket, or not? His eyes were searching mine, grey and serious, unsure. And so I took a deep breath and told him, not about the orbs or the apparition, or anything from my childhood, not even about the warnings from Zach and Bailey, but only that Letitia had known something was hidden beneath the house and there had been.

"I didn't tell you about the manuscript because I thought you might tell Belinda and... I'm sorry... I should have trusted you."

He shrugged, obviously hurt.

"I'm sorry, Glynn. It's just I felt entrusted with it and I thought you might not share my concern that no one else should know. You'd ask why and I couldn't give you an answer that would make sense to you. And Letitia was adamant no one else should know I have it."

Eventually, he said, "So, do you think you can decipher this manuscript, then? That it will shed light on your hypothesis about a coven?"

"I think so. I've done a bit."

"Where've you hidden it?"

"In the attic. I'll get it down. There was an old prayer book with it, as well."

It felt better telling him, showing him the document and sharing what I knew, along with the notes I'd made so far. We had always been a team and it was as much his as it was mine. I still didn't trust him completely, and clearly he wasn't remotely convinced there was a coven in the village, but he at least he'd agreed to meet me halfway. To see for himself.

It was midsummer, still light at ten o'clock in the evening, and we were sitting outside drinking beer, the void between us beginning to close a little.

"We're on the same side, you know?" he said.

"I know."

"Oh, by the way. I bumped into Colin Cade at the fête."

"Oh?"

"Cheeky sod tried to sting us for some cash, said we were the only ones who hadn't contributed to the village project. And then invited me to a men-only night at The Brank."

"The Brank? You're kidding! That was one of the things I meant to tell you about after we paid for the tree. I heard one of the blokes tell Keith they'd see him in there."

"Cade said there were regular meetings. Asked if I wanted to join. No women allowed."

A little knot of worry formed in my stomach.

"No, don't worry, I haven't got time for that kind of shit. But I did ask who lived there. And guess what he said?"

I shook my head.

"No one. It's empty. No locals will touch it on account of it being haunted. That's the only reason any newcomers got to come here, by the way, including us. Anyway, it's what you might call an unofficial, unlicensed drinking establishment. He said the photos on the wall would make my eyes pop."

"Oh, Glynn. Please don't go. They'd have something on you."

"That was my feeling. Bloke like that a few years ago roped some of my mates into a club that turned out dodgy – backhanders and favours, that kind of thing, stuff said when people were plastered, all recorded. Anyway, I said I'd think about it. Took about two seconds."

The little knot untied itself and he reached for my hand for the first time in weeks.

"I'm sorry, Lyds. I've not been able to think about anything except surviving. I do love you."

"I love you, too."

That love was to be tested yet, though. Seriously tested. And meanwhile, I worked on translating more of Randall Cribbs' script, not realising how important it was, or how little time there was left.

***

Chapter Twenty-Nine

I'd say things settled down for a while, but that wouldn't be quite true. Maybe they did for a week or so…

Firstly, there was an issue at work rumbling in the background like thunder circling a valley. Although the atmosphere on the ward was calmer than it had been, questions were being asked. After the incident with the violent old man, I'd taken to leaving my bag in the locked boot of my car instead of Madeleine's office. Call it instinct. It wasn't a calculated move, just that if anything was amiss she'd blame me. She had already compiled a list of petty complaints, and I was watching my back. Turned out it was one of the few smart things I've done in my life.

Everyone had noticed the unease on the ward over the past couple of months. Old people who sometimes remembered who they were and sometimes didn't, had picked up on the waves of anxiety, fear and mistrust. The atmosphere had fractured, and one by one, they'd started to act up. Where an elderly lady had been docile, she became agitated and upset. Where an old gent had slept through the night, now he kept getting out of bed, disturbed, confused, shouting. Other things went wrong, too – fluorescent lights flickered on and off, the phone rang incessantly but there'd be no caller, alarms rang, windows and doors jammed, the sluice blocked up and equipment went missing. Everyone was on a short fuse, the days were hot, agitated patients were prescribed ever higher doses of sedatives, more and more staff called in sick, and now a departmental meeting had been called.

And secondly, there was the fateful evening at Monica's. The one that brought everything to a head.

See you soon… see you again soon…

It would have been early July. A dry golden haze had settled over the village, hay baled in the fields, farming machinery whirring in the background. It was idyllic, dreamy.

When, on my way up to see Kendra, Monica stopped me on the lane.

Despite Keith's 'Keep Out' signs, I'd continued to cut through the woods, always keeping to the path and keeping Skip on a lead. We never made a sound, bothered no one. Yet, I felt uneasy in there – watched – as if Cicely Cribbs, because she really did give me the creeps, could see us. Curious, I'd searched for her books online but found nothing. Nor did I ever see her around. But her presence seemed to be everywhere.

Once or twice I could have sworn she was walking towards us on the path, and several times I glanced over my shoulder, convinced she was standing silently in the long grass, or leaning against a tree – a fleeting impression that vanished the moment it was formed, of a woman wearing a long, full skirt, shawl and boots, not the jeans and fleece she normally wore. But the face, with sharp lower teeth, square jaw and close-together doll-eyes, was unmistakeably hers. And every time it happened, a shiver breezed up my spine, the chatter of birds dying away. Lest I doubted my own senses, Skip would always glance in the same direction at the same time. Although, there was never anyone there.

On that particular afternoon as I went up to Kendra's house, the weather was sultry, hot and dusty, too uncomfortable to walk in the full glare of the sun. I'd exited the woods and was hurrying up Coach Lane with Skip, the sun scorching my face, when Monica's SUV suddenly appeared. A great tank of a car, it was roaring towards us down the middle of the road, and I leapt out of the way, yanking the lead so Skip's head was flush with my legs. Spotting us, she braked hard, so abruptly the engine cut out. Sweat was beading all over her face.

"Oh, fabulous, I've seen you! How are you, Lyddie?"

"Yes, fine. Thank you. How are you?"

"I was going to come down, but you've saved me a job. Would you like to come to dinner on Saturday? Not many, just the six of us – you two, Fay and Duncan?"

"Oh, how kind. Thank you. I'll check with Glynn but I'm sure he'll be delighted. We ought to have one next. It really is our turn."

She waved a hand, batting away the idea.

"That's wonderful. Shall we say eight?"

Continuing up to Kendra's, deep in thought, my mood picked up. I'd decided to take her up on the offer of a chat. She would know who was involved in this coven, I was sure. One way or another I'd find out what I needed to know. And I did need to know. They would be the ones to avoid, and I had to have some idea who they were. They'd be the old families who believed their demon-worshipping ancestors guarded the bridge like trolls, superstitious enough to carry on those traditions. But who? Keith? Kath

Ettrick? Belinda?

Kendra was sitting outside at a table on the patio, painting her nails glittery black, a row of cold ciders on the table ready and waiting.

"Heard you've had a time of it recently, my lovely? Come and sit down, take the weight off." Indicating a dog bowl, she added, "That's for Skip. He'll be all right there in the shade."

I was so grateful for a friend. I'd gone through life never really holding onto anyone in particular. I would get close to someone only to move on again. Kendra was easy company, funny and kind. She lit a cigarette, offered me one, opened a couple of bottles. And I never even thought to ask how she knew what I'd been through recently, how she knew I'd 'had a time of it'. Instead, I launched straight in.

"God, yes. First the incident at work and then the night of the fête."

"Ooh, go on then – what's happened?"

I told her about Madeleine, how since day one she had to keep taking me into her office for every tiny fault. About the day I was struck by a patient, that I was sure she'd missed out his meds; had possibly, in fact, missed out other patients' meds, too.

"I don't get it," I said. "She absolutely detests me and I don't know why."

"Jealous, I expect. Or maybe she dopes herself up? Might explain that gormless grin you said she had?"

"I don't know. Anyway, it's why I was off for a while when the boards were being done."

We got through a couple of bottles cider each, 7.5%, that afternoon, while she talked about the Cades, the funeral for Mallory's baby, and how there'd been a fight in the yard outside their house that night.

She stubbed out a cigarette.

"I don't know why Agnus Stipple's over there so much, either. We're supposed to be raising money for the bridge, not giving them party money for projects they keep making up. She's blowing smoke up Carrie's arse, if you'll pardon the expression."

It occurred to me then – the Cade family were part of the coven, weren't they? Of course, that would make perfect sense. It had to have been Mallory and Slim up there the other night.

"So what happened after you left the fête, then? I thought you just went home? When I said I heard you'd had a time of it, I meant with the floorboards."

"Oh, I see." I was thrown for a minute, recalling the casket under the boards, dying to confide what I was finding out. That's the thing with me, I blurt out everything I know, and it was an effort not to tell her. "Well, this is what I wanted to run by you, really. I took Skip up to the ridge that evening, and thought I saw something – a fire, smoke, down at the ruins. Anyway, I must have fallen asleep because suddenly it was dark and then Skip and I both heard someone up there behind us. I've got to admit I was spooked and ran home. I think there were two of them. They chased me down the hill."

"Oh, my God. Someone up there? What? Spying on the village?"

"More like the abbey ruins. There was a group of people down there, and it's the second time I've seen them… well, the second time I've seen smoke."

She looked taken aback. "You're kidding me?"

"No. The first time I thought I saw girls dancing in a ring, but the last two times I've been up there it was thick black smoke. Anyway, there was someone watching me. I won't be going up there alone again, that's for sure."

"Very advisable. Any idea who it was?"

I shrugged.

"Two of them, both tall and thin. At the moment I suspect Mallory and Slim."

She nodded.

"I think there's something going on."

"How do you mean?"

"Well, and don't laugh, but a coven."

She did laugh.

"No, I'm serious. I'm wondering if that family is taking traditional pagan celebrations a step too far. Or maybe they're in with some local people? Maybe that's why Agnus is there so much? The Cades are part of the coven?"

"Oh, I see where you're coming from now. You mean they're offering sacrifices and doing naked rituals? Drawing down the moon?"

I laughed. "You're right, it does sound silly."

"What do you know about that kind of stuff, Lyddie?"

I hesitated, just for a moment. "My mother dabbled," I said.

"Really?"

I told her then, the things I'd never told Glynn, how I'd been taken to a psychiatrist after seeing hooded, smoky figures in my room at night. And that afterwards my mother had told her friends and they'd laughed at me.

"But I did see them," I said. "I wasn't imagining it. They appeared in my dreams, waking me up in the middle of the night. I'd get three loud knocks in my head, jump awake, and see these things standing over my bed, staring down with furnace-red eyes, smoke instead of a face. And here I see orbs at night, coloured orbs, and a man, a ghostly, silvery man in a dark suit. I'm what you call sensitive, I think. Maybe psychic?"

"Really? A silvery man in a dark suit? Perhaps he was a late resident of the cottage?"

"Could be."

It was good to offload it all, to relate every last thing, theorising and discussing.

"It's all real, innet?" she said.

"Yes. How can it be imagination when more than one person sees it? Skip sees these figures at the same time as me, as well."

I told her about the time in the kitchen back in Yorkshire. About the shadowy man who'd peered into my face.

"And what about when a whole group of people see an entity? All of them, together? How can that be imagination?"

"A tulpa," she said, stubbing out a cigarette. "Or an egregore – that's like a spirit brought through a group of people. More than one believes in something and you have an entity, conjured by group thought and brought in by summoning. It protects the group."

"I didn't know that."

"Mmm."

I think I was a bit tipsy on cider, already cracking open a third, but I remember prattling on, just not quite sure what about.

"Something about this whole place transports me back in time, you know? I feel it ever so strongly. I've always picked up on atmosphere and undercurrents, though. Keep getting told I'm nuts. It's such a relief to talk to someone like you."

"I know what you mean. No one believes in the dark side 'til it's too late."

"Too late?"

"You know? After they become…" She seemed to flounder around for the right word. "Consumed?"

"Ah!"

"Anyway, I'd better get the lord and master's tea on or there'll be hell to pay."

I jumped up.

"Oh, yes. Sorry. I've overstayed."

"Don't be daft. Come up any time. Just ring first in case I'm out."

"We've been invited to Monica's on Saturday night."

"Nice. Enjoy!"

"Actually, I'm thinking of having a barbecue in August. I'd invite the whole village but the thought of Keith Cribbs makes my stomach churn."

"I think he makes everyone's stomach churn. Cicely's all right, though."

She was collecting the empties, had lifted up the ash tray, a half-smile on her lips, and I was bending down to untie Skip.

"Yes, she seems nice," I said, acutely aware as I spoke, of the flat note clanging discordantly in what had been a harmonious melody.

Simultaneously we turned away from one another.

Cicely was not all right. How come Kendra's intuition was so off? I thought she was highly astute? Or, was it mine that was way off? Was Cicely, in fact, nice? She could quite innocently have mentioned to Keith about meeting me in the woods. Him putting up those signs could have had nothing to do with her.

My God, how we lie to ourselves!

It wasn't until I was half way down the lane again, however, that I realised Kendra had actually told me nothing of consequence. And about a coven, I was none the wiser.

***

Chapter Thirty

By the time Saturday night came around, both Glynn and I were more than ready for a party. It had been fractious at work, with everyone eyeing everyone else suspiciously and more than the usual quota of staff off sick. Turned out Glynn had endured a stormy week, too. Someone had driven into the back of him in stop-start traffic on the motorway, badly denting the bumper. His dad had received a text asking for money, convinced it was from Glynn, even reading out the number. Yes, it was Glynn's number, but of course he hadn't sent it. Would never, ever do that. "What? By text?" he'd shouted down the phone. And his boss had accused him of not being a team player, when Glynn not only went out of his way to be in almost constant communication with colleagues, it was inherent to his nature. He couldn't be a lone wolf if he tried. To top it all, his credit card had been refused at a supermarket check-out, and in full view of a queue of people the cashier had told him he was trying to use a stolen one. He'd been wrongfully accused all week, and we both felt inordinately tired.

Perhaps that goes some way to explaining why, on Saturday night at Monica and Tim's, we gulped down gin and tonics like fruit juice. Certainly, it was a night of information-swapping like no other.

As it was a hot night, we were all sitting outside on a terrace strung with fairy lights.

"Here's to us!" said Fay, raising a glass. "Thank you for such a wonderful evening, Monica!"

"Thank you, Monica!"

"Cheers!"

I remember I had on a sleeveless white dress, the chat was amiable and easy, wine flowing, the food Mediterranean – olives, seafood, steak and salad.

"I'd love to learn about the history of the abbey," I said, halfway through the first course. "Does anyone know more about it?"

"Tim's the one to ask," Fay said. "He's the history expert. In fact, he's head of the local history society."

"Oh, really?" I said. "I didn't know that. So, was it destroyed during the Dissolution?"

I found myself looking into large, glassy blue eyes that held almost no expression.

"An understandable assumption," he said. "King Henry did order most of them to be razed to the ground. But in this case, I think not."

He cut a piece of rare steak and chewed it slowly, swallowed, dabbed at a smear of blood in the corner of his mouth with a serviette, sipped wine, swallowed again. Making me wait, patiently, still smiling, starting to feel a touch ridiculous.

"You see, there's another story here. Mostly passed down through word of mouth. I've been interviewing locals and historians in the area for my book, collecting and translating old texts from the few literate souls around at the time. There isn't much, but church records and a letter from a visiting member of the nobility, do seem to back up local rumours."

"Oh, you're writing a book?"

"Yes, history is a huge interest of mine, a passion."

"He was in the civil service with Malcom," said Fay.

"Malcom?"

"My first husband. He and Tim founded a history society together back in London. That's where we met Professor Yates."

"This was our holiday home originally," Monica said. "We only moved here permanently after Fay inherited Ashe House."

"Yes," I said. "I heard that. It's amazing you all knew each other before."

"And even more of a happy coincidence," said Tim, "when The Old Rectory became available for Team Yates. I think the old man fell down the stairs."

"Dreadful thing to have happened, of course," Monica said. "I think his poor wife passed soon after. Grief, probably."

"That can happen," I agreed.

"A twist of fate in our favour, though," said Tim. "All of us history buffs moving here at pretty much the same time. Presumably, Monica told you a little about the abbey already, Lydia?"

My mind was fuzzy with wine and I couldn't be sure what she'd said.

"It's built on a ley line cross, isn't it?"

"Who told you that?"

I frowned. "I can't remember."

He searched my eyes.

"Yes, well we think the abbey was built on the site of a druids' grove, and under the earth there's a maze. You won't find anything like this in conventional history books, by the way. Druids were spiritually advanced, as many ancient cultures were, knowledge we in the modern world have largely forgotten, or dismissed as rubbish."

"Hear, hear," said Monica.

He cut another piece of steak, chewed, dabbed at his mouth.

"The druids were gradually driven out of the South West, and the land fought over for hundreds of years. The bones in Buckholt Wood and beneath the fields are testament to the bloodshed. But matters did eventually settle, and an abbey was built over the top of the maze. However, trouble was coming again because there was a great fear of the devil sweeping across Europe in the sixteenth and seventeenth centuries, and this is where Creech Cross parts company with documented history. Local people say their ancestors witnessed women dancing naked and conjuring up demons in the grounds of the abbey. They said the nuns were not nuns but witches in disguise, and one night the mob went up there and torched the lot of them."

"Oh, my God!"

"Not only that, but they barred them in, leaving them to burn to death. The screams coming from inside were said to sound like screeching, squealing demons. And any who escaped were chased and hunted down like wild animals, strung up high on Barrow Ridge for all to see, their black robes flapping in the wind like the torn wings of a raven."

The image was graphic and, draining the remainder of

what had been a large glass of wine, I struggled with the sudden memory of the day at the ruins – the haze of smoke, grass all black, screams rending the air, of being unable to breathe.

"There would surely be no truth in the nuns being demonic?" I said.

"Of course not," said Monica, refilling my glass. "It was ridiculous, unfounded fear and superstition. People don't think. Just imagine, all that frenzied terror whipped up! Those poor women."

Tim nodded. "That said, I do believe it's been used since for, shall we say, the darker arts?"

"I thought so."

"What do you mean, Lyddie?" Fay asked.

I then proceeded to tell them what I'd witnessed from Barrow Ridge at Beltane and again at the solstice. I also told them I'd had unseen company up on the hill and they'd chased me off, finishing with the words, "I wouldn't be at all surprised if there's a coven here."

There was a small silence. I was poured another glass of wine. And continued. I'm not even sure what I said except I moved on from covens and witches to having seen several ghosts in my time, only stopping short when it came to Well Cottage. I'd have carried on, I expect, but for the fact I'd never told Glynn about either the orbs or the man in the black coat, and caught myself just in time.

"Lyddie's a bit fanciful, aren't you, love?" Glynn said.

Everyone laughed, but in that moment of embarrassment and confusion, I noticed an exchanged glance between Tim and Fay. I was drunk as a skunk and the candlelit faces were woozy, but I had, thankfully, stopped blurting out everything I could think of. And was compos mentis enough not to mention the manuscript.

Alas, to my horror, Glynn, who was also pretty well-oiled, wasn't.

"Well, you must bring it over to Tim so he can decipher it for you," said Monica. "It's his forte, darling. And besides, it's not really yours, is it? It's the property of everyone, part of our collective history."

"It is ours," I slurred. "It's in our house."

Barely perceptibly the atmosphere changed and, despite being drunk, a warning light came on in my head. All five were staring at me.

I think I laughed, saying of course Tim could have it, that I'd bring it round just as soon as I'd read it myself. I went over the top, saying I hadn't had the time but it looked like poetry and prayers, mostly. Glynn's eyebrows were rising to his hairline because only that day I'd read out huge chunks to him, and made serious headway into translating what was turning out to be not only a fascinating account of events in 1669, but also disturbing and acutely relevant.

I shot him a look and prayed it worked. *Well, you went and told them! I've got to get us out of this.*

"We'll pop round and collect it for you, dear," Monica persisted. "Tomorrow afternoon?"

I kept my voice light, innocent, drawing on survival skills honed to perfection in childhood.

"No, it's okay. I'll drop it in when I've finished. I'd really like to have the chance to read it first."

Inwardly, I was pleading with Glynn not to turn against me, for the love of God to be in my corner. Please, I silently begged him, don't tell me not to be silly, to hand it over, that Tim's far better educated and better placed to translate it than me.

Thankfully, his attention had been diverted by a conversation with Fay, leaving me to fend off Monica's loud and continued insistence that she'd call in and it wouldn't be any trouble, when I accidentally overheard a whispered conversation between Tim and Duncan. Monica was babbling on, about how he'd had the same publisher since Cambridge days with Vernon, and I found myself listening to several things all at once, thus missing key information. The impact of what was being whispered between the two men while Monica was talking, took precedence, her words only resurfacing later. How the Stipples had befriended Tim at the secret society in London...

Secret society?

Stipples?

But I wasn't quick enough to pick up the thread. Instead, I was listening with increasing alarm to the conversation between the two men on my right.

"It's an Oedipus Complex," Duncan was saying. "I never had a look-in. I realise now she only wanted me to rebuild the house."

"Must be difficult for you, old chap?"

"They've brought the woman in, you know?"

"The sex wor…"

They both stopped dead, realising I'd tuned out of the conversation with Monica and into theirs. I kept my gaze firmly fixed on the wall, at a painting, a disconcerting one, of rotund naked people in frankly pornographic poses. Porn in paintings… great art…

"Are you all right, Lyds?"

Porn in the Cades' living room. Porn in Monica's

dining room…

"Yes, fine. Bit tipsy, that's all."

I kept an expression on my face that came easily – empty, vacant, a tad stupid – and glanced over at Glynn, hoping he'd smooth over the awkward moment. But the atmosphere in the room had turned brittle, and loaded. And it struck me how right Glynn had been. We didn't know people. We didn't know them at all. The story he'd related about his neighbour with the pigeon shed full of hard porn, came to mind. The kind of filth, he'd said, that would make you physically sick, the kind of stuff that if you knew about it, you wouldn't want them even looking at your kids from across the street. And for some reason all of that resurfaced as we sat there eating tiramisu.

"We were all dreadfully sorry to hear about the accident with your dog, by the way," Monica said.

There was a glob of cream on her chin.

"Yes, thank you."

"Is he all right now?"

"Yes, recovering."

"Poor Rosamund was beside herself, absolutely in bits about it."

I had the distinct feeling of being probed for a reaction. Prodded. Poked.

"No one's fault, though, was it?" Tim added.

Of course it fucking was.

I was so angry, I could have pulled the tablecloth off from under the plates. The tiramisu was a bought one, a mess of cream and sugar and chemical chocolate. What did they want from me? What did these people want? That I go and apologise to Rosamund for the fact she ran over my dog? It was all I could do not to coldly ask them to explain how the clip on Skip's lead could have separated itself from the steel ring on his collar. Perhaps, Skip had then un-looped the lead from the post and rail fence himself, before hanging it neatly over the top? But they were peering at me, not only closely, but with glinting eyes.

That's when it dawned on me. They were excited. Wanted me to react. Suddenly, I felt like a deer caught in a sunny glade, hearing the click of a gun, searching the dark trees for where the predator was…

Fuck! Fuck! I'd got everything wrong here.

Putting down the spoon, I said, "He's almost back to normal anyway. Thank God!"

"I think Rosamund's afraid to run into you," said Fay. "At a fête or something. Super-awkward."

I looked at Glynn.

"We're going to go up there," he said.

My eyes widened. Where did that come from? What on God's green earth was he saying? 'No,' I wanted to yell at him. 'No, Glynn, no!'

"Sorry? Where?" Fay fixed him with a puzzled look.

The beady wart on her lip was pulsing like a blood-filled tick, and I tried to quell the image of her with her own son. I tried so hard, but it was obvious she knew that I knew. The veil between me and the other four was absolutely down.

Fay now focussed on Glynn.

She was actually alarmed, I realised, wrong-footed. And the moment was charged.

Then Glynn, he of the easy chat, said, "What we were talking about up to a few minutes ago – Creech Abbey Ruins. Lyds reckons there are rituals being held up there, so the next one's when, Lyds?"

"I'm not sure."

"I'll be honest," Glynn said. "I'm finding the notion of a coven a bit ludicrous, but as Lyds says, that doesn't mean it's not true. Anyway, we're going up to Barrow Ridge together next time, so I'll report back!"

He tapped his nose, oblivious to the fact that five sets of eyes were fixed on him in appalled silence.

Shortly afterwards, we walked home.

"Great night," Glynn said, arm around my shoulders.

"Yes, it was lovely."

"You telling them there's a coven here, though," he said. "They'll think we're barking at the moon. Did you see their faces?"

"You shouldn't have said we were going up there."

"Why?"

"You just shouldn't have."

"Don't start, Lyds. I'll go where I want, when I want. I can't see Tim or Duncan outpacing me, can you?"

"Not going to be them, is it?"

"Oh, you mean Slim and his sister? I'm not worried about them, either. You worry too much."

I didn't say anything. But as we approached the bend in the lane, I sensed we were being observed from within the woods. She was on the periphery of my vision. The same one, the woman in the long, full skirt and shawl, with light, frizzy hair and a gaping mouth.

Cicely's all right, though…

"There's stuff unseen," I muttered. "Glynn, you don't have to believe what you don't want to. But there are things going on here that aren't good. Don't ask me what or who or why. I don't know. But I don't feel safe anymore."

He was telling me not to be daft, that it was all my

imagination, as he unlatched the front gate and we walked up the path.

It was almost a full moon, the night clear with a zillion stars studding an inky sky.

We both saw it at the same time.

On the doorstep. A hare with its head cut clean off. Not a bite, not frayed around the neck. Clean like the chop of an axe. Laid out on the mat and perfectly in the centre of it.

A hare. No head. Oozing blood. Still warm.

***

Chapter Thirty-One

Glynn said it was 'kids'.

"What kids? At this time of night? Why?"

"Power. Scaring people. Getting their kicks, I don't know," he said, dropping the beheaded hare in a black plastic binbag.

"Don't let it get to you, Lyds. It's just a prank."

We sat in the moonlit kitchen drinking hot tea. By then, the fog of alcohol was lifting, and the conversation over dinner began to replay in fits and bursts.

"Malcom Stipple," I said, as the first wave of recollection hit me. "Apparently, Fay's first husband was Malcom Stipple."

"Suppose it stands to reason. He inherited Ashe House."

"Yes, it's just I didn't know, hadn't made the connection, and the name features heavily in Randall Cribbs' script. Tim and Vernon were at Cambridge together, too. They all knew each other. Happy coincidence when The Old Rectory came onto the market, eh?"

"So? What are you saying?"

"Nothing really, just that they all knew each other before, and–"

"And they have an interest in history and researched the area?"

I shrugged.

"You actually told them you thought there was a coven here," he reminded me.

"I know! Look Glynn, I wouldn't go there if I were you. You told them about the manuscript when Letitia expressly said it was to be kept secret, and then blurted out that we're planning to go back up to the ridge."

"No, I didn't."

"Erm… you did."

"I don't remember. Well, I kind of do but I don't remember why, or how."

"Mmm."

"Ah, shit! Sorry. Look, don't worry about it, okay? I mean, what do you think they're going to do? So, Tim wants the information to add to his book? Big deal. Read it and then give it to him."

I think I knew then, that I was on my own. He'd never believe me if I said they were the coven. That was who 'they' were. No wonder Bailey put on such an act. Or was the nervousness real in their presence?

I knew I wouldn't sleep easily anyway, so I took an antihistamine and as there was plenty of hot water in the immersion, had a bath. Glynn didn't have the same problem, being out for the count when I eventually got into bed, and I envied him the deep and peaceful sleep.

The Stipples befriended Tim and Vernon at the secret society in London…

Well, you must bring it over to Tim so he can decipher it for you… it's not really yours, is it?

You've got something they want but they don't know you've

got it yet. Keep it to yourself when the time comes…

But what if I was reading too much into it? Was I being too quick to judge, to think the worst because of my background? Perhaps, they genuinely loved history and simply wanted the truth? What if I stripped away all pre-conceived notions and pretended I'd just landed from outer space? What did that leave? My own senses. *Trust them.* My own intuition. *Trust it.*

At which point the orbs reappeared. The whole room was full of them – the deepest cobalt blue, the most shimmering sunset orange – and I did my best to process what was before my eyes. Who is to say what is true and what is not unless they see for themselves without bias, without preconceived ideas? Glynn was adamant that 'ghosts' did not exist. Because he'd never seen one. Because what he couldn't see could not exist. Like molecules, I asked him? Not the same, he said. But the truth of the matter was, we were never going to agree unless he saw what I saw, and even then he'd probably explain it as a trick of the light. All I know is I saw those orbs. Time and time again I saw them. I instructed myself, anyway, to keep calm and be in full awareness. To document as an observer. Letitia had told me to never be afraid, that if you were afraid you would get more of what you were afraid of, more dark entities, because that's the frequency in which they resided and thrived.

With each steadily counted breath, the anxiety dissipated. There was nothing menacing about them, I decided. The energy in the room was not oppressive and heavy. Nothing malign was materialising from the corners, towering over the bed, or scratching and rustling in the shadows trying to scare. I feared Madeleine at work more than this. I feared being chased down a hill alone at night more than this. In fact, they didn't feel threatening at all. And nor did the man. Who, when I next blinked, was suddenly there again.

I'd told no one about him. Except Kendra, who I felt would understand. She'd told me she once heard coat hangers rattling inside her wardrobe, had felt an evil presence in her bedroom at home, after which I'd confided in her.

No one believes in the dark side 'til it's too late... you know, after they become... consumed...

The fear she'd inspired was rekindled with the memory of her words, and I quickly blanked it out, breathing calmly, praying silently.

I wasn't sensing fear in the man's presence.

Instead, his piercing blue eyes looked upon me kindly, as if caring for a sickly child.

"What is it you want?" I whispered.

My heart was picking up pace. I should be terrified.

But I wasn't.

Nor was there an answer. But I must have instantly dropped into a deep and dreamless sleep, because next morning, there was.

'*Be the cycle breaker!*'

Those were the words I woke up with. In my head. '*Be the cycle breaker!*'

I didn't know what that meant. Break what cycle? How? Why? But as the day progressed, a sense of urgency seized hold of me, and the feeling grew. A quickening. The manuscript must be read as soon as possible and an understanding gained. Time, characters and events were now in place, history set to replay, layer over layer, like the interweaving tracks of the land, unchanging, eternally on a loop.

'Be the cycle breaker!'

But as fast as enlightenment lifted my consciousness, the darkness in the village matched it. As if, with patient anticipation, an age-old intelligence that had lain dormant for centuries, was about to resurface.

***

Chapter Thirty-Two

"Thirteen," he said. "Thirteen dead crows on the lawn."

When I next opened my eyes, it was to find Glynn standing at the bedroom window. Heavy cloud hung precipitously over the valley, the day ominously dark, stormy and close.

"You're kidding!"

Throwing back the covers, I hurried over. Sure enough, the grass was strewn with dead birds, black, shiny wings splayed out in a ring. A perfect circle.

A dull thud of recognition lumped in my stomach.

"How did this happen?"

"How should I know? I just came back upstairs with your coffee and opened the curtains. Maybe lightning last night?"

"What?"

Was he serious? Lightning that killed exactly thirteen crows and left them in a circle on our back lawn?

He turned away, stony-faced, and I realised his explanation fitted the only possibility he allowed himself to have, and therefore it was so. The decapitated hare last night had been done by kids. The crows killed by lightning.

It was frustrating. I felt blocked, snagged in the reeds,

beginning to feel like Mulder in the early days of *The X-Files*. But just as Scully had been presented with the seemingly impossible, the unbelievable, time and time again, so it was with Glynn, yet still his mind remained firmly closed. I knew as soon as I saw the hare what we were dealing with, and now my heart was thumping in sickly waves from the sight of the dead birds. My biggest fear, however, was not being believed.

"Okay, Glynn."

There was such an uncanny run of lousy luck after that, though, that even he struggled to keep coming up with explanations.

The next incident happened on Tuesday morning, just two days later. He was reversing out of the drive when a truck crashed into the Audi sideways-on, with such force that the car was shunted down the lane and tipped into a ditch. He was badly shaken, mostly because he swore there'd been nothing coming from either direction. The lane, he said, had been clear both ways. Our cottage is on a flat stretch between two bends, and from either approach a vehicle had to brake to take the ninety-degree corner. As such, the truck, like Rosamund's car when it hit Skip, could not have been travelling at speed. And Glynn was adamant there'd been nothing there. Clear sky. Clear vision. Crashed at speed.

"It came out of nowhere," he said, staggering back in. "Lyddie, I swear there was nothing there. The road was completely empty, and I don't hang about. It literally materialised out of thin air, up close in a fraction of a second."

"Are you all right?"

He raked his hair back and forth. He was shaking and

had to sit down.

"In better shape than the car. They've got to come and tow it out of there. It's nose-down in the ditch."

"What about you?"

"Banged my arm, nothing much. Bit shook up."

I'd been getting ready for work but rang in to say there'd been a car accident.

"I'll let Sister Parcet know," the night sister said. "There's a staff meeting this afternoon, though. You ought to be there if you can."

My mind, however, was on Glynn. Physically, he was all right, but the accident had diverted my worry and attention from work to him.

"It's very odd," Glynn kept saying. "I'm not kidding, Lyds – the road was empty."

"I know, you said."

But he kept going over and over it.

"There wasn't even anyone already on the bend because I wait until it's definitely clear. It *was* clear. An empty road. I backed out dead quick, tight to the nearside verge, put full lock on, then there it was. Slammed into the side like a bulldozer. And it must have crossed over to do it. You'd be able to see the tyre tracks!"

"Who was it?"

"Builder loaded up with supplies."

"What happened to him?"

"Nothing. It was a mean bit of kit – steel bars on the front."

He was ashen. He had finally stopped shaking from the adrenalin hit, but he wasn't his usual confident self for several days.

"Lyddie?"

I'd made more tea.

"Yeah?"

"He didn't brake."

"He must have."

"No. He kept pushing the car down the road and tipped it into the ditch. I'm going to sound insane but I swear he had enough time to see me and slam on the brakes. Even if he came down Coach Lane like a fighter jet, which I'm sure I'd have heard, but even if he shot down there and screamed round the bend, he would still, surely, have hit the brakes? But he didn't. Go back and look at the tyre tracks on the lane. He kept coming. Pushed the car all the way over to the ditch by Cribbs' farm. He did it deliberately."

"But why? Why would anyone do that? It doesn't make sense."

He looked directly into my eyes. I remember the moment. We were sitting at the kitchen table. A veil of fine rain had misted the garden, clouds obscuring the top of Barrow Ridge.

"I don't know why. But…"

"What?"

"There's something sinister about this. I didn't realise at the time because it all happened so fast and I was in a state of shock, couldn't believe the truck was still coming, but…" He raked his hair again, and my heart nearly stopped then with what he said. "You'll probably think I'm mad, but I got a brief glimpse of the driver's face."

"Go on."

"The bastard was smiling, Lyddie. I'm not joking. He was fucking smiling."

We were quiet for a while.

"I believe you, Glynn."

And then I told him why. I told him everything. All I'd told Kendra. More, because I could tell Glynn about Letitia and what she'd said. I told him about Bailey and Zach, how their voices and demeanour had changed, about the orbs and the ghostly vision, how I thought the past was informing the present. How important the manuscript could be in making sense of what was happening here. And finally, I told him about what happened when I was growing up. About my mother.

"I've let others tell me what's real and what's not all my life," I said. "Even convincing myself I was delusional, should take medication. But you know what? I was actually right as a child, because it turned out my mother and her friends were dabbling in the dark arts."

"Why didn't you tell me before?"

"In case you fell out of love with me, wrote me off as weird, not normal…"

He almost laughed. "But you are weird and not normal."

"Thanks. But I was right, you know? One of my mother's circle, a neighbour, told me. Said to get as far away as I could. She'd had things go wrong, the whole family got sick, husband lost his job, son diagnosed with schizophrenia. And here's the thing, Glynn – she told me they never should have done the things they did, especially not with me upstairs. She said my mother wasn't herself anymore, had lost control."

I couldn't tell him anymore, largely because I hadn't accepted that what happened to her had been anything other than an accident. There was no proof, no proof of anything.

He squeezed my hand.

"So what's going on here, do you reckon?" he said. "Do you really think there's a coven? That it's been going on for centuries?"

"Possibly, yes. Remember Fay's reaction when you said we were going up to Barrow Ridge together?"

"Hang on! You're saying Fay's involved?"

"And Monica desperately wanted the manuscript we found, didn't she?"

"Yes, but that was for Tim's book. So, who then…?"

I shook my head.

"I don't know. And I don't know how to find out, either. But the atmosphere changed when you said we were going up to the ridge, and they wanted that script really badly. Letitia warned me not to give it to anyone. She kept saying I'd got something they wanted and that was before I even found it. Then Bailey told me about the maze and the missing map. So, in all truth I don't know if there's a coven as such, or who's in it. But I do know someone wants the information I have, and they now know I've got it. And that was unquestionably Monica."

"Holy crap!"

"I recognise dark witchcraft, Glynn. I got close to a girl in my class once, made friends with her, started to tell her things. Next thing, in her desk one morning, she lifted the lid and there was a dead crow. Then her mother had an accident at work. She was a hairdresser and tripped over a wire, blinding one eye with the hot tongs in her hand. I found a poppet of her with a needle piercing one eye in my mother's dressing table drawer. After that, I deliberately cut Sally out of my life. To save her. There's light and there's dark, Glynn. Even Tim alluded to it. What I don't know is why the events in 1669 are relevant to the present day yet. All I know for sure, is that they are. Nor do I know what the cycle is I'm supposed to break, or how to do it. Why would I hear those words – first about the maze, then being the one to break a cycle?"

He shook his head.

"The only thing I can clearly see to do is carry on deciphering this script. And then there's Cicely Cribbs. She's creepy as all fuck. She's involved, I know it. But how would she fit in with Fay and Monica? As far as I can see, she has nothing to do with them."

And Madeleine. Madeleine Parcet.

"Well, we've both got the day off so why don't we work through this thing together? I'm more intrigued now. And to be honest, it'll help take my mind off everything else. I can't relax. I keep going over and over the accident."

"Good idea. I'm not going into work this afternoon, anyway. Can't think of anything worse than sitting in a meeting with Sister Parcet."

Madeleine Parcet. Madeleine Parcet. Cicely Cribbs. Madeleine...

It was with relief that I went to get the script from the attic. He was going to help me. At long last, we were a team again. Now there'd be progress.

"Could still be coincidence?" Glynn said, unravelling the sheaf of papers.

"Glynn!"

"All right, all right. It's just there's no proof of anything that would stand up legally or logically at the moment." "Correct. That's why I need you, Agent Scully! There could be something here that makes sense of it all. So, let's give it a chance. They certainly want it, that's for sure."

We each took separate sections, working through the text word for word, padding out the story and cross-checking on his laptop. I made an early lunch and then we continued working through, because as the story finally came together, we were thoroughly engrossed. Like a meadow of glow worms, one by one a plethora of tiny lights began to flick on in my head. I was excited. Glynn was excited.

Vaguely, I remember him going out to speak to the driver of the tow-truck, sometime mid-afternoon.

"I can carry on with this, if you want to get some air?" he said, coming back in. "They've taken the car. Should get a courtesy one sometime tomorrow, although the office said to take a few days out; and to go get a medical check-up."

I'd been deep in the seventeenth century, following fifteen-year-old Cicely Cribbs down a lane called Thorne Hollow, and for a minute struggled to grasp what he was talking about.

"Oh, that's good."

"Now the shock's over, I can feel my shoulder's jarred and my neck aches a bit. Anyway, if you want to go take Skip out, I'll carry on with this."

"Probably whiplash. Do you want me to have a look?"

"No, it's all right. It's not broken, I've had worse."

"Okay, if you're sure?"

There was a soft rain that day, the scent of the earth sweet and the flowers heady. Clipping on Skip's lead, I took him through the garden gate into the woodland, glancing back at Glynn in the kitchen. Head bent, he was working on the last couple of paragraphs before piecing together what we'd done and typing it up, after which we could read it back and hopefully make sense of it all.

It was Skip who sensed them.

My mind had been running amok, had just flicked back to the situation at work, to missing the enquiry meeting. How suspicious did it look that I'd taken the day off? When I realised Skip had stopped dead in his tracks.

For several minutes, I stared unseeingly into the woods, trying to see what he could see, the only sound that of rain pattering on the canopy of leaves.

And then they stepped out. Two tall, thin figures with hoods pulled low.

"Don't be scared. Don't run, Lyddie," said Bailey. "Me and Zach just need to talk."

***

Chapter Thirty-Three

My first instinct was to do exactly that, to run like hell. I'd never outpace them, though.

Through the trees I could see the cottage roof. Would Glynn hear if I screamed?

But this was Bailey. Crouching down, he was ruffling Skip's head.

"Hello, old friend. You gonna roll over for me, are you?"

I was frozen with indecision. Couldn't believe it.

"You know why we've come," Bailey said. "We were going to talk to you the other night on the ridge, but you ran off."

"That was you? Oh, my God!"

Bailey stood up and instinctively I stepped back.

"Why were you there? What were you doing? You chased me!"

He looked at Zach.

"No, we never chased you. We're the ones watching out for you."

"Someone did."

They both seemed perplexed. Shook their heads.

"Lyddie, there was no one up there but us and we

didn't chase you. We wouldn't do that. I told you, we're watching out for you and it looks like you need us more than ever."

My heart was pumping hard, palms in a sweat. I didn't know what to believe any more.

"We need to talk."

"What about?"

"My grandma, for one thing. She did her best to tell you as much as possible, but as you know, as you must have guessed, someone was knocking her out."

I put my hand to my mouth. "Oh, my God. I thought—"

"She asked me to bring you to her, so I put on an act, how I couldn't cope. Anyway, long story short, my mother didn't like you being in the house, Lydia. She didn't want Letitia talking."

I felt my face blanch.

"At first, I thought Letitia had just taken a turn for the worse, but it happened almost as soon as you started visiting. My mother remarked on it several times, in front of everyone, and for a while I didn't know what was going on, but then Letitia blurted out, 'No more injections,' remember?"

I nodded.

"I knew it was a cry for help. To both of us. Anyway, that's when it fell into place. You saw my face that day! Soon as I got the chance, I went into my mother's room and there in the back of her wardrobe was a box containing a syringe and a brown glass bottle half full of tablets, a mixture of stuff, a concoction."

Holy crap! The drugs issue at work! Patients who should have had medications but had been going up the wall, instead. The same ones who'd now miraculously calmed down again. And there I'd been, asked to go in and look after Letitia, who'd then rapidly deteriorated. My heart was a lead weight in my chest. I felt sick.

"Does your mother know a woman called Madeleine Parcet, by any chance?"

"Madeleine, yeah. Why? She's in the history society, for want of a better term."

"Flaming hell!"

"Why? What?"

"She's the sister on the ward at work." I quickly filled them in. "There's an enquiry going on."

"So, that's how they got supplies," Zach said, his voice again that of a much older man, far less emotional than us. He stood slightly apart, watching the path both ways, squinting into the haze of the woods.

"But it stopped, didn't it? The last time I saw your grandma, she was completely lucid. How did you manage it?"

"Took the stash and lost it somewhere in town."

"Didn't Fay suspect you?"

"She went mental. It was a risk. There was nothing she could do, though, and Letitia woke up enough for your next visit, so it was worth it. Nerve-racking few days, to be honest."

"Let's keep it down," Zach hissed. "Come on, we need to get off the path. Let's go to the ring, mate."

"I've seen Cicely in here," I whispered.

"Don't even think about her. Block her from your mind."

They led me deep into the woods, to a cluster of large stones shrouded in ferns.

"Safe in the ring," said Bailey, marking out a circle in the dirt, then trailing salt around the perimeter.

"You have no idea what you're dealing with, Lyddie. And that's why people get hurt," Zach said.

"Hurt?"

"You've made a big mistake. Robin got hurt. Your predecessor. He was doing what you've been doing – going up to the ridge, finding stuff out. His mother watches her, see?"

"Hang on, back up. What mistake?"

"Snooping about and then telling them," said Zach.

"Sit down, Lyddie," Bailey said. "We're going to have to bring you up to speed quickly because you cannot hand over what we found. You told them, didn't you?"

"I'm confused. Robin's mother watches who? You're talking about Kath Ettrick, then?"

"Kath Ettrick had to sell that house quickly because Robin had the crap beaten out of him one night; and before that they killed his dog and he nearly lost his mind. They were going to kill him. Worse. You don't want to know. So, once you two were here, the plan was to suss you out and then, shall we say, absorb you both into the situation, in different ways. But Letitia managed to tell you about the manuscript, despite them doping her up. They had no idea how much she knew or how much she told me, either. They didn't even know for sure if any information still existed, they only suspected. But now you've gone and told them. So, you're not safe, you and Glynn. You know that, right?"

I shook my head, lost. "Who attacked Robin? Who is Kath watching?"

They looked at each other.

"Tell her," Zach said. "We need mutual trust. And we need to know what's in the manuscript."

"My dad was Malcom Stipple," Bailey said. "They disclosed that information to you deliberately the other night to see if anything clicked with you. To see if you understood the significance. And Zach's dad was Malcom's brother."

"You're cousins?"

They nodded.

"Both of them died young, though," Bailey said. "Completely 'unexpectedly'." He made air apostrophes with his fingers. "Our family have owned Ashe House for centuries. You've seen the painting on the stairwell? Well, he was known as Master Stipple. Nathaniel."

"Oh, of course! And he was the one who had Randall Cribbs hanged, the man who used to live in our cottage."

Zach, who'd been keeping watch, swung round sharply.

"Really? We need this information, Lyddie. It's really important."

"We're nearly done. It's been painstaking work, but I'm convinced there's a parallel between then and now. As if things here are being re-enacted. It's very strange. I kept thinking my imagination was in overdrive again but... I don't know, I'm still missing something."

"So are we," Bailey said. "So, it would have been in the sixteen-hundreds when Stipple ruled the roost round here. He owned the big house, all the tenant farms, the inn, and the mill. The family even presided over the two churches. But he was a greedy, nasty piece of work who wanted all the power, all the land, all the food, all the trade from the stagecoaches passing through, and all the money from the tolls. No one else was to have a foothold in this valley unless it was to work for him, and that included the nuns, who he detested. They didn't have to pay him tithes, and they had prime farmland, the best spot. He hated that.

"He was also the local judge. But behind the respectable veneer, he raped women, blackmailed people, and anyone who resisted or challenged his authority was falsely accused of a crime and burned at the stake, or hanged. It was him who whipped up a local mob to raid the abbey and then burn it to the ground, citing the nuns as witches."

"I heard that, yes."

"Nathaniel was really after the maze. That's where the nuns used to pray. Afterwards, he used it for darker purposes, but this is the missing bit of the story, Lyddie, and we really need it. Who helped him? Because it wasn't Elspeth Cribbs, the local witch."

"Who helped him? How do you mean?"

"They come from far and wide to dance on that maze, see?"

"Who?"

"Members of the cult. The club. It's not a witches' coven like in Stipple's day. It's a secret society based in London and Cambridge. You can't join a club like that, you have to be invited, go through initiations, do incriminating things, swear allegiances. Nothing is written down. They have codes and symbols to identify each other.

"These are clever people, into studying the mechanics of the occult, alchemy, energy manipulation and remote viewing, getting excited when they find out entities can be channelled into earthly hosts. They work with witches but they're not adepts themselves. So, imagine what they found here! One of the most powerful energy grids on earth. Plus three age-old adepts. Dark witches."

My mind was on overdrive. Three adepts…Three girls in white dresses dancing on the embers of a maze in the ruins…

"But they don't have what they really want, and they're desperate for it. They cannot unlock the maze. Not without the original map and the information on astrological alignment. This is all hearsay, there's nothing, no proof of anything. Only that Elspeth Cribbs was said to have it, and was suspected to have given it to the nuns to safeguard."

"Remember, they still don't know for sure a map exists," Zach said, in that curiously deep voice that sent shudders rippling across my back. An ancient soul, was what came repeatedly to mind. He was an ancient soul.

I frowned, shook my head.

"From what we can glean," Bailey said, "Elspeth wouldn't work with Nathaniel Stipple, refused to give him what he wanted. But someone helped him do what he did to this valley. Imagine what would have happened if he'd had the map of the maze, because it was bad enough! Also, we believe the person who helped him was a dark witch. He or she passed down that knowledge through family, and they now suspect what we've found. Buried for nearly four hundred years, that map would enable them to resurrect an unprecedented level of horror. In other words, they're pretty sure you have what they've been looking for, and now they know where it is. And that was your mistake."

"I only have a manuscript," I said. "I told them that. Just a manuscript. There's no map–"

"Wasn't there something else in the casket?" Bailey said. "I thought there was a book?"

"A prayer book. A leather-bound prayer book."

He glanced at Zach.

"Look again," Zach said. "Check carefully. You know what you're looking for now."

"There might be clues in it," Bailey said. "Maybe even code? That's why we've had to come and find you. Remember, we need to be brought up to speed, too. We need the missing pieces of the picture if we're to watch the right people. We need the connection in order to work that out."

"So, who sent the hare? And the crows? Who are the adepts? The same ones who attacked Robin?"

No one's lived there since her son went doo-lally...

Had to buy a place for Robin, see, that's in a sort of sheltered complex. Got to have special psychiatric supervision...

"The locals are frightened, aren't they?" I said.

"Very. They're never quite sure who among them works for the club... Who sold out, you might say. You never truly know someone else, especially when money's involved. And they don't know for sure who the adepts are. The dark witches. That's bloodline."

"Do you know?"

"Not a hundred percent," said Bailey. "We know two, but this is where the information you've got comes in. It's going to be hereditary. Evil like this only works if it's done in total secret. They find each other. Thing is, if those three get hold of the map, and Randall Cribbs might disclose that in the manuscript, then the lights go out. That's what's scaring people, because they don't want a repeat of what happened hundreds of years ago, with murders and suicides, madness and infestations. It really happened, and it's the real reason they won't allow the bridge to come down – the necromancy, the rituals, would bring it all back. The cult doesn't actually know what they're dealing with.

Zach, you tell her, mate."

Zach looked straight into my eyes.

"In this day and age, they can't sacrifice someone, say they disappeared in a bog or fell down dead in the woods and a fox ate them. Nor can they accuse someone of witchcraft, or rape, or whatever they want, and get the village mob whipped into a murdering frenzy. They're got to be a bit more subtle when they want to get rid of a person. This is how mad and dangerous this village is. My mother, my bat-shit crazy mother, had my father killed. When he found out what was going on."

"Killed?"

"Nothing you could prove. He found out she was involved with the club. The situation here is relatively new, or resurrected you might say. It's been dormant a long, long time. But now the dark witches have focus."

Three of them... My mind was ticking over. Cicely. Definitely Cicely. But the other two...

Well, think about that one though, because we do need a new bridge. It's not far off collapsing...

Just the club so far. So, you enjoying yourself? How's it going down there at Swamp Manor?

No, surely not Kendra! She was an incomer, anyway. This was hereditary...

"There was a terrible row between my parents one night. Up until then, I'd been blissfully unaware. But a few days after my dad threatened to tell the village what she was up to, that they had a right to know she'd given away secrets that should never have been shared with people like that, book or no book, fat cheque or no fat cheque, he started to get nightmares, claimed something was sitting on his chest at night and he couldn't breathe."

"Hag-ridden? It's in the manuscript!"

"Yes. And one day he got infested by horseflies when he was working in the barn. Thousands of them. He was badly bitten, angry swellings all over his face, eyelids and hands, throat constricting, had to go to hospital. And then came the hallucinations. He'd walk into a room and nearly die of fright, said there was someone watching him everywhere he went – in the woods, by the river, standing in the lane. There were sudden, violent, crippling headaches. One time he lost his sight. And not long afterwards he died in a car accident."

"Psychic attack?"

"Yeah."

"I'm so sorry, Zach."

"Yeah. Anyway, I'm awake to it now. Here for a reason."

"You said we're not safe?"

I told them then, about the hare and the crows, about Glynn's accident that morning.

"The intention will be to drive you out and there'll be nothing you can prove. Who, these days, is going to believe hexes and poppets, astral projections and blood sacrifices cause illness and accidents?"

The more they told me, the more I kept seeing Kendra.

"Who, though?" I heard myself ask. "Who are the three?"

***

Chapter Thirty-Four

"There's one very powerful dark witch in our midst, not to be underestimated, and two acolytes," Bailey said. "She's under total possession. Pure evil, not herself."

Not herself...

I had a violent flashback then, to my mother having a heated row downstairs, with the same neighbour who later told me what I knew was real.

She's totally lost control. She's not herself, Lydia. Is there somewhere you can go?

"And how do you eliminate an evil spirit once it's completely in the body?" Bailey was saying. "Where does it go? Into a bottle like they'd have you believe?"

"Fire," I said, remembering the blaze when I came home from school one day, the house I grew up in a cauldron of flames. "You said it yourself. Burn the host. Leave not one drop of blood."

There! I'd finally admitted it to myself. It had been no accident. The rest of her little group had burned her out of existence to save themselves, to save me. Burn the host!

"Are you all right, Lyddie?"

"Yeah, sorry..."

Very few people had ever suspected my mother. Pretty,

friendly, funny, with a wicked sense of humour. Always had beautiful nails, stick-on false ones in those days, hair piled high, make-up perfect…

A bottle like they'd have you believe?

I couldn't get her out of my head. Who'd gone to great lengths to tell me about bad things happening after bottles were uncorked? Who lived high on the hill with a bird's eye view of the village, of Ashe House and where I tied up Skip? Who had I seen the day before Cicely told Keith about me walking in Horseman's Wood? Come to think of it, what had she been doing walking down the lane on her own at the exact moment I exited the woods?

His mother watches her, see?

Robin's mother watches who? You're talking about Kath Ettrick?

The ghost of Mrs Ettrick sits and watches me…

It couldn't be Kendra. They were just quips, her being witty and amusing, a friend, a friend I'd so badly wanted. And besides, she wasn't local. No…

They had to be talking about Cicely Cribbs.

I want to be cremated when my time comes.

I don't. Or how will I keep coming back?

"My brother stands at the foot of the stairs in our house and bows to that picture of Nathaniel Stipple. Can you believe that? Never passes it without a glance. Always bows."

I barely heard him.

"Aiden? Why?"

"Too much of a narcissist to read people, that's why he failed with you, but he's bloody good at hypnosis, feeds off a lot of energies like the parasite he is. There aren't many women in this village he hasn't screwed, and that includes

Kendra, by the way."

Not Kendra, no!

I refused to believe what was hidden in plain sight: Kendra scrutinising my face after pointing out Aiden's 'fancy piece'. She was trying to find out if I'd had an affair with him. If I'd succumbed. If I was as jealous as she was.

"You didn't tell me who crippled Robin?"

Zach sighed. "Mark," he said. "Come on, Lyddie. You know! You must know. Mark does what she tells him to do. Him and a mate kicked him almost to death, and that came after he'd been sent half-mad. That's why Kath and Tony got him out of the village as fast as they could. It doesn't excuse them doing you over, by the way, but they were genuinely desperate and in a hurry."

"What can we do?" I heard myself saying.

"Don't add to the negative energy with fear or anger, for a start," said Zach. "You don't fight the dark with more darkness. Remember it's mostly illusion, dark magic. They'll conjure up delusions and hallucinations, so you feel, for example, chased down a hill alone at night. They'll invoke fear and superstition, manifest accidents and illness using poppets and astral projection. But once you see the trick–"

"'See the trick… and the magician will fail.' That was the last thing your grandma ever said to me, Bailey."

"That's right," he said. "Keep the vibes high and know what's going on so you're not literally in the dark. Maybe think about selling up, though. Seriously. Especially you, Lyddie, because you're way too much of a channel, mate. They see you coming. They can use you. Didn't Letitia say?"

You have a crystal aura… crystal child…

But all I could see was Kendra magically appearing at my elbow, Kendra serving drinks for the Cades, knowing something about everyone, needling me about Aiden, subtly putting me down. I'd got it all so, so wrong. How? And that was after being warned.

"I remember her telling me to watch how people made me feel. Not what they said. But how they made me feel. I guess that one went over my head, too."

It just couldn't be Kendra. There wasn't a link between Randall's account and the present day. Maybe she just played all sides? Yes, that was it. She was one of those who knew but said nothing, a kind of double agent.

The rain was coming down hard by then.

"What about the Cades? Are they in it?"

"God, no! It's just money with them," Bailey said. "They weren't supposed to come here but Zach's grandfather at The Old Rectory sold off the land. That would have been before he fell down the steps, obviously. Anyway, the Cades only had caravans on it because there wasn't any planning permission until Yates turned up a few years later and wangled his way onto the parish council."

"Bought his way onto it," Zach said.

"Why did he give them planning permission?"

"Long story short – they're not part of the club but they do dirty work for them, kind of paid gatekeepers, facilitators. Bit like Keith. And the community project for planting trees is also a racket. Silence money. That's why the club keeps an eye on them, but they can't stand them, and neither can local people."

Three maidens with waist-length hair in white dresses. She was on my mind.

"Please tell me Kendra isn't one of the three?"

"Come on, Lyddie," said Zach. "You know the answer."

"I told her everything."

I was staring at the bark of a tree in front, seeing with new eyes, noticing so many things I never had before. Sigils carved into tree bark, pieces of knotted string hanging from branches, catching shards of sunlight through drops of rain.

"She gives what you ask for," said Zach. "What you lack, she gives."

I shook my head.

"I can't believe she's a Satanic witch."

"What is it about Kendra?" Zach said. "You're protecting her. Did the need for friendship blind you?"

Letitia's words about preconceptions painfully replayed.

"Friendships don't necessarily come in the packages you expect or want," he said, his voice mellowing with kindness. "Sometimes the best friends you'll ever have can be who you least expect."

"A couple of gormless lads, for example," said Bailey.

I nodded, smiled. "Or an elderly lady."

"Exactly."

"It's just… well, Kendra was really kind to me, so hospitable, gave me so much."

They both waited patiently as the rain drummed down.

I took a deep breath.

"Okay, did Mallory Cade sexually assault a girl when she was fourteen?"

Bailey's mouth dropped, eyebrows shooting up to his hairline.

"What? No way!"

"I've got a reason for asking. Did she recently have a stillbirth? With a funeral at the church?"

"No. Hundred percent."

"And Robin. Is he under psychiatric supervision?"

"No," said Zach. "He's in sheltered housing on disability benefits at the age of twenty-five because Kendra's husband put him in a wheelchair and kicked his head in so badly, he no longer knows who he is."

"So, Kendra lied to me?"

Despite the horror of the situation, my eyes filled up. Some things did, indeed, run deep.

"We're going to have to go in a minute, mate," Zach said.

"I need to ask a couple more things. On the equinox at Carrie Cade's party, your mother, Zach, slapped Mervin Yates across the face. Really hard. And the odd thing was, no one else present, which included Fay, seemed remotely shocked. So, I'm curious. What was that about?"

"They're all insane, you know?" said Bailey. "It would have been an initiation ritual for your benefit. They were bringing you in at that point."

I remembered how staged it had felt. The sly smile from Mervin Yates. And Kendra taking me straight out, no one batting an eyelid.

"And the adept who's perfectly possessed, the one everyone's terrified of? It has to be Cicely. Kendra wasn't local, and she wouldn't be able to behave like she does. Because it seems, with hindsight, that Kendra was maybe assigned to me? Gave me what I wanted."

Zach nodded.

"That's good. You've got clearer sight now. Found your own way. Yes, Cicely is the one. You even think about her and she'll be in your head. Astral projections everywhere. Here in the woods in particular, but also up at the ruins and sometimes on the bridge. Even in your dreams.

Especially in your dreams."

"She doesn't look like she does now, does she? She's in a long skirt, shawl, boots. Same face, though. Same as Randall Cribbs' daughter."

"That's her," said Zach.

Bailey nodded.

"But if she's reincarnating through the bloodlines, then the other two would be reincarnated, as well. There are three in that manuscript. And Kendra is not from this village."

"We're going to have to go, mate," Zach said. "Cicely will be here soon, I can feel her."

"Quickly then. Who else have we got to watch out for? Keith?"

"He's just a nasty old git – does the kills for them. And he ain't going to say anything about any of it with Cicely being his daughter. At least not in this life."

"Your mother doesn't like him, Bailey."

"She can't stand him. He's got zero respect for women, you must know that? I won't tell you what he did to his late wife."

"What about Kendra's husband? Does he know?"

"No," Bailey said. "Mark assaulted Robin because she told him to, probably said he made a move on her or something. But he doesn't know what she really is. And like the rest of them, he doesn't want to. Willow's only seven, you'll rarely see her, and luckily she's got a big family on the Ettrick side. Ettricks don't get on with the Cribbs, by the way. Story goes that one of the Ettrick lads was tried and hanged for murdering Cicely Cribbs in the sixteen hundreds. After that, your cottage was razed to the ground. We really would like to read Randall's account, Lyddie. We don't know who the third one is, see?"

"Come on, mate," said Zach. "We've got to get going. Can you get a copy to us, Lyddie?"

We were standing up by then, brushing away the protective circle, beginning to set back towards the path, and I spoke while walking.

"There were three girls who 'danced with the devil' according to Randall. One was his daughter, Cicely. The other two were the Parcet sisters at The Tollhouse – Loveday and Winifred. Thing is, when you read the descriptions, you'll see what I mean about reincarnation. If that's the case, then I'm going to guess the third one is Madeleine Parcet, the ward sister. But she doesn't live here, and Kendra isn't from this village, either, so it doesn't make sense."

"You've said that twice," said Zach. "But Kendra was originally from around here," said Zach.

"No, Tim said, or was it Monica? They said she'd married in."

"What did he actually say, though?" Zach said. "Listen to what he actually said. Not what you think he said. That's what they do – power of suggestion, using words as you would expect to hear them. What did he actually say?"

"That she married Mark Ettrick."

"Exactly." He looked across me towards Bailey. "That's it, mate. That's the connection. Kendra and Madeleine. Both Parcets."

My heart nearly jackhammered into my ribs.

"What Kendra, gob on a stick, didn't tell you…"

Kendra Parcet.

Her name. She'd never told me her maiden name.

Suddenly the resemblance was there… the heart-shaped

face, dark roots beneath the platinum blonde, the twitch of the smile. Wily, comely…

"Why didn't you tell me her family name?"

Bailey was staring at Zach.

"Well, I suppose we didn't think it was relevant."

Zach frowned.

"Why would we? We'd never have thought of Madeleine Parcet if it hadn't been for you. Now we see it. Only now."

"Except Kendra isn't from this village."

"Marnhull," said Bailey. "Her family's in Marnhull. But Kendra came back. She came back here. Can you find out where Madeleine lives?"

"I'll try."

"Then we'll know."

"Got to go!" Zach said. "See you tomorrow with the manuscript, Lyddie. Same time, yeah?"

"Yes, of course."

"Keep your word, it's important. And watch your back between now and then. Seriously. There's a quickening. A lot can happen in twenty-four hours. Remember how badly they want this."

***

Chapter Thirty-Five

During the final few weeks of July, both Glynn and I came to accept we weren't safe there and couldn't stay. It was harder for him to come to terms with than me, mostly because there was no tangible reason, no single incident – nothing he could see or explain. Rather, it was an escalating awareness that brought us to that point. And all intentions for going up to Barrow Ridge at Lammas, so he could see with his own eyes what he didn't truly believe, were dropped. This is what happened.

After parting from Zach and Bailey, that night I lay in bed turning over what I now knew. Or thought I knew. The air was muggy, thunder rumbling around the basin of the valley, and a distant flash of lightning briefly lit up the room.

Cicely Cribbs' image kept looming into my head and it was an effort to shut her out.

You even think about her and she'll be in your head. Even in your dreams. Especially in your dreams…

And if it wasn't her, it would be Madeleine's sly smile. Or Kendra twiddling an earring with glittery, pointed nails. I did my best to blot them out, to think of other things, but conversations and confrontations replayed, and having finally written out Randall's confession, I saw the three of them quite clearly. Exactly as they had once been.

Three girls in white dresses, sitting on wooden stools outside the cottage, whispering and giggling, chanting a rhyme over and over, winding string, winding and binding all day long...

And the attacks, when they came, were swift and vicious.

The first happened in the early hours of the following morning, just as I'd drifted into shallow sleep. Not me, but Glynn. He woke with a great lunge for air, grabbing my arm, gasping for breath.

"There's a weight on my chest, I can't breathe."

"Try to keep calm, slow it all down." I switched on the lamp. "I'll call an ambulance."

"No! No, it's not my heart. There's a lead weight on me. A ton weight, crushing my lungs. I can't... I can't..."

His face was ashen, skin coated in sweat.

"Any pain in your left arm? In the neck?"

"No!" He looked at me, puzzled. "It's going now. Lifting off. That was the worst nightmare I've ever had. Fucking hell!"

I ran for a glass of water and a towel, and when I came back he was sitting up.

"It was a woman, a heavy, squat woman hitching up full skirts, all dirty and wet, crawling onto my chest. She smelled rank, staring into my eyes with a sort of inhuman dead stare... long, lank hair, sopping wet... it was so real, so bloody real..."

"Stress," I said, trying to calm him down. "You just had a car accident and we've been working on frightening stuff all day. Maybe it's your subconscious mind making sense of it all?"

He shook his head. "Can't you smell her? The room stinks like a rancid swamp. Didn't you see her in the mirror when I was telling you there was a weight on me? She was still there. I woke up and saw her in the mirror. And then she was on my chest and I couldn't wake up. It was like I was dreaming but awake…"

Eventually, we managed to get back to sleep again, albeit with a lamp on. And then next day, I took a copy of the translated manuscript, folded up in my skirt pocket, into the woods without Skip. This would be a rapid handover. I was very wary, on guard. I, too, felt there was a quickening.

The storm hadn't freshened up the weather any – the afternoon hot and close, sun dappling through the canopy in fiery rays, and not a sound, no birds singing, no breeze stirring in the leaves. On reaching the old oak tree where we'd met the day before, I broke a sweat. God, the humidity was intense, an oven. I checked my watch. Waited a quarter of an hour, constantly vigilant. Each minute felt like an age.

Then it occurred to me: had they meant us to meet by the boulders? Was that what they meant by the same place? We'd headed into the woods directly opposite the tree, and remembering it clearly, I set off in a straight line. There were no traces, however, of anyone ever having been there – no flattened grass, no footprints – and when I came across the boulders, there was no sign of a ring. Or the boys. For a while I waited, confused. It was definitely the right place. Surely they wouldn't have let me down?

When a voice cracked the silence.

"Looking for something?"

She'd materialised out of nowhere.

Cicely Cribbs was standing a matter of feet away, blocking the way back to the path. Wearing denim shorts and a tight pink T-shirt, she eyeballed me, her face taut, no flash of those sharp lower teeth.

"Only Dad said you've no right to be in these woods. This is private property."

"There's a public right of way."

"There's such a thing as asking permission, common courtesy."

Not wanting to antagonise, feeling hate vibes coming off her, I nodded, moving away in the direction of the cottage, giving her a wide berth.

"My apologies. Thought I saw orchids, that's all. You have beautiful woodland, you're so lucky."

"No dog today?"

"Not today."

She watched me walk all the way back to the cottage gate, standing in the path, making sure I'd gone; and instinctively I pictured a bubble around me, a bubble of protection, praying it worked. Refusing to look back.

That night in bed I did the same, and the next and the next. But Glynn was subjected to repeated night terrors, murmuring feverishly, sometimes shouting, in his sleep, covered in sweat, fighting off an imaginary attacker. And then early one morning, about three o'clock, he woke and shouted, "No!"

The lamp went on and I shot to the surface from a deep, unconscious sleep.

When he was finally able to speak, he said there'd been fingers pressing into the hollow of his throat.

"Someone's in the house," he said, gasping for air. "I

was fast asleep when I felt fingers digging in, pushing into my windpipe, strangling me. There's someone in the house!"

We checked every room, making sure all the windows and doors were locked, that no one had been in.

"Another shit dream," he said, eventually. "But it felt real. And look…"

We both stared at his sheet-white face in the hall mirror. There were red marks on his throat.

We sat up for the rest of the night, drinking hot tea. I'd told him already what Zach and Bailey had said, about Robin being beaten up after being sent half mad, about Zach's father's demise, even the suggestion we might have to move. But he couldn't accept it, still preferring my original explanation that he was stressed, having bad dreams. Despite the marks on his neck. 'No way,' he kept saying. 'No way' could people make things like that happen.'

But there was a whole lot more to come.

The phone would ring in the middle of the night, just once or twice. Enough to wake us up, to question if we'd dreamt it or not. We'd drift off and then it would happen again. No record of a call having been made. One night, around midnight, all the smoke alarms went off one by one, ear-piercing screeches. First the landing, then the hall, then the kitchen. Black mould appeared one morning in the kitchen, plaster crumbled from the walls. And then there were the noises. A loud crash downstairs as if a bookcase had toppled, sledgehammer blows against the walls. And every night without fail, just as we got into bed, seconds after, there'd be three taps on the window pane.

"D'you hear it?" Glynn asked, lying stock still, eyes

wide.

"Yes."

"Again. Every night."

There'd be knocks on the front door, too – in the early hours, so loud they reverberated through the house. Blinds rattled in the bathroom as if by the wind, except the window was shut and it was night; shadows darted across mirrors and crowded around the walls, and cold air would breeze into our face. One of the most horrible things was the clock speeding up. It doesn't sound frightening but the tick-tock-tick-tock from the carriage clock on the mantelpiece would get faster and faster and faster, and somehow it caused the heart to pump faster along with it.

We were losing sleep.

And day after day, always going together after Cicely's appearance, we tried to deliver Randall's manuscript to Zach and Bailey, but without success. I agreed with Glynn that I shouldn't be alone with her, and he'd taken a few days off work following the accident. We never left the path, but waited in the same place I'd met them before, by the oak. If they were in there they'd find us, we reasoned.

Each time we waited fifteen minutes. But no one came.

And then about a week later, around two o'clock in the morning, Skip started howling.

Glynn sat straight up and flicked the light on. I was already half out of bed.

Skip, who usually slept soundly through to six or seven, was howling like a wolf.

We both tore downstairs.

Shattered glass lay all over the utility room floor in a thousand starlit fragments.

There'd been an attempted break-in.

That pushed Glynn to the edge faster than anything else. Running for one of the fire irons, he ran outside ready to take someone's head off, but there was no one in the garden. All the sensor lights were on and I had the torch flashing into every corner. But the place was deserted, the woods still and dark beyond the gate, the fields in shadow.

By then, I'd already accepted we may have to leave the village, had begun to mentally prepare. Nothing had gone well since we'd moved there. I think Glynn had had enough, too. He was getting tired, had just gone back to work, and was beginning to concede that yes, there had been far too many coincidences for it to be mathematically possible.

He sat on the foot of the stairs that night, raking his hair back and forth, dark circles under his eyes for the first time.

"I don't know what to do, Lyddie. Do we stay and root this out or find pastures new? I don't see why these bastards should get their way, but this is beyond a joke. I can't live like this. *We* can't live like this. What do we do?"

"If we gave them what they want, it would be far, far worse," I said. "For everyone, not just us. And we can't stay even if we burnt it, because they know we know who they are and what they are. That's how it works, can you not see? You have to see through things if you want the truth. Through to the unbelievable."

After we'd cleared up the glass, nailed boards across the window and brought Skip into the lounge, Glynn went back to bed and I stayed up, thinking. How did it get better for us? This was our life! Perhaps the sole reason for coming here was to unearth this information and get it to Zach and Bailey? Mission almost concluded, was it time to move on?

Where did we go?

I was lying on the sofa when I saw them for the last time. Relief rose in me at the sight, so much my eyes stung. Electric blue, sunset orange, orbs and spheres of every size and shape, danced in the darkness, quivering and alive. And almost as soon as they appeared, I fell asleep, thinking about those questions.

The answers came next day.

I'd had to go to work, of course. The atmosphere on the ward was calmer by then, and when I asked about the team meeting I'd missed, I was told nothing had been found that was untoward. Dr Christian had repeatedly refused the SHO's toxicology requests, citing them unnecessary, and when, out of curiosity, I had chance to look at the nursing reports, I found no mention of increased agitation on the ward during May and June. To view the matter objectively, based purely on evidence, would be to find absolutely nil of note, except for higher doses of risperidone and nitrazepam across the board, to be titrated up or down according to need, a detail I now saw had been added retrospectively. No one was found guilty of anything, the stock-take episode ascribed to a miscalculation by Pharmacy.

The way Madeleine worked people over was clever. Observing, I watched her confuse them, reflect questions with new ones, divert attention, and plant select words into minds, usually three times – 'That would be best. I think it would be best. The best thing to do, yes.' Always, she elicited three 'yesses'. I'd never noticed before.

It was almost impossible to avoid her, but by then I was picturing myself in a bubble and it seemed to work. Once or twice I caught a frown on Madeleine's face and inwardly grinned. Maybe it did?

And then our luck turned.

First, I'd wanted to find out where Madeleine lived, and the chance came at the end of a staff handover meeting, in front of everyone, and I grabbed it.

The subject of good walks around Creech Cross had come up in conversation.

"Don't you live near there, Madeleine?" I said. "You'd know about the walks better than me."

Everyone turned to look at her, including the SHO who'd been as suspicious as I had about drugs not being given.

It was the first and last time I ever witnessed her completely thrown.

"Not anymore, I live in a flat in town, Nurse Spicer. It's just my elderly parents who live there now."

"Oh, really? Are they in Creech Cross?"

Everyone was looking at her. There was nothing she could do.

"They have a farm near Upper Creech."

"But you'd know the walks if you grew up there?" said the physiotherapist who'd been keen to know where they were.

"Yes, of course."

I had to look down at the floor, unable to keep the excitement out of my eyes. *Please God,* I thought. *Please, let Zach and Bailey be there today.*

Because the final piece had just slotted into place. The picture we hadn't been able to see.

Fortunately, it was my half day and when I got home Glynn was already there. I was bursting to tell him what I'd just found out, but his news was greater than mine. In a state of shock, he grabbed me as soon as I walked in.

"You're never going to believe this," he said.

Completely unexpectedly, he'd been offered an overseas assignment. Two years in Auckland, New Zealand, helping set up a new office there.

We hugged for a long time. Then sat outside on the lawn with Skip, and a few beers.

"Are you sure you're okay with this?" he said. "We don't have to do it. I said I'd discuss it with you because it's a big move."

Oddly, I could already see the packing boxes, and the For Sale board.

"Yes, I'm more than okay with it."

For the first time in months we were on a high, propelled onto a new trajectory. And on a whim, that afternoon at five, we set off into the woods once again with the manuscript.

"They'll be here today," I said.

And they were. Approaching our usual place by the old oak, a dark shape separated from the myriad of tree trunks, and we were able to hand over the document.

The following is our best interpretation of what it said:

***

Chapter Thirty-Six

Randall Cribbs
13th May, 1669
Old Creech Cross Cottage

I set down here the particulars of certain events and persons known to me afore my fate, which awaits me in the form of a public hanging on the morrow morn. I write in feverish haste, for I have been gravely sick, and this confession, together with the prayer book entrusted to my keeping, must by necessity be hidden deep inside the stones of the well lest they fall into the wrong hands, this being a trial to me as I am sorely weakened. I am much determined, however, that the truth be known. Aye, that this place is a sinful place, rife with the deeds of the wicked and those who commit violations against their eternal souls.

Now I must hurry afore my daughter, Cicely, returns. The clock ticks ever faster, heralding my approaching death, for at sunrise they will come. The men of this parish, led by Master Stipple of Ashe House, will take me to the top of Barrow Ridge and from there I will be hanged by the neck. The crime of which I am falsely accused is that of rape, the woman affronted being Loveday Parcet, a maid of fifteen years and friend of my daughter, Cicely Cribbs. She of the sly, secret smile. No man or woman will see that smile of hers, not unless it is intended. For it is meant solely for thee, to feel the malignant and diabolical influence of everything she touches, and then thou wilt see that smile. This is meant for thee, it is to say, for thine eyes and thy soul, so that only thee will know. And be powerless.

I did not see that smile of Cicely's until it be too late to save myself, for I was blind to the truth, to the painful knowledge that the terrible evil committed in this place was at the hands of my own child. Was there ever such a maid? An only child, of flaxen curls and gentle manner, who would sit quietly baking bannock in the crock over the fire for her widowed father? I am not a wealthy man. Although educated to that of a clerk, the family fell on hard times and I have since taken work such as I am fit. It has been a comfort to me that there be barley cake and potatoes waiting on arrival home, a sprig of hare parsley, maiden's honesty and cowslips in a jug on the table. Cicely be a good daughter after her mother died, softening the water with burnt lye wood, washing, cooking and sweeping. I never saw ought else, it being heartening to me the days she spent in the company of the other young maids, Loveday and Winifred Parcet, laughing while they wound string to make a few pennies, singing rhymes and telling stories. She was a child to me. A child. I saw nothing untoward. Not afore she set a glad eye on Ethan Ettrick.

Master Ethan Ettrick be a lad of eighteen, with farmland and a prosperous future laid out before him. My Cicely be fifteen, same as Jack Parcet's daughter, Loveday. Now I look back on it, I ought to have heeded how she took to wandering along the pathways of Lower Creech; been mindful she'd visited Elspeth Cribbs, a crone who put the fear of the devil in all who be overlooked by her. A clay pipe-smoking witch, there were those who saw her riding an old wooden hurdle along the path by Buckholt Woods, a place ill-reputed, of blood-sodden earth and desolation. A sudden rise of rooks from the trees and the pursued knew the fate to come, if not that night then the next – an iron weight on the chest, hag-ridden to an early death. It is said if she overlooked a man he would see the corpse lights, hear the clock ticking ever faster, spurring on the beat of the heart until he would pass out of this world, quickly and in terror. What was my good daughter doing visiting such a crone? Such were my thoughts, such were my fears.

It seemed Elspeth enchanted the young with what they craved the most, attending her for love charms, and it was she who taught them how to bind a lover, to knot string and wind him in. Alas, a darkness hath descended on this parish, becoming worse with each passing month, until there be a ring of them at the abbey ruins. Perhaps I thought no ill would come of it, that it be a maid's fancy and nought else? And it ought to be remembered the dancing maidens be our daughters, our kin. 'Doan go up there,' folk said. 'They be dancing on the ashes.' Thus the village kept it secret, for these are dangerous times to be called a witch. Aye, and my daughter sups with the devil. For Elspeth Cribbs' love potion failed her, and Cicely was scorned in favour of another.

I have seen with my own eyes, can no longer deny the malevolence and deviousness residing within my own child, and the master she now serves. Cicely has chosen to walk a dark path and worship the dark lord. The day I confronted her with my knowledge, she had until then been a child with a sweet countenance, her actions kindly, her words gentle. Not wily, sly and knowing like Loveday and Winifred Parcet. Nor indeed as comely. Instead, she had about her an innocence, eyes the colour of cornflowers, a spirit of hopefulness within. But Ethan Ettrick had passed her over most publicly for another, his betrothed an incomer, a young woman whose family had wealth, who was pretty and had caught his eye. Cicely is neither pretty nor wealthy. I doubt Master Ettrick ever laid eyes upon her, considering her, if indeed he saw her at all, to be a simple local girl who wound string and sometimes worked in the fields. To him she was invisible.

I must come, however, to the others, for this is the greatest of her mortifications, those maidens she had kept company with, winding string, sitting in circles, singing and laughing. She kept the humiliation to herself for some time. The only maid left un-betrothed. Many months passed. Nothing outwardly seen. I came home to baked bannock as usual, to nettle tea, potatoes and berries, a jug of bluebells on the table. But it was then, around that time, perhaps Beltane, that the sightings first began.

It is a witches' coven and in the space of one year I came to see clearly it had nought to do with poor Elspeth Cribbs of Lower Creech. I know that now, yet it be too late, for Elspeth was hanged for a witch at the crossroads on the border road, where no county be forced to claim the body as belonging to them. After which the head was severed from the body with an axe, followed by the hands and the feet. Her bones lie beneath the old bridge on Cutty Lane, from where she cannot arise and walk the earth again, those boulders holding the bridge being for such a purpose, as there have been many such as she accused in this parish. Many murders, too. Not in the way, however, as was said. But I will come to that.

Sickness and disease began to plague this village around the time of the last Summer Solstice. Elspeth, it was said, led the dancing at the abbey on the mizmaze, there being a whole lamb as was sacrificed, singing and whistle pipes carrying on the thick night air, there being a hot fire and a purple haze over the marsh fields. That August was hot and dry, and the brook ran to nought, a trickle under the rocks was all. Then came a mighty infestation. Mice scurried around backdoors, running on the lanes, a heaving mass on barn floors, in outhouses, eating all the grain, scratching inside house walls.

There is an alehouse here, The Cat and Chapel Inn, and the master took against his wife, accusing her of witchcraft, having her locked into a brank, her jaw chained to the mantel so all could witness her humiliation, her tongue held still, said he, 'til she broke the curse. He beat her in front of drunken, goading menfolk, until one night the poor woman died, of exhaustion, of infection, of misery. A matter of days later a farmer was stabbed at his own field gate. Another fellow dropped dead on the path near Lower Creech, and later a fox was seen trotting briskly along the lane with a human hand in its mouth. Thereafter, at the turn of Samhain, Ethan Ettrick's new wife fell down one day on the path by Buckthorn Woods, clutching at her head, screaming in pain. Terrible headaches plagued her thereafter, until within a few weeks she be stone dead in the ground, heavy with child.

Thereafter, a multitude of fires broke out on farms, in barns, blazing through fields, and before October was out, a tremendous storm broke, after which there were toads. Toads pulsed on the lanes, in the ditches, surging out of wells and streams. Folk collapsed with fever, writhing in pain, there being great pustules on the skin, and blood in the eyes. Complaining of a great weight on their chest, at the point where each hag-ridden wretch would struggle to draw another breath, there would be seen an ugly crone, dripping wet with sodden hair lank around her face, standing outside the door, come to collect the soul. Young maids became greatly afeared to walk home after dusk or to venture into the woods or fields, and doom spread across the valley. Folk took to leaving crossed iron knives on the stairs, and a bishop brought forth from town to bless the earth, departed quickly, too frightened to complete the task.

Elspeth Cribbs, it was demanded, must be removed from this parish lest there be not one soul left standing and she took us all to the devil. Let the witch's neck crack like a nut and her flailing limbs be seen by all who passed the turnpike. Thus, she was dragged from the house and hanged before dawn.

But I know now, far too late, that the fools took an innocent woman. I did not truly know her, had believed the reputation, understanding only when delusion fell from my eyes, that her misfortune had been simply to be unsightly, with a disconcerting fat, round wart on her lip. But there should be no doubt an evil atmosphere presided in Creech Cross. Elspeth's death, however, had done nought to stop its spread. Instead, it passed through the villagers one to another like a contagion, smothering all in a dark cloud of fear and suspicion; led, always led, by the rousing, fire-mongering Master Nathaniel Stipple of Ashe House.

Let me come now to Nathaniel, standing in the church pulpit in Lower Creech his dark eyes glinted, face much reddened, as he thumped the wooden rail. Were they blind? Had they not seen the heinous creatures at the abbey dancing with the devil? Why, Elspeth Cribbs was a regular visitor, was she not? They had seen. Seen with their own eyes. Smelled the burning flesh of living sacrifices, witnessed the black smoke billowing from the chimneys, heard the demonic chants carried on the wind. Had they not had their fill of malevolence, murder, sickness and death? Were we all to die, one by one? Was every farm to be bankrupted? Many had been decimated by illness, with men too sick to work, failed crops, and the ravages of fire and rodents. Evil pervaded the entire valley, and must be swiftly stamped out. Elspeth Cribbs may, even in death, have infested these women's souls. Masquerading as angels, they were, in fact, demons. Demons who carried on evil work and who must be burned, the evil curse on this village snuffed out, never to return. They must rise up in haste, rise up at once.

Stipple gathered together a frenzy of men and women armed with fire, and that very day they marched up to the abbey. I need not recount what happened. The abbey now lies in ruins. And in the early hours I wake even now, to the sound of screams reverberating around the valley. The screams of good and holy women locked and barred inside.

My suspicions regarding Cicely were, however, aroused shortly afterwards. I had taken a walk up to the abbey, to pray for the souls of those innocent women, when at once it came to me. How could it have gone unnoticed? Nathaniel Stipple's harvest had survived all ravages of storm and pestilence. All but his, and a handful of estates owned by the Ettrick family, had been driven to disaster. Much of the land from the smaller farms which had fallen to bankruptcy, had subsequently been acquired by them, and subsequently their own assets had expanded significantly. Indeed, the farmer who'd been stabbed at his own field gate, had been the owner of a particularly thriving establishment, now sold by his widow to Nathaniel; and the poor man who'd recently returned from a war, a soldier who'd stopped at the Cat and Chapel Inn, had too much to drink and fallen asleep in a field, had been heir to the mill, now also owned by Nathaniel.

Most of all, however, I recalled the expression in my daughter's eyes on hearing Ethan Ettrick's new wife had dropped to her knees in the field by Buckthorn Woods, and that she had later died in a great terror. A fever of the brain was diagnosed by the local doctor, who had been summoned from Sherborne. However, the woman had screamed most fervently there be a demon inside her head, its eyes ablaze with malice. On imparting this information to my daughter, in some distress myself, it was therefore a hammer to the heart, when I caught, in the glint of the mirror as she turned from me, a smile.

After the terrible fire, the year turned from Samhain into Yule, Imbolc to Ostara, the fervour of fear that had once gripped the parish, fading to memory, to grief, to sadness. And finally to acceptance. I had thought it was over. It was, therefore, of great surprise to me, when Cicely once more took to walking over to Lower Creech, along the higgledy-piggledy weave of paths towards the farm of the young widower, Ethan Ettrick.

I had been following Cicely for some time. To the idle eye she was gathering flowers for the advent of Spring. Alas, she was collecting other items, too. With mounting horror I observed her scraping up dirt with her nails from beneath the hanging post at the crossroads, and from within Buckholt Woods. I saw her strangle a raven, her small white hand squeezing its neck, hot ruby red squirting down her arm as the bird's eyes bulged. She worked quietly, at first light or dusk, snipping hemlock, carving sigils into tree bark, marking, I realised, a territory, a net, singing softly to herself, a maiden with a basket of flowers and a sweet smile on her face should anyone cross her path.

Fear chilled my soul. Upstairs abed, I would wait for the

click of the door latch, for her to step into the mists of dusk and begin her work. Who had taught her such evil? Elspeth Cribbs, I was certain, had taught her little but love potions, and it was clear they had not worked. So, who, I asked myself, as I trailed her into the woods at dusk, across fields and over streams, was teaching Cicely? For I could scarce believe she worked alone. The village was relatively settled then, as survivors recovered, the air one of recovery, of hope, as the wheel turned once more and the days grew warmer. It was then the notion came to me. She was going to try again. She intended Ethan Ettrick to be her husband. I confess part of me wanted her to attain her prize, for it pained me to see her so unhappy. There was still some hope in her, then. Still some light.

This brings me to the evening of the nineteenth day of March this year, 1669. I had followed her into Horseman's Wood, through the garden gate and onto the bridlepath as far as Jack Parcet's fields. I hung well back, wondering where Cicely might be going, when I saw Loveday emerge from the cottage with her younger sister, Winifred. Waving to Cicely, they appeared as wraiths through the mist and met with her at the stile. From there, the three, dressed in long cloaks with hoods, linked arms, each holding a basket. On they walked, quickly and quite purposefully, skirting Jack's land towards the crossroads at Upper Creech, whereupon they stepped onto the lane, walked past The Old Rectory, then vanished into the dusk.

It was difficult. The light was such that I could be seen and, with no tree to dart behind, I felt quite exposed, but after a short hesitation, I guessed they were heading towards the abbey ruins, and my heart lurched a little at the sound of revelry. I continued to walk behind them, but on drawing nearer, veered off towards the opposite bank from where I could swiftly escape without being seen. I must confess I was fleetingly hopeful all would be well, the celebration being one for renewal, hope and rebirth. I needed only to reassure myself of that. The Parcet girls were courteous and respectable, and the evening passed as it should have, with pipe whistles and concertinas. There was a fire, singing, dancing and much merriment. Even then, I pushed to the back of my mind that they were dancing on ashes, on the grave of the holy sisters, and that the elders in the village had cautioned against being there.

The night cooled, my coat was heavy, the undergrowth soft, and it had begun to drizzle. And so it was through a veil of rain, and the fog of confusion, that I woke from what must have been a brief and fitful doze, and I woke so abruptly it was a struggle to believe what was then afore me.

Thirteen of them in number. A monotonous chant now filled the air, discordant and flat of key. Approximately six feet apart one from the other, they swayed, chanting, the drone increasingly hypnotic as they circled widdershins around a smoking fire that stank of burning flesh. I recognised the stench at once, recalling the night of the fire, aware the screams of pain renting the night air were human, when into my appalled senses came the sound of laughter, a horrible muffled laughter that echoed around the valley. I felt then, rather than saw, a swirling vortex, as if a great corruption had occurred, and all that had been beautiful was now an abomination. Blades flashed in the firelight, the spinning dance ever wilder, the roar murderous and most heathen. I put my hand over my mouth in an effort not to vomit, attempting to blank the evil from my sight as each in turn fell writhing and convulsing to the ground.

I do not know how I kept my counsel. I only knew that if I ran, I would be seen, a fleeing, terror-stricken man hunted down like quarry. And so I waited, cold, shivery, frightened, knowing I must find out, by following where they went, who they were. Most of all, who; and I prayed it would not be so, if Cicely was the leader.

I can now state with confidence that the grandmaster of the coven is Master Nathaniel Stipple of Ashe House. That he is the scandalous one accusing others of what he does himself, but to a degree others never knew existed. I saw him take back his hood as he walked into Ashe House with his son. He had held the staff and raised the sword, read aloud from the infernal book in his hands, and plunged in the blade. Alas, as I eyed him from the gloom of Horseman's Wood, he paused, before suddenly swinging around, staring straight into my eyes. Even though, behind the great oak, I could not be seen.

I list here the others. Ethan Ettrick's father, Ambrose. The pretty wife of the farmer who'd been stabbed. She had made a good fortune from the sale and I saw her scurry back up the track behind the Green. The innkeeper who'd tortured his wife and left her to die. He sauntered into the stable courtyard, cackling to himself. Another was Silas Cribbs, my cousin, the clue being his build, the curve of his stoop a sinister outline in the drizzly pre-dawn as he walked over the fields towards Creech Farm. I know not the others. But I suspect they were those who'd fared well from the spate of fires and bankruptcies. And then there were the three maids, Loveday, Winifred and Cicely.

The events I witnessed on the night of the Spring Equinox defy explanation from a simple man such as I. However, it is my belief that the coven headed by Master Stipple, turned all that was good, bad. To any man doubting my account, pray bring forth an explanation for the whirling black vortex rising above their heads, spiralling into the air, on the night they sacrificed another human being to whatever demon they summoned to fulfil their desires.

Alas, however, I was seen, and the next day fell into a fever. I lay in a pool of sweat, greatly fatigued, chest weighted, shivery, with skin furnace-hot. Cicely stood at the bedroom door, her face fading in and out of focus. I could not lift my head, for it be heavy as lead.

"You have been out in the rain, Father?"

My throat was parched, scorched to acid, scratched as if with a thousand nettles and thorns, and I could not rest.

I heard her walking around the cottage, thought I heard a soft lilting song, felt the cold dampness ooze in, as one by one, she opened windows and no fire was lit. I begged, nay pleaded, for her to tell me who had taught her such evil, but there was no light in her then. Only the cold, blank stare of contempt. I could not tell you how many days or even weeks later it was, when the thundering knock came on the door and Stipple's men broke in. Loveday Parcet had been raped, brutally raped. The girl was beside herself, in a terrible state. And she had, under great sufferance, for not wanting to betray a man deemed a good man, the father to her dearest friend, finally confessed to my name.

"What say thee, Randall Cribbs?"

I turned my head, the fever having wrung me out to a feeble bundle of aching bones. My throat and mouth were sanded dry, lips cracked, vision a blur. The only drink Cicely had brought was on the table, a small glass containing fluid cloudy and moss green.

"Look to thy master. Nathaniel Stipple. I am an innocent man."

They shook their heads. I would be hanged.

Night closed in before she bent and whispered in my ear,

the voice quite unrecognisable, and which sent unto me a deep chill.

"Thy curiosity led thee to thine own miserable end. Thee wishes to know? How badly thee wishes it…"

She tortured me until the first grey streaks of dawn appeared over Barrow Ridge.

"Winifred Parcet," the voice said. "Pretty little Winifred brought Cicely to me, and now I have her soul."

I will soon hear her steps upon the path. Light and gleeful. It is a beautiful morning, the song of a blackbird loud and clear, a scent of violets on the air. It is to be my last. I pray to God Almighty now for my deliverance. May God grant me courage to face what cometh, to depart this earth with dignity, and may God rest my eternal soul.

Amen.

Randall Cribbs

***

Epilogue

2003

We left Creech Cross before August was out. And most of that time was spent organising and packing. There was a tremendous amount to do. We'd decided to sell up and have our belongings shipped out to us, and with annual leave to take, we were able to spend most of August in a hotel on the Devon coast. Once everything had been crated up and taken to the docks, it felt... freeing. It was over. The club would be pleased they'd driven us out so quickly, and we'd already had an offer from an anonymous buyer, who we suspected was connected to them. However, without the elusive map, they would never get what they truly wanted. And no one, including myself, until I read and re-read our translation of what Randall had said, knew I had it. Not for sure.

For a year, I wondered what to do with it, stashing the prayer book inside a crate full of crockery and household items no one would ever sift through. There it lay, wrapped in a tea towel somewhere on the Indian Ocean, riding the waves in its casket. I didn't even unpack it when the crates were delivered to the bungalow in Auckland. The house was on stilts, there were lemon trees in the garden, and I was sitting on the balcony with Skip, overlooking other bungalows on stilts, most with pools, when the subject of the map came to mind once more.

So many times I wondered about Bailey and Zach, about how they quietly navigated a path through dark waters, systematically undoing dark works, sabotaging rituals, confusing the players. And all the while they blessed the earth, protected the animals, and lifted the energies. It seemed like an insurmountable battle, yet I had a feeling that eventually they would win. How strange it all was. At least the two boys would now know who to watch. I had been able to help with that.

It did puzzle me though, trying to work out if I'd ever been connected to Creech Cross in some way. I don't think so. Obviously, I can't say for sure, but maybe some of us are catalysts, needed for change to take place? With the passing of time, I've noticed I never seem to stay anywhere for long, and after I've left there's been a shift in the dynamics. Who knows how the cosmic dance is orchestrated? I can say for sure, however, that without events at Creech Cross, I might never have broken free of what Letitia called the prison of my mind, and seen past fear to the truth. Would never have known I'm one of the crystal children. It explained such a lot.

Glynn chose to erase the memory completely, to write it off as a bad patch he would never revisit, and to a large extent, so did I. But there was still the question of the map. And what to do with it.

In the end, I made myself re-examine the papers that had been carefully folded into the prayer book so many centuries before. The maps, for there were several, were complex, displaying an intricate knowledge of astrology, numbers, sequences, and dates. The most extraordinary thing was pulling out the diagram of the maze. For there before me was precisely what Bailey had described – a sixteen-petalled flower, each with three parts, a star in the middle and a cube at the heart; a four-dimensional cube it was difficult to comprehend because it looked futuristic, like something from a quantum physics book. And yet it was ancient. Not hundreds but allegedly thousands of years old. From another epoch. Buried for so long. Almost lost.

For such a long time I deliberated. It was historical. Sacred. Then again, perhaps in a previous age there had been no evil?

And now there was.

'Yes, in people,' Letitia had said. 'Of course, in people. And the really clever ones will pretend to serve the light.'

Pretty little Winifred…

We both loved New Zealand, and after six months we moved to another place on stilts, out of the suburbs of Glenfield, to the Bay of Plenty. We'd sit on the beach until midnight, looking up at the stars. Sometimes I'd think about the orbs. I kind of missed them. What had they been? And what of the silvery ghostly man? Randall? Had they been there to watch over me, to make sure I did the right thing? I never saw orbs again, but I asked the question, out loud as I had in Creech Cross. What was I to do with this map? Was its very existence a bond, a focus for those who waited with intent? If it did not exist, would they themselves be set free from a mission assigned long ago?

The answer came the next day.

Break the cycle…

It had not made sense to me before, but that morning,

all at once, it did. And so, trusting my instinct, I went out onto the balcony and burnt them. But as the flames took hold, I swear this is what I saw. I hadn't thought of them, not once, in all that time since we left. If any of their faces, including Monica's, Aiden's or Fay's, ever came to mind, I'd pull down an imaginary black roller blind and block them out. But in the flames that day came Cicely Cribbs' face. It stared directly into mine, the close-together, doll-blue eyes gleaming with a special kind of hatred, and close by, hovering like a ghostly attachment, were two others shimmering in the smoke. One of another girl, with dark wavy hair brushed over to one side, the other of a smaller, prettier one with an impish smile. There was a scent of violets in damp sweet woodland, and then they were gone.

***

Acknowledgements

Thank you to Lorna Read for proof reading, Candice Wright for sending so many wonderful photos of abandoned abbeys, and all the advance readers who gave their time so generously.

References

Dorset. Up Along Down Along.

A Collection of History, Tradition, Folklore, Flower Names and Herbal Lore.

Edited by Marianne R. Dacombe

Bannock: barley bread as referenced in the above book.

More Books by Sarah England

Father of Lies

A Darkly Disturbing Occult Horror Trilogy: Book 1

Ruby is the most violently disturbed patient ever admitted to Drummersgate Asylum, high on the bleak moors of northern England. With no improvement after two years, Dr Jack McGowan finally decides to take a risk and hypnotises her. With terrifying consequences.

A horrific dark force is now unleashed on the entire medical team, as each in turn attempts to unlock Ruby's shocking and sinister past. Who is this girl? And how did she manage to survive such unimaginable evil? Set in a desolate ex-mining village, where secrets are tightly kept and intruders hounded out, their questions soon lead to a haunted mill, the heart of darkness... and the Father of Lies.

***

Tanners Dell – Book 2

Now only one of the original team remains – Ward Sister Becky. However, despite her fiancé, Callum, being unconscious and many of her colleagues either dead or critically ill, she is determined to rescue Ruby's twelve-year-old daughter from a similar fate to her mother.

But no one asking questions in the desolate ex-mining village Ruby hails from ever comes to a good end. And as the diabolical history of the area is gradually revealed, it seems the evil invoked is both real and contagious.

Don't turn the lights out yet!

***

Magda – Book 3

The dark and twisted community of Woodsend harbours a terrible secret – one tracing back to the age of the Elizabethan witch hunts, when many innocent women were persecuted and hanged.

But there is a far deeper vein of horror running through this village, an evil that, once invoked, has no intention of relinquishing its grip on the modern world. Rather, it watches and waits with focused intelligence, leaving Ward Sister Becky and CID Officer Toby constantly checking over their shoulders and jumping at shadows.

Just who invited in this malevolent presence? And is the demonic woman who possessed Magda back in the sixteenth century the same one now gazing at Becky whenever she looks in the mirror?

Are you ready to meet Magda in this final instalment of the trilogy? Are you sure?

***

The Owlmen

If They See You, They Will Come for You

Ellie Blake is recovering from a nervous breakdown. Deciding to move back to her northern roots, she and her psychiatrist husband buy Tanners Dell at auction – an old water mill in the moorland village of Bridesmoor.

However, there is disquiet in the village. Tanners Dell has a terrible secret, one so well guarded no one speaks its name. But in her search for meaning and very much alone, Ellie is drawn to traditional witchcraft and determined to pursue it. All her life she has been cowed. All her life she has apologised for her very existence. And witchcraft has opened a door she could never have imagined. Imbued with power and overawed with its magic, for the first time she feels she has come home, truly knows who she is.

Tanners Dell, though, with its centuries-old demonic history… well, it's a dangerous place for a novice…

***

The Soprano

A Haunting Supernatural Thriller

It is 1951 and a remote mining village on the North Staffordshire Moors is hit by one of the worst snowstorms in living memory. Cut off for over three weeks, the old and the sick will die, the strongest bunker down, and those with evil intent will bring to its conclusion a family vendetta spanning three generations.

Inspired by a true event, *The Soprano* tells the story of Grace Holland – a strikingly beautiful, much admired local celebrity who brings glamour and inspiration to the grimy moorland community. But why is Grace still here? Why doesn't she leave this staunchly Methodist, rain-sodden place and the isolated farmhouse she shares with her mother?

Riddled with witchcraft and tales of superstition, the story is mostly narrated by the Whistler family, who own the local funeral parlour, in particular six-year-old Louise – now an elderly lady – who recalls one of the most shocking crimes imaginable.

***

Hidden Company

A dark psychological thriller set in a Victorian asylum in the heart of Wales.

1893, and nineteen-year-old Flora George is admitted to a remote asylum with no idea why she is there, what happened to her child, or how her wealthy family could have abandoned her to such a fate. However, within a short space of time, it becomes apparent she must save herself from something far worse than that of a harsh regime.

2018, and forty-one-year-old Isobel Lee moves into the gatehouse of what was once the old asylum. A reluctant medium, it is with dismay she realises there is a terrible secret here – one desperate to be heard. Angry and upset, Isobel baulks at what she must now face. But with the help of local dark arts practitioner Branwen, face it she must.

This is a dark story of human cruelty, folklore and superstition. But the human spirit can and will prevail… unless of course, the wrath of the fae is incited…

***

Monkspike

You are not forgiven

1149 was a violent year in the Forest of Dean.

Today, nearly 900 years later, the forest village of Monkspike sits brooding. There is a sickness here passed down through ancient lines, one noted and deeply felt by Sylvia Massey, the new psychologist. What is wrong with Nurse Belinda Sully's son? Why did her husband take his own life? Why are the old people in Temple Lake Nursing Home so terrified? And what are the lawless inhabitants of nearby Wolfs Cross hiding?

It is a dark village indeed, but one which has kept its secrets well. That is, until local girl Kezia Elwyn returns home as a practising Satanist, and resurrects a hellish wrath no longer containable. Burdo, the white monk, will infest your dreams… This is pure occult horror and definitely not for the faint of heart…

***

Baba Lenka

Pure Occult Horror

1970, and *Baba Lenka* begins in an icy Bavarian village with a highly unorthodox funeral. The deceased is Baba Lenka, great-grandmother to Eva Hart. But a terrible thing happens at the funeral, and from that moment on everything changes for seven-year-old Eva. The family flies back to Yorkshire but it seems the cold Alpine winds have followed them home... and the ghost of Baba Lenka has followed Eva. This is a story of demonic sorcery and occult practices during the World Wars, the horrors of which are drip-fed into young Eva's mind to devastating effect. Once again, this is absolutely not for the faint of heart. Nightmares pretty much guaranteed...

***

Masquerade

A Beth Harper Supernatural Thriller
Book 1

The first in a series of Beth Harper books, *Masquerade* is a supernatural thriller set in a remote North Yorkshire village. Following a whirlwind relocation for a live-in job at the local inn, Beth quickly realises the whole village is thoroughly haunted, the people here fearful and cowed. As a spiritual medium, her attention is drawn to Scarsdale Hall nearby, the enormous stately home dominating what is undoubtedly a wild and beautiful landscape. Built of black stone with majestic turrets, it seems to drain the energy from the land. There is, she feels, something malevolent about it, as if time has stopped…

***

Caduceus

Book Two in the Beth Harper Supernatural Thriller Series.

Beth Harper is a highly gifted spiritual medium and clairvoyant. Having fled Scarsdale Hall, she's drawn to the remote coastal town of Crewby in North West England, and it soon becomes apparent she has a job to do. The congeniality here is but a thin veneer masking decades of deeply embedded secrets, madness and fear. Although she has help from her spirit guides and many clues are shown in visions, it isn't until the senseless and ritualistic murders happen on Mailing Street, however, that the truth is finally unearthed. And Joe Sully, the investigating officer, is about to have the spiritual awakening of his life.

What's buried beneath these houses, though, is far more horrific and widespread than anything either of them could have imagined. Who is the man in black? What is the black goo crawling all over the rooftops? What exactly is The Gatehouse? And as for the local hospital, one night is more than enough for Beth... let alone three...

***

Groom Lake

A Dark Novella

Lauren Stafford, a traumatised divorcee, decides to rent a cottage on the edge of a beautiful ancestral estate in the Welsh Marches. But from the very first day of arrival, she instinctively knows there's something terribly wrong here – something malevolent and ancient – a feeling the whole place is trapped in a time warp. She really ought to leave. But the pull of the lake is too strong, its dark magic so powerful that it crosses over into dreams... turning them into nightmares. What lies beneath its still black surface? And why can't Lauren drag herself away? Why her? And why now?

***

The Droll Teller

A Ghostly Novella

1962, and on Christmas Day at precisely 6pm, a mysterious old man by the name of Silas Finn, calls on the new owners of an ancestral home in Devon and asks which they'd prefer to hear – a story or a song. Ten-year old Enys Quiller is adamant they must have a story, just as Cousin Beatrice instructed.

'You'll be sure to tell me dreckly, won't you?' says Beatrice. 'What the droll teller says?' But the strange and macabre tale of Victorian poisoning and madness that follows, has far-reaching repercussions for Enys and her family, and after the droll teller has finished, any notion of staying there, or even together, is shattered.

***

The Witching Hour

A Collection of thrillers, chillers and mysteries

The title story, *The Witching Hour*, inspired the prologue for *Father of Lies*. Other stories include *Someone Out There*, a three-part crime thriller set on the Yorkshire moorlands; *The Witchfinders*, a spooky 17th century witch hunt; and *Cold Melon Tart*, where the waitress discovers there are some things she simply cannot do. In *A Second Opinion*, a consultant surgeon is haunted by his late mistress; and *Sixty Seconds* sees a nursing home manager driven to murder. Whatever you choose, hopefully you'll enjoy the ride.

***

www.sarahenglandauthor.co.uk

Printed in Great Britain
by Amazon